coolcamping
kids
SECOND EDITION

Sophie Dawson, Jonathan Knight, Andrea Oates, Hayley Spurway, Clover Stroud,
Alexandra Tilley Loughrey, Ally Thompson, Harriet Yeomans

with additional contributions by
Dixe Wills

KEY

CDP – chemical disposal point
1W, 1M – one women's, one men's (for loos and showers)
Public transport options are only included where viable

Introduction   4

Campsite Locator   8

Cool Camping Top 10   10

Campsites at a Glance   12

A Mum's Guide   **18**

South-west England   24

Camping Games   **58**

West Country   72

Campfire Cooking   **92**

South-east England   96

Home Counties   114

Welsh Borders   132

Residential Camps   **146**

Brecon Beacons   150

West Wales   154

Mid and North Wales   176

Central England   188

East Anglia   196

Peak District   220

Family Festivals   **226**

Lakes and Dales   230

Scottish Lowlands   254

Scottish Highlands   268
and Islands

Index   286

Acknowledgements   288

introduction

Parents. We know you love holidays. But chances are that since the kids arrived the very concept of holidays has been redefined. Tears, tantrums and tiredness can mean an exhausting experience for all, leaving you in need of – well, another holiday.

Luckily, camping and children go together like marshmallows and hot chocolate. The idea of racing around in the outdoors, building dens, making friends, getting muddy and sleeping under the stars is, quite frankly, far more agreeable than a week at a hotel or at Aunt Mary's. And as your kids busy themselves with worms and frisbees and fairies, not only does it take the pressure off you, but actually witnessing them have so much fun is one of the great, underrated pleasures of being a parent.

Picking a campsite that will keep you and your children happy, however, is not always as straightforward as it might seem; children, rather like adults, bring with them a long list of their own specific demands. It is with this in mind that we have travelled around the UK once again to bring you the second edition of *Cool Camping: Kids*, designed and written specifically for you and the children in your life. We have steered clear of the big corporate sites with chicken-in-a-basket and fruit machines in the clubhouse, wave machines in the swimming pool and karaoke until dawn. Your children would have probably loved that, but we have a hunch that you might not. Instead we have picked a stellar cast of some of the most family-friendly sites on offer in the country, all of which exemplify the certain free-spirited sense of adventure that *Cool Camping* is all about.

This latest edition has been redesigned and now features a whopping total of 75 fantastic

family campsites, every one of which has been visited by us and, wherever possible, by our kids: each of them, from newborn babes-in-arms to surly teenagers, has given our selection their very own version of a thumbs-up. We think that you and your children, whatever their age, are going to love the sites covered in these pages, too.

We want you to have the most fun possible with your kids, wherever you are camping, so we have given you a thorough section for each site detailing all the practical aspects of your holiday. This includes extensive info about onsite and offsite fun, with listings for local attractions that children are bound to enjoy. And because this is the UK, we've included an If it Rains section, too, so even if it is chucking it down, you should be able to find a nearby castle or two to cavort in until the weather brightens up again.

In the name of serious research, we've tested the best places for local homemade ice cream, the tastiest fish and chips and the most luscious pick-your-own strawberries to add to the Food and Drink sections. If you are already a fan of the *Cool Camping* books, then you'll probably be a pretty independently minded traveller anyway, but because we want you and your family to be safe, we've included a Nanny State Alert section, too (where necessary), briefly outlining any potential hazards you should be aware of.

Part of the pleasure of camping with children is dispensing with the domestic clutter of everyday life. Without sounding too Zen about it, there's a purity to camping that's hard to replicate in 'normal' life, giving you time to completely connect with your children, rather than having

to worry about what you are going to put into their lunchboxes, if they've learnt enough for their spelling tests and whether they've got nits or not.

The focus of 'all-in-this-together' fun is food and mealtimes, so we've included a cooking section (p92) with some yummy treats you can easily put together on a barbecue or campfire, and which your children will love to help out with, too.

There's also a games section (p58), so you can make your own fun on site, and we've picked a selection of our favourite festivals (p226) that are just as enjoyable for kids as they are for parents. Finally, we've assembled a list of the best residential kids' camps in the country (p146), so even if you're chained to a hot keyboard over the summer, there's no reason why your kids shouldn't be having fun around a crackling campfire.

And because we've chosen a wide geographical spread, whichever part of the country you are in, we're pretty sure you'll find some place in *Cool Camping: Kids* that you and your children will love.

A few final words to those undecided readers that haven't tried camping before – just give it a go! The worst that could happen is a weekend of wet weather and a wasted few quid. But on the other hand, it might just be your best ever holiday together – and the start of a wonderful, new family adventure in the great outdoors…

Happiest camping!

campsite locator

MAP	CAMPSITE	LOCATION	PAGE
1	Noongallas	Cornwall	24
2	Westerley	Cornwall	28
3	Higher Pentreath Farm	Cornwall	30
4	Tregedna Farm	Cornwall	34
5	Arthur's Field	Cornwall	38
6	Higher Moor	Cornwall	42
7	Ruthern Valley	Cornwall	44
8	Mayrose Farm	Cornwall	46
9	Cornish Yurts	Cornwall	50
10	Cerenety	Cornwall	52
11	Maker Camping	Cornwall	56
12	Devon Yurt	Devon	62
13	Runnage Farm	Devon	66
14	Highfield Farm	Devon	68
15	Coombe View Farm	Devon	72
16	Caffyns Farm	Devon	74
17	Cloud Farm	Devon	78
18	Somerset Yurts	Somerset	82
19	Rocks East	Wiltshire	84
20	Eweleaze Farm	Dorset	88
21	Rosewall	Dorset	90
22	Stoneywish	Sussex	96
23	Wapsbourne Manor Farm	Sussex	100
24	Safari Britain	Sussex	104
25	Cobbs Hill Farm	Sussex	108
26	Nethergong Nurseries	Kent	110
27	Swiss Farm	Oxfordshire	114
28	Britchcombe Farm	Oxfordshire	116
29	Cotswold Farm Park	Gloucestershire	120
30	Viaduct Barn	Gloucestershire	124
31	Dome Garden	Gloucestershire	128
32	Tresseck	Herefordshire	132
33	Wriggles Brook	Herefordshire	134
34	Yellow Wood	Herefordshire	138
35	Astro Clear View	Herefordshire	142
36	Pencelli Castle	Powys	150
37	Erwlon	Carmarthenshire	152
38	Tir Bach Farm	Pembrokeshire	154
39	Dale Hill Farm	Pembrokeshire	158
40	Trehenlliw Farm	Pembrokshire	162
41	Celtic Camping	Pembrokeshire	164
42	Naturesbase	Ceredigion	168
43	Denmark Farm	Ceredigion	172
44	Woodhouse Farm	Powys	176
45	Gwerniago	Powys	180
46	Treehouse	Powys	184
47	The Green Caravan Park	Shropshire	188
48	Bosworth Water Trust	Warwickshire	190
49	The Dandelion Hideaway	Leicestershire	192
50	Cliff House	Suffolk	196
51	Clippesby Hall	Norfolk	198
52	TheCanoeMan	Norfolk	200
53	Nature's Path	Norfolk	204
54	Manor Farm	Norfolk	206
55	Kelling Heath	Norfolk	210
56	Wild Luxury	Norfolk	212
57	High Sand Creek	Norfolk	216
58	Haddon Grove	Derbyshire	220
59	Rowter Farm	Derbyshire	224
60	Rosedale Abbey	North Yorkshire	230
61	Masons	North Yorkshire	232
62	Rukin's Park Lodge	North Yorkshire	236
63	Holme Open Farm	Cumbria	238
64	4 Winds	Cumbria	242
65	Wild in Style	Cumbria	246
66	Fisherground	Cumbria	250
67	Solway View	Dumfries and Galloway	254
68	Balloch O' Dee	Dumfries and Galloway	256
69	Tibbie Shiels	Selkirkshire	260
70	Culzean Castle	Ayrshire	264
71	Seal Shore	Arran	268
72	Comrie Croft	Perthshire	270
73	Iona Campsite	Iona	274
74	Calgary Bay	Mull	278
75	Borlum Farm	Inverness-shire	282

cool camping top 10

Choosing a top 10 out of this bunch of gorgeous sites is a little like being asked to pick your favourite child. Impossible. They're all different but we love them just the same. Somebody had to show a bit of tough love, though, so here we go...

3

Naturesbase, Ceredigion
Each of the 10 precious pitches has been carefully mown into wild-flower strewn meadows at this friendly eco site, a short drive away from Wales' best beach. **p168**

4

Noongallas, Cornwall
It might be the sheltered valley location with the sea in the distance, or it could be the delightful idiosyncratic way the site is run, but we know there's magic at Noongallas. **p24**

7

Celtic Camping, Pembrokeshire
A picture is worth a thousand words. Just take a look at that view! It's real and waiting at this stunning West Walian site with direct access to a beach and coastal path. **p164**

8

Yellow Wood, Herefordshire/Powys
Go 'bush' and camp under a tarp in the middle of ancient woodlands. No electricity here, just the sound of twigs snapping as the local wildlife scuttles around. **p138**

1 Wapsbourne Manor Farm, Sussex

Like a favoured blankie, Wowo becomes more special with each year. The communal pizza nights, kids' courses, campfires, rope swings and relaxed philosophy earn it top spot. **p100**

2 Comrie Croft, Perthshire

With onsite fun and actvities galore, this Scottish eco site is a wee gem for families in need of a rural escape to the breathtaking scenery of Perthshire. **p270**

5 Dome Garden, Gloucestershire

Grand Designs meets camping. All the freedom that kids need in a magical garden inhabited by geodesic domes, with funky sleeping pods. Plus tree-swings galore and a pizza oven. **p128**

6 TheCanoeMan, Norfolk

Just you, your canoe and the open river. Spot wildlife and enjoy the leisurely paddle to your very own tipi on the reeded banks of Norfolk's marvellously meandering Upper Bure. **p200**

9 Fisherground, Cumbria

An adventure playground and a rafting pond are just the start of the thrills at Fisherground. When you want some seaside fun, just hop on the steam train to the Cumbrian coast. **p250**

10 Treehouse, Powys

A kid's dream. A tree house – with bunkbeds – that you can stay in. Doze off to the sounds of the wind in the trees, owls hooting and the crackling of the wood-burner. **p184**

campsites at a glance

COOL FOR TOTS   page

1 Noongallas   24
2 Westerley   28
3 Higher Pentreath Farm   30
4 Tregedna Farm   34
5 Arthur's Field   38
6 Higher Moor   42
7 Ruthern Valley   44
8 Mayrose Farm   46
9 Cornish Yurts   50
10 Cerenety   52
12 Devon Yurt   62
14 Highfield Farm   68
16 Caffyns Farm   74
17 Cloud Farm   78
18 Somerset Yurts   82
20 Eweleaze Farm   88
21 Rosewall   90
22 Stoneywish   96
23 Wapsbourne Manor Farm   100
24 Safari Britain   104
25 Cobbs Hill Farm   108
26 Nethergong Nurseries   110
27 Swiss Farm   114
28 Britchcombe Farm   116
29 Cotswold Farm Park   120
30 Viaduct Barn   124
31 Dome Garden   128
32 Tresseck   132
33 Wriggles Brook   134
35 Astro Clear View   142
36 Pencelli Castle   150
37 Erwlon   152
38 Tir Bach Farm   154
39 Dale Hill Farm   158
40 Trehenlliw Farm   162
42 Naturesbase   168
45 Gwerniago   180
47 The Green Caravan Park   188
48 Bosworth Water Trust   190

49 The Dandelion Hideaway   192
51 Clippesby Hall   198
53 Nature's Path   204
54 Manor Farm   206
55 Kelling Heath   210
59 Rowter Farm   224
60 Rosedale Abbey   230
62 Rukin's Park Lodge   236
63 Holme Open Farm   238
64 4 Winds   242
65 Wild in Style   246
66 Fisherground   250
67 Solway View   254
68 Balloch O'Dee   256
69 Tibbie Shiels   260
70 Culzean Castle   264
71 Seal Shore   268
72 Comrie Croft   270
73 Iona Campsite   274
74 Calgary Bay   278
75 Borlum Farm   282

COOL FOR INBETWEENERS

all of the sites in this book

COOL FOR TEENS

1 Noongallas   24
2 Westerley   28
3 Higher Pentreath Farm   30
5 Arthur's Field   38
6 Higher Moor   42
10 Cerenety   52
16 Caffyns Farm   74
17 Cloud Farm   78
19 Rocks East   84
20 Eweleaze Farm   88
22 Stoneywish   96
23 Wapsbourne Manor Farm   100
24 Safari Britain   104
26 Nethergong Nurseries   110

27 Swiss Farm   114
29 Cotswold Farm Park   120
30 Viaduct Barn   124
31 Dome Garden   128
32 Tresseck   132
34 Yellow Wood   138
35 Astro Clear View   142
36 Pencelli Castle   150
38 Tir Bach Farm   154
40 Trehenlliw Farm   162
41 Celtic Camping   164
42 Naturesbase   168
45 Gwerniago   180
46 Treehouse   184
48 Bosworth Water Trust   190
49 The Dandelion Hideaway   192
50 Cliff House   196
51 Clippesby Hall   198
52 TheCanoeMan   200
55 Kelling Heath   210
60 Rosedale Abbey   230
70 Culzean Castle   264
71 Seal Shore   268
72 Comrie Croft   270
75 Borlum Farm   282

BEACH WITHIN REACH

1 Noongallas   24
2 Westerley   28
3 Higher Pentreath Farm   30
4 Tregedna Farm   34
5 Arthur's Field   38
6 Higher Moor   42
8 Mayrose Farm   46
9 Cornish Yurts   50
10 Cerenety   52
11 Maker Camping   56
15 Coombe View Farm   72
16 Caffyns Farm   74
20 Eweleaze Farm   88

21	Rosewall	90
22	Stoneywish	96
39	Dale Hill Farm	158
40	Trehenlliw Farm	162
41	Celtic Camping	164
50	Cliff House	196
54	Manor Farm	206
56	Wild Luxury	212
57	High Sand Creek	216
67	Solway View	254
70	Culzean Castle	264
71	Seal Shore	268
73	Iona Campsite	274
74	Calgary Bay	278

COOL FOR CAMPFIRES (whether open, communal or in designated spots, firepits, chimeneas, etc)

1	Noongallas	24
2	Westerley	28
5	Arthur's Field	38
8	Mayrose Farm	46
9	Cornish Yurts	50
10	Cerenety	52
11	Maker Camping	56
12	Devon Yurt	62
13	Runnage Farm	66
14	Highfield Farm	68
15	Coombe View Farm	72
16	Caffyns Farm	74
17	Cloud Farm	78
18	Somerset Yurts	82
19	Rocks East	84
20	Eweleaze Farm	88
22	Stoneywish	96
23	Wapsbourne Manor Farm	100
24	Safari Britain	104
26	Nethergong Nurseries	110
28	Britchcombe Farm	116
30	Viaduct Barn	124
31	Dome Garden	128
32	Tresseck	132
33	Wriggles Brook	134
34	Yellow Wood	138
35	Astro Clear View	142
38	Tir Bach Farm	154
40	Trehenlliw Farm	162
41	Celtic Camping	164
42	Naturesbase	168
44	Woodhouse Farm	176
45	Gwerniago	180
49	The Dandelion Hideaway	192
52	TheCanoeMan	200
53	Nature's Path	204
56	Wild Luxury	212
62	Rukin's Park Lodge	236
63	Holme Open Farm	238
64	4 Winds	242
65	Wild in Style	246
66	Fisherground	250
67	Solway View	254
68	Balloch O'Dee	256
69	Tibbie Shiels	260
71	Seal Shore (on beach only)	268
72	Comrie Croft	270
74	Calgary Bay (on beach only)	278

FOR FIRST-TIME CAMPERS

5	Arthur's Field	38
6	Higher Moor	42
8	Mayrose Farm	46
9	Cornish Yurts	50
12	Devon Yurt	62
15	Coombe View Farm	72
18	Somerset Yurts	82
21	Rosewall	90
23	Wapsbourne Manor Farm	100
24	Safari Britain	104
27	Swiss Farm	114
31	Dome Garden	128
33	Wriggles Brook	134
36	Pencelli Castle	150
37	Erwlon	152
38	Tir Bach Farm	154
41	Celtic Camping	164
42	Naturesbase	168
46	Treehouse	184
49	The Dandelion Hideaway	192
50	Cliff House	196
51	Clippesby Hall	198
53	Nature's Path	204
56	Wild Luxury	212
64	4 Winds	242
65	Wild in Style	246
70	Culzean Castle	264
72	Comrie Croft	270
75	Borlum Farm	282

FOR CAR-LESS CAMPERS

6	Higher Moor	42
10	Cerenety	52
14	Highfield Farm	68
24	Safari Britain	104
27	Swiss Farm	114
30	Viaduct Barn	124

31	Dome Garden	128
35	Astro Clear View	142
37	Erwlon	152
46	Treehouse	184
48	Bosworth Water Trust	190
49	The Dandelion Hideaway	192
54	Manor Farm	206
58	Haddon Grove	220
61	Masons	232
62	Rukin's Park Lodge	236
64	4 Winds	242
65	Wild in Style	246
70	Culzean Castle	264
71	Seal Shore	268
72	Comrie Croft	270
73	Iona Campsite	274
75	Borlum Farm	282

DOG FRIENDLY (on leads mostly)

1	Noongallas	24
2	Westerley	28
3	Higher Pentreath Farm	30
4	Tregedna Farm	34
5	Arthur's Field	38
6	Higher Moor	42
11	Maker Camping	56
13	Runnage Farm	66
14	Highfield Farm	68
15	Coombe View Farm	72
16	Caffyns Farm	74
17	Cloud Farm	78
21	Rosewall	90
22	Stoneywish	96
23	Wapsbourne Manor Farm	100

25	Cobbs Hill Farm	108
28	Britchcombe Farm	116
29	Cotswold Farm Park	120
30	Viaduct Barn	124
32	Tresseck	132
35	Astro Clear View	142
37	Erwlon	152
38	Tir Bach Farm	154
39	Dale Hill Farm	158
40	Trehenlliw Farm	162
41	Celtic Camping	164
42	Naturesbase	168
44	Woodhouse Farm	176
45	Gwerniago	180
47	The Green Caravan Park	188
48	Bosworth Water Trust	190
49	The Dandelion Hideaway	192
50	Cliff House	196
51	Clippesby Hall	198
53	Nature's Path	204
54	Manor Farm	206
55	Kelling Heath	210
56	Wild Luxury	212
57	High Sand Creek	216
58	Haddon Grove	220
59	Rowter Farm	224
60	Rosedale Abbey	230
61	Masons	232
62	Rukin's Park Lodge	236
66	Fisherground	250
67	Solway View	254
68	Balloch O'Dee	256
69	Tibbie Shiels	260
70	Culzean Castle	264

71	Seal Shore	268
72	Comrie Croft	270
73	Iona Campsite	274
74	Calgary Bay	278
75	Borlum Farm	282

STUNNING VIEWS

1	Noongallas	24
3	Higher Pentreath Farm	30
4	Tregedna Farm	34
5	Arthur's Field	38
6	Higher Moor	42
8	Mayrose Farm	46
10	Cerenety	52
11	Maker Camping	56
12	Devon Yurt	62
16	Caffyns Farm	74
17	Cloud Farm	78
20	Eweleaze Farm	88
21	Rosewall	90
24	Safari Britain	104
29	Cotswold Farm Park	120
30	Viaduct Barn	124
33	Wriggles Brook	134
35	Astro Clear View	142
38	Tir Bach Farm	154
39	Dale Hill Farm	158
40	Trehenlliw Farm	162
41	Celtic Camping	164
42	Naturesbase	168
43	Denmark Farm	172
44	Woodhouse Farm	176
45	Gwerniago	180
46	Treehouse	184

47	The Green Caravan Park	188
54	Manor Farm	206
57	High Sand Creek	216
58	Haddon Grove	220
59	Rowter Farm	224
61	Masons	232
62	Rukin's Park Lodge	236
63	Holme Open Farm	238
64	4 Winds	242
68	Balloch O'Dee	256
70	Culzean Castle	264
71	Seal Shore	268
72	Comrie Croft	270
73	Iona Campsite	274
74	Calgary Bay	278
75	Borlum Farm	282

COOL FOR CAMPERVANS

1	Noongallas	24
2	Westerley	28
3	Higher Pentreath Farm	30
4	Tregedna Farm	34
5	Arthur's Field	38
6	Higher Moor	42
7	Ruthern Valley	44
8	Mayrose Farm	46
11	Maker Camping	56
14	Highfield Farm	68
15	Coombe View Farm	72
16	Caffyns Farm	74
17	Cloud Farm	78
19	Rocks East	84
20	Eweleaze Farm	88
21	Rosewall	90
22	Stoneywish	96

23	Wapsbourne Manor Farm	100
25	Cobbs Hill Farm	108
27	Swiss Farm	114
28	Britchcombe Farm	116
29	Cotswold Farm Park	120
36	Pencelli Castle	150
37	Erwlon	152
38	Tir Bach Farm	154
39	Dale Hill Farm	158
40	Trehenlliw Farm	162
41	Celtic Camping	164
44	Woodhouse Farm	176
45	Gwerniago	180
47	The Green Caravan Park	188
48	Bosworth Water Trust	190
50	Cliff House	196
51	Clippesby Hall	198
54	Manor Farm	206
55	Kelling Heath	210
57	High Sand Creek	216
58	Haddon Grove	220
59	Rowter Farm	224
60	Rosedale Abbey	230
61	Masons	232
63	Holme Open Farm	238
66	Fisherground	250
67	Solway View	254
68	Balloch O'Dee	256
69	Tibbie Shiels	260
70	Culzean Castle	264
71	Seal Shore	268
75	Borlum Farm	282

SPLASHING ABOUT (campsites with lakes, swimming pools, rivers or streams that can be played in)

13	Runnage Farm	66
14	Highfield Farm	68
17	Cloud Farm	78
23	Wapsbourne Manor Farm	100
27	Swiss Farm	114
28	Britchcombe Farm	116
32	Tresseck	132
38	Tir Bach Farm	154
42	Naturesbase	168
44	Woodhouse Farm	176
46	Treehouse	184
47	The Green Caravan Park	188
48	Bosworth Water Trust	190
50	Cliff House	196
51	Clippesby Hall	198
52	TheCanoeMan	200
60	Rosedale Abbey	230
61	Masons	232
62	Rukin's Park Lodge	236
63	Holme Open Farm	238
64	4 Winds	242
65	Wild in Style	246
66	Fisherground	250
68	Balloch O'Dee	256
69	Tibbie Shiels	260
72	Comrie Croft	270

ANIMAL MAGIC

5	Arthur's Field	38
7	Ruthern Valley	44
8	Mayrose Farm	46
9	Cornish Yurts	50

10	Cerenety	52
12	Devon Yurt	62
15	Coombe View Farm	72
18	Somerset Yurts	82
22	Stoneywish	96
24	Safari Britain	104
25	Cobbs Hill Farm	108
26	Nethergong Nurseries	110
29	Cotswold Farm Park	120
31	Dome Garden	128
35	Astro Clear View	142
38	Tir Bach Farm	154
42	Naturesbase	168
44	Woodhouse Farm	176
45	Gwerniago	180
47	The Green Caravan Park	188
49	The Dandelion Hideaway	192
52	TheCanoeMan	200
54	Manor Farm	206
56	Wild Luxury	212
59	Rowter Farm	224
63	Holme Open Farm	238
67	Solway View	254
68	Balloch O'Dee	256
72	Comrie Croft	270
73	Iona Campsite	274

LUXURY CAMPING

8	Mayrose Farm	46
9	Cornish Yurts	50
12	Devon Yurt	62
18	Somerset Yurts	82
23	Wapsbourne Manor Farm	100
24	Safari Britain	104

28	Britchcombe Farm	116
31	Dome Garden	128
33	Wriggles Brook	134
38	Tir Bach Farm	154
46	Treehouse	184
49	The Dandelion Hideaway	192
53	Nature's Path	204
56	Wild Luxury	212
64	4 Winds	242
65	Wild in Style	246
72	Comrie Croft	270

PLAYIN' AROUND (campsites with playgrounds)

4	Tregedna Farm	34
5	Arthur's Field	38
7	Ruthern Valley	44
21	Rosewall	90
25	Cobbs Hill Farm	108
27	Swiss Farm	114
28	Britchcombe Farm	116
29	Cotswold Farm Park	120
31	Dome Garden	128
36	Pencelli Castle	150
37	Erwlon	152
38	Tir Bach Farm	154
47	The Green Caravan Park	188
48	Bosworth Water Trust	190
50	Cliff House	196
51	Clippesby Hall	198
54	Manor Farm	206
55	Kelling Heath	210
60	Rosedale Abbey	230
63	Holme Open Farm	238

64	4 Winds	242
65	Wild in Style	246
66	Fisherground	250
67	Solway View	254
69	Tibbie Shiels	260
70	Culzean Castle	264
72	Comrie Croft	270

SURF'S UP

3	Higher Pentreath Farm	30
6	Higher Moor	42
9	Cornish Yurts	50
10	Cerenety	52
11	Maker Camping	56
16	Caffyns Farm	74
40	Trehenlliw Farm	162
41	Celtic Camping	164
67	Solway View	254
71	Seal Shore	268
74	Calgary Bay	278

a mum's guide

Kids just love camping. There are few phrases that elicit more delight than 'let's go camping!' 'Want some chocolate?' might come a close second!

the best fun

You'd be hard pressed to find a child that doesn't jump at the chance to forgo baths, cook on campfires and spend the night sleeping in a field. Whether you are entertaining your own children, or some you've borrowed for the weekend, camping is some of the best fun that children and grown-ups can have together – out in the fresh air, without all the trappings of modern life and taking a break from the daily routine. And the great thing is that it doesn't really need all that much planning in advance, doesn't have to cost very much and pretty much anyone can do it, regardless of where they live or whether or not they drive a car.

reconnecting with kids

Breaking out of the normal routine of everyday life is also a brilliant way to reconnect with your children and spend some quality time together away from the usual distractions and necessities of life at home. And children really love the fact that, for a few days, you can all kick back and dispense with those phrases that drive us all mad: 'If you don't put your shoes on now we're going to miss the bus/Where's your book bag?/You didn't forget your lunch box again did you?/Is that the time? We're going to be late' that govern most parents' and kids' lives. Camping and children are a match made in heaven – just keep a few basic rules in mind and you'll have some very, very happy, fun-sized campers on your hands indeed.

cutting the clutter

We don't want to start *Cool Camping: Kids* with a long list of complicated items for you to rush out and buy. Camping isn't about a retail experience: it's about a real experience. Of course, if you want to go to a camping shop and spend a hefty sum on lots of plasticky nylon bits of camping equipment then go ahead; there's no doubt such retail therapy can be a lot of fun. Just remember that it's not strictly necessary and it's certainly not essential. Camping is all about cutting a lot of clutter out of life. So break free from the screen addiction that dominates our lives and leave the plastic at home. Certainly, you can, if you are very well organised, equip each child with a torch, a disposable camera and a backpack full of favourite toys and books, but it might be much more sensible to reckon on the fact that they'll probably lose all those things the moment they get out of the car.

getting your tent legs

A happy camping trip should be framed by the experience of getting out into a beautiful part of the country, perhaps somewhere you've never visited before, throwing up a tent, perhaps borrowed, and then getting down to some serious fun with your kids. It's as simple as that: homemade fun, like homemade food, is our favourite variety. As well as saving money, cutting back on kit will make your trip a lot less stressful. Squeezing everything you own, plus the kitchen sink, into

your car is probably not that much fun for you, or your family. There are a few basic things to bring, or to do, when you are planning a camping trip with children. If you're first-time campers, then it's probably best to borrow kit and head out for a night or two, not all that far from home. This way you can work out exactly what you need to take for a longer trip further afield. Don't start your inaugural trip with a 10-hour drive to some far-flung spot, because camping close to home is best until you really get your tent legs: long car trips are tiring and, wherever you live, there are sure to be some tip-top campsites nearby.

choosing a site

When it comes to site selection, remember that pre-warned is pre-armed. Find out what facilities are available beforehand. We all have different tastes, and so do our children, and while some kids will love the lack of boundaries of the more basic sites, others will respond very positively to play facilities and spanking-clean showers being laid on. Try to arrive at your site in plenty of time before dark, so that your kids have time to orientate themselves, explore new surroundings and perhaps even make a new friend or two. Pitching a tent in the dark, while trying to placate hungry, car-tired children, isn't the best start to your holiday. Arriving just after

lunch, perhaps having stopped for a picnic on the way, is ideal; you can then choose a lovely spot, get your camp sorted out and be cheffing up a tasty teatime treat by late afternoon. You might even be able to fit in a trip to the seaside/run through the woods/walk on the moor as well.

putting safety first

You'll probably find that your children will make friends, fast, with your site neighbours. Free from adult social hang-ups, kids eye each other up and get stuck into a game of football pretty quickly. Make sure you've checked out the site beforehand, so that you are aware of any cliff-top paths or meandering streams, and know exactly how close the site is to the nearest road. We don't go in for huge municipal sites in this book, so if you're staying on a site listed here, we hope that it'll be a small, friendly site with lots of other children for yours to play with. Having said that, it's easy to lose sight of a child, quickly, between tents. Camping should give your kids a chance to push the boundaries a bit, in a safe environment, but the younger your kids are, the more nerve-wracking this can be. Knowing about potential hazards can help you relax and make you feel less of a headless chicken when you're squawking round the site trying to locate them for tea.

cooking up a storm

Campfire cooking, or cooking on a barbecue, is one of the great delights of camping with kids. If you're lucky enough to find a site where you can have a fire (and, happily, there are lots about – see p14 for listings), educate your children to respect the flames. Children and fires are a dangerous combination, but part of the pleasure of camping is that it gives them a chance to learn practical skills that they might be missing in normal life. Lots of us don't have open fires at home, but being able to light and understand a proper fire is a handy life skill. Teach them to cook on that fire, and you might have a budding camp chef on your hands. But whether they are cooking mackerel or toasting marshmallows, teaching them how to respect a fire is a lot more useful than banning them from going anywhere near it. And there are few things more pleasurable in life than sitting round a glowing campfire with your kids, drinking mugs of steaming hot chocolate.

getting a lie-in

Don't get your knickers in a twist if your children break their usual night-time curfew. That's half the fun of camping. And you can take consolation from the fact that if they are knackered in the morning, you might get a good extra half hour of sleep or more in your own sleeping bag.

having wet-weather fun

We know that our great British weather can make or break a camping trip and we really hope that you're camping under glorious sunny skies, but if you aren't, don't despair, as certain strategies can help you cope. A bit of pre-trip research, checking out the forecast and, if it's looking grim, genning up on local museums, castles, activity centres, swimming pools and cinemas will be time well spent. If you're feeling energetic, just brave the rain and relish the fact that you can run around on an empty beach, where you would have been getting wet anyway.

keeping dry

One of the first rules of scouts is that in wet weather you must keep your top half dry and there's no need to worry about your legs. A mac over shorts and wellies is a good combo: long trousers stay wet all day, but skin dries in no time. It's always nice to make your tent cosy, but it's essential when the weather's grim. An extra blanket under sleeping bags will keep kids warmer than one on top, as cold comes up through the ground, and have a no-shoes rule in the tent. The last thing you want is to curl up in a sleeping bag coated with mud. It's also a good rule to keep one set of dry clothes for each child down their sleeping bag. And when packing, you can never take too many socks. But don't let rain spoil your fun; remember that your children probably mind about it a lot less than you do. Most children relish the anarchy of wet weather, and its mud-sliding opportunities.

take a play tent?

Packing a football or rounders bat means you've always got a game handy for your children to occupy themselves with. Board games and cards are useful for wet weather, but fiddly little counters and pieces will quickly get lost. Wink murder (see p61) is probably much simpler, and it doesn't cost a penny. If your sleeping tent isn't capacious, why not take along a little extra tent for playing in, especially if your children are small? It can become a base for games and means that muddy or wet children don't sit on top of their lovely dry, clean bedding. It also gives them a sense of having their own space and can easily become a Wendy house, space rocket, magic castle or witches' den, depending on what mood your children are in.

Most of all, just have fun. Camping is all about spending time together: cooking together, playing together and, at the end of the day, snuggling up together. It's that simple.

last but not least...

■ It's easy to forget… a water container, matches, towels, anoraks, tin openers, corkscrew, washing-up liquid and sponge.
■ Camping will be easier with… fold-up chairs, wind-up torches, chopping board, foil, coolbox, chocolate.

noongallas

If you happened to see a real-live hobbit sitting on a grassy knoll at Noongallas, we really wouldn't be at all surprised. This site is full to the brim with fairy glens and mystical glades, where you can make camping magic all of your own.

There's something a little magical about the owner John Line and his campsite, the curiously and wonderfully named Noongallas. JRR Tolkien, famed author of imagination-firing books *The Hobbit* and *The Lord of the Rings*, would have probably loved it here, and the two of them could have traded their expert knowledge, too.

He can tell you, for example, how many fledglings have hatched in the dance hall he built. He might then show you the best place to pick chanterelle mushrooms (which sell for a small fortune in a fancy deli), and he will help you find the footpath through nearby Trevalyor Woods, where beech trees hang over a bubbling stream.

And the site, sitting on croft land, is pretty special, too, nestled at the edge of a fairly steep area divided into five fields by gorse hedges and waist-high bracken. It's the perfect spot for children to shake off term-time traumas: and the fact that families tend to stay on site during the day tells you a lot about how convivial and peaceful it is.

Acoustic musicians love it here, and you'll often hear a didgeridoo or guitar around the campfire of a balmy summer evening. In the mornings, a pop-up shop appears in the form of Adrienne in her campervan with a host of fresh pastries, bacon sandwiches and coffees.

Ask John what he likes best about running the site and he'll chuckle and tell you that it makes him feel like he's on holiday all the time. One night here, and you can see why.

Noongallas, Gulval, nr Penzance, Cornwall TR20 8YR; 01736 366698; www.noongallas.com

THE UPSIDE With the sea in the distance and fields surrounding you, there's a real sense of space and harmony on the site, assisted by John's idiosyncratic entertainment in the dance hall.

THE DOWNSIDE The facilities might be too wild for some.

WHO'S IN? Tents, small campervans, groups, dogs – yes. Caravans, motorhomes – no. Campfires (wood £5) allowed.

THE FACILITIES Unmarked pitches are scattered across several of the 6 fields. There are flat alcoves and terracing to make pitching easier, as the site is on a slope. Two clean, basic showers and 6 loos can be found in a block divided into male and female. John provides a washing-up sink that he describes as 'quaint'; so don't expect brand-spanking-new facilities but a mellow, low-impact site. There's a recycling area and fridge-freezers in the dance hall for campers.

ONSITE FUN Gangs of very happy children roam the site, as this is a place that families return to again and again. There are a few 'crash pads' for kids to jump about on in one of the fields, but most of the fun is of their own invention. There's a stream running through a mystical beech glade at the bottom of the field, where children lose track of the day creating camps and making dams. Noongallas's gloriously dilapidated dance hall attracts a lot of musicians; you'll find a party for all ages in full swing most summer evenings.

OFFSITE FUN The best local beach is at Treen. Go there for low tide and you will find two islands and a lagoon to mess around in. There are other beaches at Mounts Bay, Long Rock and Marazion, and at the beach at Porthcurno you might even see a dolphin. Penzance is almost at the bottom of the hill. There are fake pirate ships to explore there, but don't expect

non-stop entertainment as you can exhaust the town in a couple of hours. Trevarno Gardens (01326 574274; www.trevarno.co.uk) are worth a visit on a sunny day. At Gweek there's the National Seal Sanctuary (08714 232110; www.sealsanctuary.co.uk). Head south-west and you'll find the famous, and rather fabulous, Minack Open Air Theatre (01736 810181; www.minack.com). Ancient mysticism can be found at Chysauster Iron Age village at New Mill and the Merry Maidens stone circle at St Buryan, further down the coast.

IF IT RAINS Young children love the animals and bird shows at Paradise Park wildlife sanctuary in Hayle (01736 753365, www.paradisepark.org.uk), which also boasts the excellent indoor Jungle Barn soft-play area. All ages ought to love St Michael's Mount (01736 710507; www.stmichaelsmount.co.uk); the guides there are especially good at recounting the house's ghost stories.

FOOD AND DRINK There's an ice cream shop on the bridge at Newlyn called Jelberts, and the ices there are fantastic. The Coldstreamer Inn (01736 362072; www.coldstreamer-penzance.co.uk), 2 miles away, does good food; but if you don't mind a drive, the Gurnard's Head hotel (01736 796928; www.gurnardshead.co.uk) serves excellent meals and has folk-music nights on Mondays. You could always buy a bit of haddock (smoked and undyed) at Tesco in Penzance and ask John for his truly delicious chowder recipe.

NANNY STATE ALERT At the bottom of the hill in the trees there's a little stream.

GETTING THERE Follow the A30 from Hayle through Cockwells and Whitecross to Crowlas. At a crossroads after the pub turn right. Follow the road through Ludgvan and bear left after the sign to Vellanoweth. This road runs parallel to the A30 for 2 miles, when you come to Gulval Churchtown. Do not bear left at the church, but pass it on your left. At the junction signed to the B3311 turn left to Penzance, then immediately right, signposted 'Rosemorran and Polkinghorne'. Noongallas is just over a mile up the narrow lane.

PUBLIC TRANSPORT Train to Penzance, then either walk the 2 miles to the site or catch the irregular bus (towards New Mill) which stops near the site, or just hop in a taxi (journey of around 10 minutes).

OPEN July–August.

THE DAMAGE Adult £6 per night; child (under 14) £3.

westerley

A faraway field, a fire and a friendly farmer. And that story of the Emperor's new clothes. Everyone came out to see him parading through the town, and they clapped and cheered, even though he had nothing on!

Do you remember that traditional story about the Emperor's new clothes? Well, this site, Westerley, is rather like that when it comes to dispensing with the frills and embracing what's purely natural.

We love it even though there's actually nothing there. And that's quite a rare phenomenon in this justifiably popular part of Cornwall – the coast around St Ives is pretty much heaving with places to pitch your tent. If, that is, you want to stay on a characterless municipal site with tent wall to tent wall, bingo and all-night karaoke. At Cool Camping, that's not our idea of fun.

But, in fact, we do like Westerley a lot, because although it's essentially just a couple of fields separated by a gorse hedge, it's well set back from the road, you can pitch wherever you like and the beach is just a walk away; so you can leave the masses of Babylon behind.

Dare we say this? But the fact that it's so basic actually makes Westerley feel rather exclusive – in a funny sort of way. And there's also the not-inconsiderable fact that the farmer, Mr Stevenson, is a bit of a diamond, who really wants everyone to have a good time here. He'll deliver logs to your tent if you want a little fire and has been spotted helping the uninitiated and newcomers struggling with a tangle of guy ropes.

Even the Emperor couldn't complain about that, now, could he?

Westerley Campsite, Balnoon, St Ives, Cornwall TR26 3JH; 01736 794853; www.westerleycampsite.co.uk

THE UPSIDE Your kids will be within sight all the time, but there's enough room for onsite fun. The beach is a walk away.

THE DOWNSIDE It might be a bit basic for first-timers.

WHO'S IN? Tents, motorhomes, campervans, groups, dogs – yes. Caravans – no. Campfires and barbecues allowed.

THE FACILITIES There are 3 new wetroom-style showers and 6 toilets, hot water for washing-up, mobile-phone charging, a fridge-freezer, washing machine and 8 hook-ups.

ONSITE FUN Space to run around in and geese to feed.

OFFSITE FUN You can get to Carbis Bay Beach by walking down the lane and along a footpath. St Ives isn't far. Ponies can be hired at Penhalvin riding school, a 10-minute walk away.

IF IT RAINS Paradise Park bird sanctuary is open all year (see p27). Head underground at Geevor Tin Mine (www. geevor.com) or Poldark Tin Mine (www.poldark-mine.co.uk).

FOOD AND DRINK The Countryman, at the end of the lane, does cream teas and is only a 10-minute walk away. Bill and Flo's Farm Shop (01736 798885) in Lelant is good.

NANNY STATE ALERT A main road at the top of the track.

GETTING THERE From the A30, take the bypass for St Ives when you get to the Hayle roundabout. At the next roundabout turn right. Go to the second mini roundabout past the garden centre and take a sharp left. Pass the Balnoon Inn and go up the lane on your right, 45 metres past the inn (signposted 'Balnoon'). The site is 650 metres along on the left.

PUBLIC TRANSPORT Train to St Ives and catch Western Greyhound bus no. 508/516 to Balnoon. Walk to the site.

OPEN August, but application has been made to extend this.

THE DAMAGE Adult £6 per night; child £2–£4. Dogs free.

St Ives

higher pentreath farm

Beach, beach, beach. It's all about the beach. And what a very lovely beach it is, too – all big and golden and sandy – just crying out for an energetic game of kiss-chase, kick-the-can or frisbee. And did we mention the beach?

In a county of pretty good beaches, Cornwall's Praa Sands is right up there, waving its blue flag with pride and helpfully cleaning its own sands every day with a gentle tide. Its wide, flat reach and safe waters mean it's popular with families; the reliable waves are popular with surfer-dads, while the athletic surfers and bronzed lifeguards are popular with the mums. Yes, it's a popular old place, but there's plenty of room here for everybody.

From its bird's-eye vantage point above all this hubbub, Higher Pentreath Farm surveys the day. It observes the crack-of-dawn surfers, the pre-breakfast dog-walkers and the café coffee-sippers. It watches the daytrippers come and go and the evening joggers run to and fro. And as the setting sun lights the bay with the red and golden tones of summer evenings, those lucky campers at Higher Pentreath need only step outside their tents to appreciate this special cove.

The three fields that form the site offer increasingly better views the higher up you go; but the price you pay for this amazing hillside location is the sloping ground, so be prepared. It's also worth noting that the slope to the beach makes it quick and easy to get to, but exponentially harder to get back from. Better just to sit and watch it all from the camping chair. Another beer, anyone?

Higher Pentreath Farm, Praa Sands, Penzance, Cornwall TR20 9TL; 01736 763222

THE UPSIDE The view, the beach, the excuse that it's just too difficult to get back up that hill.

THE DOWNSIDE It can get pretty crowded in summer, and the facilities aren't the greatest.

WHO'S IN? Tents, campervans, caravans, motorhomes, groups, dogs (on leads) – yes. No campfires allowed, but barbecues off the grass are permitted.

THE FACILITIES The main block has 12 loos and 4 showers for ladies and just 1 shower, 3 toilets plus some urinals for gents. But don't feel like you're the victims of sexism here guys, as there's a smaller block behind the farmhouse with 3 toilets and another shower. They can get a bit mucky during busy times, so have your flip-flops and spare loo roll to hand. There's also a washing machine and ironing board available in the laundry room, 3 large sinks for dishwashing, electric hook-ups and waste-disposal facilities.

ONSITE FUN Loads of lovely space in the main field to run around and around and around in – till everyone's really dizzy.

OFFSITE FUN The beach. Surfboards are available to hire and there are rockpools at either end of the mile-long sands. A pub, café and beach shop are all within easy reach. Further afield, Perranuthnoe Beach, on the edge of Mounts Bay, has surfer- and swimmer-friendly waves and gorgeous golden sands that back on to higgledy-piggledy rocks. Stroll across a causeway (though please check tide times first) to fairy-tale-like St Michael's Mount (01736 710507; www.stmichaelsmount.co.uk) to explore its castle and beautiful subtropical gardens.

IF IT RAINS Flambards in nearby Helston (01326 573404; www.flambards.co.uk) is a vast adventure ride, activities and

exhibitions attraction. The rides are outdoors, but the popular Victorian Village is inside, and there's a brilliant new indoor play zone for 1–11-year-olds. A more cultured alternative would be the Tate – plus the cafés, restaurants and shops – at St Ives, about 20 minutes' drive from here.

FOOD AND DRINK The Sandbar Pub and Restaurant (01736 763516; www.sandbarpraasands.co.uk) is just off the beach and has incredible views. Relax with a beer or healthy smoothie while the kids play pool or air hockey; then tuck into an organic wrap, baguette or fresh beach bite. Further afield, the Bay Restaurant, Café and Gallery (01736 366890; www.thebaypenzance.co.uk) in Penzance has a constantly changing menu featuring freshly caught fish and crabs from the local market, and it also boasts its own gallery and marvellous balcony views.

NANNY STATE ALERT Make sure your bicycle brakes work before spinning off down the hill to the beach.

GETTING THERE From the A30, take the turning for the A394. After approximately 5 miles, turn right onto Pentreath Lane and follow the road for almost ½ mile. Look out for the sign for 'Higher Pentreath' by the second track on the right. Reception is just down the track on the right.

PUBLIC TRANSPORT Train to Penzance then hop onto a First Western National bus no. 2, 2A or 2B to Praa Sands. (If the bus driver's a good 'un you may be lucky enough to get dropped off at the campsite.)

OPEN Easter/1 April (whichever comes first)–31 October.

THE DAMAGE Family of 4 with a car and a large tent £12 per night. Dogs free. Electric hook-ups available for £3 a night.

Praa Sands

tregedna farm

While maritime Falmouth dazzles visitors with a heap of harbour-side attractions, the Maen Valley waits quietly for them to stumble across its treasures. In its midst Tregedna Farm, close to one of Falmouth Bay's finest beaches, has little reason to be shy.

From its dip within the valley, Tregedna Farm is surrounded by countryside as far as the eye can see. Yet daily life here revolves around the nearby beach. And what a beach it is: wedged between the yachty buzz of Falmouth and the peaceful waterway of the Helford river, Maenporth is one of the best-located beaches on Cornwall's south coast. But being a 40-minute walk from Falmouth town, it's far enough to deter the maddening crowds. Putter along the coast towards the Helford and you will usually be rewarded by a deserted nook of sand.

It's a simple life at Tregedna Farm. While the smell of bacon and coffee still lingers, families set off along the footpath on a pilgrimage to the beach. Children skip ahead with buckets and spades; parents straggle behind pushing buggies laden with picnics and wetsuits. When teatime approaches, the pilgrims return, Hansel and Gretel trails of sand in their wake, the children lagging behind sporting salt-water mops and ice-cream-smudged smiles.

During the evenings, barbecue smoke fills the air and the chatter of children swirls around the tents until long after school-day bedtime. But as the sun drops so do the kids, leaving just the chink of wine glasses and the patter of footsteps to and from the dishwashing area. This easy routine greets day after day, broken only by rainy spells and sightseeing excursions that see the beach gear abandoned as parents scrabble around for the car keys and spin into Falmouth for a dose of arty, maritime culture and a spot of retail therapy.

Tregedna Farm Holidays, Maenporth, Falmouth, Cornwall TR11 5HL; 01326 250529; www.tregednafarmholidays.co.uk

THE UPSIDE The footpath to Maenporth Beach, a stunning bay between Falmouth and the Helford Estuary. Plus there's plenty of room on the site for ball games, bikes and kites.

THE DOWNSIDE The field is slightly sloped, so pick a pitch on one of the flatter edges or on the central ridge.

WHO'S IN? Groups, campervans, caravans, tents, dogs – yes. No campfires; barbecues permitted if raised off the grass.

THE FACILITIES In the 12 green pitch-where-you-like acres there's a refurbished toilet block with male/female loos and a separate stone hut with showers (2 male, 2 female), a large indoor washing-up area, local information, washing machine and tumble dryer.

ONSITE FUN There is a play area with swings and a see-saw, but the main appeal is the masses of space for ball games and running around.

OFFSITE FUN Maenporth Beach is the reason for camping here – a sheltered sliver of pebble and sand perfect for bathing and rockpooling. Don't forget your wetsuit, as this is a haven for water sports including swimming, snorkelling and kayaking. Arvor Sea Kayaking (www.askc.org.uk) runs sit-on-top- and sea-kayaking sessions from the beach and along the Helford Estuary. You can beach hop around the headland to Swanpool, where Elemental Adventures (01326 318771; www.elementaluk.com) holds dinghy sailing, windsurfing and coasteering sessions among its beach activities. Stroll along the coastal path and within 45 minutes you can be in the hubbub of Falmouth one way, or on the serene and green banks of the Helford the other way.

PATH to BEACH

Maenporth Beach

IF IT RAINS Whether or not it rains, Falmouth is worth taking a day to explore. Its key family attraction is the National Maritime Museum (01326 313388; www.nmmc.co.uk), where you can delve into maritime history, check out the underwater gallery and take the helm of a model sailing boat. Other tempting attractions include the cinema (01326 313072; www.merlincinemas.co.uk), Pendennis Castle (01326 316594; www.english-heritage.org.uk) and boat trips to St Mawes, Truro and Flushing (www.falriver.co.uk).

FOOD AND DRINK You can get seasonal produce including organic potatoes from the onsite farm shop. For snacks, burgers and ice cream bang on the beach, head to Life's a Beach at Maenporth (www.maenporthbeach.co.uk) or, just behind the beach, the Cove (01326 251136; www.thecovemaenporth.co.uk) serves gourmet cuisine made from the best local ingredients. A 20-minute walk around the headland, the Swanpool Beach Café (www.swanpoolbeach.co.uk) sells legendary ice creams and simple alfresco fare and, if you want a trendy beach hangout for a cocktail or milkshake, step further towards Falmouth to the Gylly Beach Café on Gyllyngvase Beach (01326 312884; www.gyllybeach.com).

NANNY STATE ALERT Be aware that the entrance track for cars slices between the play area and the camping field.

GETTING THERE From Truro, take the A39 to Falmouth, staying on it until you pass Asda, then turn right at the next roundabout (with the black anchor). Go straight across the next 2 mini roundabouts and continue on this road for about 2 miles, following signs to Maenporth. Tregedna Farm is on the right, about ½ mile before the beach.

PUBLIC TRANSPORT Take the train to Penmere on the Truro to Falmouth branch line. The station is about 1½ miles from the campsite.

OPEN Easter–October.

THE DAMAGE Adult £8 per night; child (aged 3–13) £3.50. Hook-up (best to book in advance) £3.

arthur's field

With three little beaches and a heritage farm just outside your tent, it's not hard to see why kids absolutely adore Arthur's Field. Just be ready for hissy fits at going-home time. Well, you can always come back here next year.

You could call site owners Debs and Peter Walker's relationship with Arthur's Field something of a love affair. And a pretty passionate one at that. Just one visit and they were smitten. And when you venture to this point on the south coast where Cornwall dips her heel into the dazzling waters of Falmouth Bay, you can see why.

It's not just because the Roseland Peninsula lives up to, and indeed exceeds, its title as an area of outstanding natural beauty that Arthur's Field is so special. It sits atop the cliffs where verdant pastures tip onto shingle beaches, making you feel so relaxed and fuzzy inside that you want to capture the feeling in a poem or a painting and never let it go. And it's this creative edge that makes the site so much more than a stunning cliff-top field with a few farm animals for the kids to feed.

During the 70s, when Arthur himself ran it, there would be concerts, games and fancy dress parties. Today, with Debs and Peter at the helm, there are fireside storytelling sessions, feast nights celebrating local food, and activity workshops from making stained glass to foraging.

Within strolling distance of three beaches and postcard-pretty Portscatho, Arthur's Field is the sort of site that stressed-out urbanites dream about. Once you pitch your tent there really is little need to get into your car again. The problem is, you'll probably never want to go home. Just like Debs and Peter, you'll end up wanting to live the dream.

Arthur's Field, Treloan Coastal Holidays, Treloan Lane, Gerrans, nr Portscatho, Roseland Peninsula, Truro, Cornwall TR2 5EF; 01872 580989; www.coastalfarmholidays.co.uk

THE UPSIDE A hop and a skip across a field and you can jump straight into the sea, with fantastic walks along the South West Coast Path.

THE DOWNSIDE The site isn't huge, so pitches get booked quickly at peak season.

WHO'S IN? Everyone is welcome as long as you respect other campers and remember it's a family site. Dogs (on leads) – yes. Barbecues are allowed in trays. Braziers can be hired for campfires and there's a communal firepit in a corner of the field.

THE FACILITIES Fifty-seven pitches, all with hook-ups, are spread over 1 field. These days you'll also find an eco-snug and a yurt on the site, both with wood-burners and futons. There are 8 showers, including 3 family, and 6 sinks, including 1 at kid-height, so Junior has no excuse for not washing up his or her hot-chocolate mug.

ONSITE FUN Every morning Debs rings a bell, Pied Piper-like, and children come running to help her collect eggs and feed the sheep, pigs, guinea pigs and rabbits. In summer the cow's field is mown to create a football pitch, and there are cricket stumps, too. Every Wednesday in summer storytellers, poets and musicians gather for a fireside gathering run by Caravanaserai (www.caravanserai.info). Bring a guitar and something for the barbecue, and join in all sorts of workshops, from windsock-making to stained-glass tutorials.

OFFSITE FUN There's private access to 3 secluded beaches, all great for swimming, fishing and diving, especially Treloan Cove and Peter's Splosh. Slightly further are Carne and Towan beaches, both about 1½ miles away, but worth it for the sand.

Porthcurnick beach is walkable from the other side of Portscatho, and seals are regular visitors. Portscatho (www.roseland-online.co.uk) is a lovely place to spend the afternoon fishing or rockpooling; if you're lucky you might spot the distant flipping tails of dolphins. Wander along the coastal path and you may see buzzards, badgers and foxes.

IF IT RAINS Don waterproofs and take a ferry from Place to St Mawes. Catch another to Falmouth. The National Maritime Museum (01326 313388; www.nmmc.co.uk) will keep kids amused for hours. The town's not bad for quirky shopping, especially in charity shops, if you or your teenagers are in urgent need of retail therapy. Local castles include Pendennis Castle (01326 316594) and St Mawes Castle (01326 270526); see www.englishheritage.co.uk for both.

FOOD AND DRINK A fish-and-chip van serves fresh local catches once a week. The Walkers also invite local chefs to come and cook their specialities for campers to eat together or as takeaway, such as paella, chilli and mussels – just bring along a bowl and a drink. Tesco will deliver and the Plume of Feathers and the Royal Standard are within walking distance, as is the Harbour Club (01872 580387; www.theharbourclub.co.uk), which also puts on events such as film showings. Locally caught fish lifts their menus above standard pub grub. The Boathouse (01872 580326; www.theboathouserestaurant.co.uk), in the village, is nice for cream teas, and you can buy fantastic seafood from Ralph's Shop.

NANNY STATE ALERT The site is within walking distance of the cliffs, so little ones should be accompanied.

GETTING THERE Follow the A3078 to Trewithian. Turn left at the 'Treloan Coastal Farm' sign towards Gerrans and Portscatho. Stay on this road until you reach Gerrans Church Square and stop beside the church, opposite the Royal Standard inn. Treloan Lane is marked on the wall here and runs directly to Arthur's Field.

PUBLIC TRANSPORT Catch a train or coach to Truro (about 19 miles from the campsite) then take a bus (no. 50/51) towards St Mawes. Hop off at Portscatho and walk from there.

OPEN All year.

THE DAMAGE Pitch for 2 adults from £13.50 (October–March, excluding Christmas) to £21.50 (summer holidays). Child (over 4) £3.50 per night; dog £1; hook-up £2.30.

higher moor

Abandon the car and don your beach gear. Paddle in Atlantic rollers, tramp along the coastal path and feast on veg from the market garden. With its cracking location and fantastic facilities for kids, Higher Moor is an all-round family winner.

Pristine and preened aren't often words used to describe a campsite. After all, it's just a field to pitch tents in, isn't it? Well no, actually, not in this case. At Higher Moor the grass is so green, the pitches so wide and flat and the landscape so manicured that you feel like guests in a rather large garden.

As a family-friendly location goes, this place is pretty tough to beat: Cubert Common rolling southwards and the secluded sands of Porth Joke just a short (off-road) stroll away. The terrain's buggy-friendly if you've got a three-wheeler, so you can dump the car, pack a picnic and sling a surfboard under your arm. You don't even need to bring your own beach toys – there's a pile of crabbing nets, boogie boards, buckets and spades on site for you to borrow.

Higher Moor is quite simply made for families. The field is safe and enclosed, days are so fun-packed that lights are usually out by 10.30pm, and in the spotless amenities block you'll find baby baths, potties, children's books and steps to help little people reach the sinks. Each pitch comes with its own picnic table for easy alfresco dining.

As well as outdoor chess, clock golf and draughts, families make the most of the space at centre-field and club together for cricket and rounders matches. Many return year on year to try and reclaim victory – at least that's their excuse – and no doubt once you've experienced the quiet seduction of Higher Moor, you'll be finding excuses to come back, too.

Higher Moor, Crantock, Newquay, Cornwall TR8 5QS; 01637 830928; www.highermoor.co.uk

THE UPSIDE Spacious pitches just a stroll from the beach.
THE DOWNSIDE Timer cords on the showers.
WHO'S IN? Groups (not the sort who want nightlife in Newquay), tents, campervans (no electric hook-ups), dogs – yes. No campfires; barbecues raised on blocks provided okay.
THE FACILITIES A 2-acre level field with 22 pitches. Two well-kept amenities blocks have baby baths, potties, steps for toddlers and a disabled/family shower room. Washing-up area, freezer and laundry plus local info, books, games, toys, ironing equipment and a trough for dunking sandy wetsuits.
ONSITE FUN Outdoor draughts, chess and clock golf; there's usually a communal game of cricket or rounders going on.
OFFSITE FUN Access to the coastal path. A 15-minute trot takes you to Porth Joke, a sandy nook between low-lying cliffs.
IF IT RAINS Newquay is just a drive around the headland.
FOOD AND DRINK As well as veg from the market garden, you can pre-order a delivery of fresh fish. Local pubs with good food and real ales: the Smugglers' Den at Cubert, St Pirans at Holywell Bay and the Bowgie Inn overlooking Crantock Beach.
GETTING THERE Come off the A30 at the main Newquay exit and follow the A392 onto the A3075 – the first exit at Trevemper roundabout. Take the first right following signs for West Pentire and, bypassing Crantock, turn left into Treago Farm. Higher Moor is on the right, at the bottom of the hill.
PUBLIC TRANSPORT Bus from Truro (no. 585) or Newquay (no. 587) to Crantock, from where it's about ½ mile to the site.
OPEN Easter–September.
THE DAMAGE Adult £6–£9 (depending on season) per night; child £3–£4.50, under-2s free. Dogs £1.

Porth Joke

Holywell Bay

ruthern valley

Cornwall isn't all about sun, sand and surfing. What about rabbits, woodpeckers, squirrels and trees? Woody, green Ruthern feels a million miles from the bustling Cornish coast, but it's actually only a short drive away.

After a nice day on the beach at Polzeath or Rock, surrounded by surfers and Sloane-rangers, Ruthern Valley is somewhere you can escape to, deliciously hidden among the green canopy of Cornwall's countryside interior.

Close to Bodmin Moor, this secluded, beguiling little site is humming with wildlife, so children can have plenty of fun spotting rabbits and squirrels, and budding ornithologists can look out for woodpeckers a-pecking and listen for owls a-hooting. Having said that, they'll probably enjoy feeding the chickens just as much, too.

It's a top location, with the wild delights of Land's End an hour or so away, and Bodmin Moor, the perfect place for stomping around with children, as you regale them with heady stories about smugglers and highwaymen, isn't far. Or you could cycle to Padstow for a crabbing session on the quay and perhaps a slap-up portion of Mr Stein's famous fish and chips, which is a pretty-much perfect way to while away an afternoon.

Since our last visit, the ugly statics have been replaced by sturdy wooden wigwams that sleep up to five people and come cosily equipped with foam mattresses on bunks, a microwave, kettle and fridge as well as heating, if you'd rather glamp than camp.

Grogley Woods are close to the site and lovely for shady walks. So, at the end of a busy day, when you've had your fill, and more, of sun, sea and sand, what could be better than returning to the peaceful, leafy shade of Ruthern Valley?

Ruthern Valley Holidays, Ruthern Bridge, Bodmin, Cornwall PL30 5LU; 01208 831395; www.ruthernvalley.com

THE UPSIDE A magical place to escape the beach crowds.
THE DOWNSIDE Not ideal for those without wheels.
WHO'S IN? Tents, campervans, caravans – yes. Groups – by arrangement. Dogs – no.
THE FACILITIES Beautifully flat pitches (26), 6 with hook-ups, spread over 4 camping areas. There are 4 solar-powered showers and 2 washing-up sinks plus laundry facilities. There are also timber camping pods that can sleep a family of four.
ONSITE FUN There's a small play area and a football space. In the woods there are lots of places for making dens. The family keeps pigs and chickens, which children can help to feed.
OFFSITE FUN Ruthern Valley is close to the Camel Trail, great for walking or cycling. Riding stables at St Breward.
IF IT RAINS Pencarrow House (www.pencarrow.co.uk) is fun for a day out. Find out about King Arthur at Tintagel Castle.
FOOD AND DRINK The site sells basics and local produce including award-winning curries, Roskilly's ice cream, Rattler cider and fresh baguettes. Cycle 3 miles along the Camel Trail to the child-friendly Borough Arms (www.theborougharms.com).
NANNY STATE ALERT There's a stream by the site.
GETTING THERE On the A30 past Bodmin head for Lanivet (A389). Go through Lanivet until you see Presingoll Pottery on the left. Just before the pottery turn left, signed for Nanstallon. Turn left again, for Ruthern Bridge (chalets), and continue for 2 miles, turning left immediately before the small bridge.
PUBLIC TRANSPORT Train to Bodmin Parkway then taxi on, OPEN All year.
THE DAMAGE Tent from £12.50 for 2 adults plus £3.25–£4.25 per child, per night. Pod from £37.50; wigwam from £45.

Padstow Harbour

mayrose farm

A tent in a greenhouse. This sort of ingenuity you can truly appreciate after a soggy camping trip with kids. Made for the most camping-shy families, this is all-weather camping in Eden. And there's a regular campsite for any non-glampers, too.

Can we really class this as camping? Well, you're staying under canvas. You can light a campfire. And you're surrounded by nature. So it must be. But with an indoor garden, wood-burner, real beds and an all-weather shell, this place takes even the term 'glamping' to another level.

It was a visit to the Eden Project that inspired the creation of the 'glamppod'. After all, if Cornwall's top tourist attraction can pull in the punters in every sort of weather, why can't a campsite do the same? It can, if you erect a family-size safari tent within a large polytunnel. Simply roll up the sides when the sun shines, or hunker down in your cosy canvas cottage when it doesn't. In the glamppod the days are balmy, even when rain is beating down and it's blowing a hoolie. What with a secluded location, valley views, an undercover subtropical garden and more panache than your average country cottage, here you've hit the glamping jackpot.

Down-to-earth campers needn't despair. The beauty of Mayrose Farm doesn't stop at the gate of the private glamppod paddock. Home to a green and pleasant camping field with just a handful of pitches, tent life here comes with full use of the heated courtyard pool, a poolside games room and acres of land tumbling into the Allen Valley. Throw in the farm animals, duck pond and a lush campfire-cum-picnic area, and whether you're glamper or camper, you can't deny this little gem is a camping paradise.

Mayrose Farm Glamppod and Camping, Helstone, Camelford, Cornwall PL32 9RN; 01840 213509; www.glamppod.co.uk; www.mayrosecamping.co.uk

THE UPSIDE All-weather glamping, rolling valley views and toasted marshmallows on the campfire.

THE DOWNSIDE As with all glamping sites, the glamppod is expensive in comparison to camping prices – but worth it.

WHO'S IN? Groups (the glamppod only sleeps 4, but add-ons can shack up in the campsite or cottages), tents, campervans, caravans – yes. No dogs (Collans Cross Kennels is just 5 minutes away, though: 01840 213410; www.collanscross.co.uk).

THE FACILITIES The 4-bed glamppod is split into a double room, bunk room, kitchen/dining room, subtropical garden and shower room. Facilities include a stove, kettle, barbecue, coolbox, wood-burner and firepit. The chemical toilet is in a separate hut. Communal amenities include the outdoor pool and courtyard, a games room (think Jenga, pool table, skittles, books, DVDs and children's toys) and acres of land with a picnic/campfire area by the pond. There are 2 family shower rooms by the poolside for campers. A small honesty shop sells an eclectic range of goodies, from farm-fresh veg and eggs, and home-baked bread and cakes, to hand-painted plaques and crockery.

ONSITE FUN Picnic by the pond and spot ducks, moorhens and wild Canadian geese. Play on the rope swing, explore paths around the farmland and meet the sheep, chickens and rabbits. Alternatively, take a dip in the pool or kick back with a book while the kids raid the toy store.

OFFSITE FUN Mayrose is conveniently wedged between moorland and beaches, so Cornwall's greatest assets are minutes in either direction. Scale the peaks of Brown Willy

and Rough Tor on Bodmin Moor, or take a spin along the flatter terrain of the Camel Trail (www.sustrans.org.uk) as it wends from Poley's Bridge back towards Bodmin. For golden sands and craggy coastline you're spoilt for choice. The closest beach is Trebarwith Strand, a 10-minute drive away, and an excellent spot for mussel picking, surfing and a sundowner. Fanning to the south there's surfy Polzeath, chic Rock and pretty Port Isaac, while to the north stands the dramatic edifice of Tintagel Castle (01840 770328; www.english-heritage.org.uk).

IF IT RAINS Light the wood-burner and get cosy in the glamppod, chill in the poolside lounge or it's just 40 minutes' drive to the bigger biomes of the Eden Project (01726 811911; www.edenproject.com).

FOOD AND DRINK Joint owner Jane Maunder (she runs the site with David Lee) bakes fresh croissants to order and her homemade bread and cakes are available in the shop alongside fresh farm produce. Ten minutes along the road towards Polzeath, at St Endellion, is Trevathan Farm Shop and Restaurant (01208 880248; www.trevathanfarm.com) – a celebration of Cornish fare where you can pick your own berries, stock up on local produce and gorge on award-winning ice cream. It's only 20 minutes' drive to the Camel Valley vineyard to sample world-class wines (01208 77959; www.camelvalley.com) and about the same to Stein's gastronomic delights in Padstow (www.rickstein.com). Closer to the site, both the St Kew Inn (01208 841259; www.stkewinn.co.uk) and the Mill House at Trebarwith (01840 770200; www.themillhouseinn.co.uk) boast excellent reputations for gourmet pub food. Local supermarkets will deliver to the site.

NANNY STATE ALERT Rope swing, (gated) swimming pool and pond to be aware of.

GETTING THERE Coming from the north, follow the A39 through Camelford and into Helstone. Mayrose Farm Cottages and Camping is signposted down a country lane on your left.

PUBLIC TRANSPORT There is a bus into Helstone, but you don't want to camp here without a car.

OPEN April–October.

THE DAMAGE Glamppod £450–£800 per week for 4 people. Camping £16–£26 (depending on season) per night for 2 adults, plus £4–£4.50 per child.

cornish yurts

Campfires. Stargazing from bed. Home comforts under canvas. No wonder yurts are the accommodation of choice in the Mongolian desert. And with a camel farm nearby, Cornish Yurts could be in a foreign land were it not for the British weather.

For a slight and magical peninsula, the Lizard packs in scores of holiday parks. At first glance there seems little in between these caravan cities and a handful of basic camping fields. Thankfully Cornish Yurts bucks the trend with a little more class – and a solution for all the weathers that whip across this sea-ravaged landscape.

Arrive to scones, jam and a copy of the local rag and you immediately feel you've been given the nod to relax and sink onto one of the futons. In such a cosy abode, decked out in furry throws, antique-style furniture, and with a log-burning stove, it's difficult not to kick back and make yourself at home. There's a fully equipped communal kitchen, which even boasts a washing machine and books and games, while a cooking shelter has gas barbecues and hobs. Each yurt even has its own shower room and loo – no, it's not en suite, but this is supposed to be camping, after all.

The yurts being based on a working farm, you can don your wellies and take a tour. Or even better, let the farmer's daughters whisk the kids off to see the calves being milked while you book in for a reflexology treatment with Polly, the farmer's wife, in the farmhouse (£25 per treatment). You may not have chosen an organic beef and dairy farm expecting a romantic holiday, but by night, huddled by the campfire or log-burner, with the candles lit and stars glinting through the roof panel, even with the kids in tow there's an unmistakable note of romance in the air.

Cornish Yurts, Tregeague Farm, St Martin, Helston, Cornwall TR12 6EB; 01326 231211; www.cornishyurts.co.uk

THE UPSIDE Luxury yurting on the magical Lizard Peninsula.

THE DOWNSIDE Camp is set out across 3 separate areas, which can be a little inconvenient in inclement weather.

WHO'S IN? Groups – yes. Tents, dogs, camper/caravans – no.

THE FACILITIES Two yurts, each with its own firepit, garden furniture and family shower room/loo. Interiors are decked out with futons (sleeping up to 6), a log-burner, furniture and electricity. Bring your own sleeping bags or hire bedding.

ONSITE FUN Check out the farm and watch milking time, play on the swings and run around the car-free field.

OFFSITE FUN Meet the camels at Roscuick Organic Farm (www.cornishcamels.com) or take a Segway tour around Goonhilly Earth Station (www.cornwallsegway.co.uk). There's a string of secluded bays and pearly beaches within easy reach.

IF IT RAINS Sound the foghorn and learn morse code on a tour of the Lizard Lighthouse (www.lizardlighthouse.co.uk).

FOOD AND DRINK Roskilly's Farm is the place to buy ice cream, and offers homemade local fare at its family-friendly Croust House Restaurant (www.roskillys.co.uk/croust).

NANNY STATE ALERT There is an axe by the log pile and the field is beside a country lane. It's a working farm, too.

GETTING THERE Head to Traboe Cross on the B3293, continuing through Traboe until you come to a T-junction with a grass triangle and a granite post. Turn right, take the next left and Cornish Yurts is the first farm on the right.

OPEN Easter–end September. Yurts are available during winter by arrangement.

THE DAMAGE £320–£470 per week (Fri–Fri). Off-peak short stays available at 70 per cent of the weekly booking fee.

cerenety

'Happy eco camping' brags the tagline. And happy is just what you'll feel here if you're eco-minded and wild about camping. Just a short walk from the kiss-me-quick seaside at Bude, at Cerenety tent life is all about being green and taking it easy.

In the eyes of the wild camping tribes, campsites are for softies. But wild camping with kids — well, it can just be a bit of a hassle. At the very least it's nice to know there's running water to deal with potty mishaps and stacks of dirty dishes. So with its no-frills, close-to-nature approach, Cerenety proves you can still enjoy the wilder side of camping in a uniform campsite.

With just a smattering of tents permitted across Cerenety's seven sprawling acres, first and foremost there's plenty of space to run around like wild things. Every feature is as squeaky green as the surrounding countryside: from compost loos, a wind turbine and solar panels, to recycled materials ingeniously put to use in rustic, efficient amenities. There's even a veggie patch where you can head to pick your own.

Animal lovers roll-up. Children flock to bottle-feed orphan lambs, and alpacas roam a few feet shy of the tents. Where nature rules and campfire smoke spirals lazily into dusky skies, it comes as a surprise that the surfer dudes, amusement arcades and retro cafés of Bude are just a mile's easy stroll along the canal. So kids can get a seaside fix without you so much as having to hunt down the car keys. Once they've hit the waves, gorged on ice cream, hired a pedalo or taken a dip in the tidal pool, you might even experience a rare moment of serenity when they rest their tired little heads back at camp.

Cerenety Eco Camping, Lower Lynstone Lane, Bude, Cornwall EX23 0LR; 01288 356778; www.cerenetycampsite.co.uk

THE UPSIDE Serene, green and no overcrowding. Even at full capacity you'll find just a handful of tents in each paddock.
THE DOWNSIDE If you're not into compost loos and eco-living then it's not for you.
WHO'S IN? Family groups, single-sex groups, small campervans, tents – yes. Dogs – by arrangement. Caravans, large campervans – no. Campfires and barbecues a definite yes.
THE FACILITIES Three sprawling fields with no set pitches – just don't cramp your neighbours' style and check with the owners which meadow to pitch in. A field shelter houses 2 showers, 3 compost loos and a washing-up sink (hot water is powered by the wind turbine and solar panels). Owner Jake will freeze iceblocks for you in the house, if you ask. A small shed-shop sells basics such as toothpaste and loo roll.
ONSITE FUN Pick your own fresh veggies from the market garden. Spot butterflies, moths and the visiting heron on the wildlife pond. Feed the orphan lambs (in lambing season) and pet the animals – Flipper the dog, Torry the pony and Red the rescue horse, as well as rabbits, ducks and chickens.
OFFSITE FUN It's a 20-minute stroll to the seaside – Bude's stunning Summerleaze, Crooklets and Widemouth beaches serving up a heady cocktail of surf, sand, cool waterfront cafés and amusement arcades. Hit the waves with Raven Surf School (01288 353693; www.ravensurf.co.uk), Big Blue Surf School (01288 331764; www.bigbluesurfschool.co.uk) or take a dip in the tidal pool, or row a boat along the canal (boat hire at Lower Wharf; 07968 688782) Cyclists can opt for a gentle route along the canal towpath, or freewheel all the way from Bude to Land's End along the Cornish Way (www.sustrans.org.uk).

IF IT RAINS Bude's popular Harlequinns Leisure Centre (01288 355366; www.harlequinns.com) has tenpin bowling and a huge indoor soft play area, and the Splash Leisure Pool (01288 356191) has a wave machine and flumes.

FOOD AND DRINK For the best local ingredients, served with gob-smacking sea views, head to Life's A Beach, overlooking Summerleaze beach. A casual family café by day (think burgers and bruschettas) and swanky seafood bistro by night (famous for its salt-baked bream), it's worth straying from the campfire for (01288 355222; www.lifesabeach.info). For a splash of seaside retro, Rosie's Kitchen serves hearty sarnies, breakfasts and milkshakes beside Crooklets beach (07966 684940; www.rosieskitchen.co.uk).

NANNY STATE ALERT Watch little ones around the campfires and beside the wildlife pond. There was also an electric fence around the horses paddock during our visit (this is only up when there are new ponies in the field, though).

GETTING THERE From the A39, turn onto the A3073 following signs to Bude. When you approach the mini roundabout signposted right to the town centre, instead head straight on towards Widemouth Bay. When you reach Upper Lynstone Caravan Park on your right (at the top of a hill), turn left – there is a small wooden signpost for Cerenety. At the end of the lane turn right and the entrance to Cerenety is about 50 metres further, on your right.

PUBLIC TRANSPORT Take a coach to Bude. Or, local buses (for Widemouth Bay) will drop you off at the end of the road if you ask nicely. If there's just one of you, owner Jake will come and pick you up.

OPEN All year.

THE DAMAGE Prices vary according to season and the size of your tent: £4–£6 per person, per night (£2 for under-3s) plus £4–£8 per tent, per night. Dogs £1–£2. It costs £2 per day to pick your own veg.

maker camping

When your children have grown up, all their most cherished memories of roaming free, having fun, making new friends and creating their own worlds will revolve around this site. But only if you take them there, of course.

If campsites were graded by how chilled their vibe was, Maker Camping would fall into the category marked Permafrost. To say it's laidback here would be like describing Michelangelo as a half decent painter-decorator, 'if you're into cherubs and that'.

An army barracks in a former life, there's now a certain hippyness to the way the Nissen huts at Maker's entrance have been reinvented as workshops and a café by various arty types and the 'rules are the province of squares and bureaucrats' ethos continues on the camping area itself.

Two very large fields – one set aside for families – sprawl over a hilltop blessed with alarmingly panoramic views of Plymouth, the sea and the under-explored Rame Peninsula. If things get busy, two more fields magically open up, so there's never any cheek-by-jowling. Kids love exploring the gun emplacements (their guns, happily, long since gone), bunkers and redoubts left here from the last war, or rushing off to make mischief in the woods. And if their parents can't muster the energy to put up a tent, there are four simply furnished and cheap-as-chips yurts in which to crash.

The site's own shabby-chic bar, the Random Arms, opens on Friday and Saturday nights and a museum and alternative café have just been built. The camping land is owned by the groovy Rame Conservation Trust and managed by Maker Events; monies raised from the campsite go towards preserving the area for future generations, thus making those who camp here unwittingly virtuous.

Maker Camping, Maker Heights, Millbrook, nr Torpoint, Cornwall PL10 1LA; 07900 994231; www.makerfestival.co.uk

THE UPSIDE Carefree camping with lush coastal views.
THE DOWNSIDE There's little shelter for windy nights.
WHO'S IN? Tents, campervans, caravans, dogs, fires in designated pits – yes. Large groups – by prior arrangement.
THE FACILITIES There are 4 small compost toilets in the fields (6 more by the time you read this, and solar showers are in the pipeline, too), with 4 women's and 8 men's conventional loos in the onsite buildings and 4 showers (£1 or 20p coins).
ONSITE FUN A tipi to play in; piles of scrap wood with which they can be as inventive as they like; a couple of horses to admire; and a huge amount of space for games. Or come in June/July for the music festival organised by Maker Events.
OFFSITE FUN Swimming, snorkelling and beach-based fun are a 10-minute walk away in Kingsand – a grassy path runs there from the site. Whitsand Bay's waves are ripe for surfing.
IF IT RAINS Nearby Plymouth boasts the National Marine Aquarium (www.national-aquarium.co.uk) for fishy fun.
FOOD AND DRINK Within easy walking distance are the delightful Old Boat Store café at Kingsand, serving veggie offerings and fresh seafood, and Cawsand's Cross Keys Inn.
NANNY STATE ALERT There are some World War II bunkers on the site and an electric fence around the horse field.
GETTING THERE A38 to the Trerulefoot roundabout then take the A374, following the brown signs towards Mount Edgcumbe. Maker is on your right, a mile past Millbrook.
PUBLIC TRANSPORT Train to Plymouth then the Cawsand Ferry to Cawsand Beach; walk or take bus no. 81C to the site.
OPEN April–September.
THE DAMAGE A maximum for any family of £15 per night.

camping games

Part of the reason why kids love to go camping so much is because it feels like one long party.

Away from all the techno intrusions into almost all areas of our lives, camping encourages a high degree of parent–child interaction. Put bluntly, you can't escape to the living room to read the Sunday papers, or to your office to check your emails and update your Facebook profile.

Chances are that you'll find yourself playing the sort of ridiculous, hilarious and sometimes occasionally humiliating games that you were always desperate for your parents to play with you when you were a child.

There's always plenty of room in every camping trip for the usual ball games such as rounders or French cricket, so don't forget to fling bats, balls and rackets – and anything else that you think might be useful – into the boot of your car when you are packing. However, for wet weather (which is bound to happen), when you are confined under canvas, board games and playing cards are worth their weight in gold. But there's also something delightful about homemade games that are just plucked out of the ether.

What follows is a selection of some of our favourite games. They don't involve a single piece of kit, but they do involve a lot of fun.

letter chaos

Choose a single category, such as animals, girls'
names, sweets or food. The first player calls out a
single item from that category, and the next player
has to use the last letter of that word to make
the first letter of the next word. For example, if
you choose animals, a round might go like this:
horse, elephant, tiger, rhinoceros. You can make
the game more complicated for older children,
if you like, using more challenging categories,
such as rivers or foreign cities. You might even
find that you can trick a teenager into doing
some geography revision, without him or her
even realising it! This is also a good game to play
on long car journeys, particularly when you are
driving to a far-flung campsite.

scavenger hunt

This is a brilliant game to while away an
afternoon on the beach. First, agree on a search
area around your site, tent or beach-base. Then
devise a list of possible treasures that each child
has to go and hunt for. For example, the list could
include a bottle top, a feather, a piece of sea-
smoothed glass, a completely round stone, and so
on. Provide each child with a bucket (or an old
yogurt pot or similar container) to carry their
treasures in and send them off to hunt for them,
while you stretch out with a good book. For the
game to last longer, make the items a bit harder
to find, like a stone with a hole in it, a starfish
or a crab's claw. The winner is the one who
has collected the most treasures after an
agreed period of time.

kick-the-can

Choose an open space, but ideally one with
some natural hiding places. The best place is in
a wood, or on sand dunes. One person is made
'king'/'queen', and must stand in the middle
of the space beside the 'can'. This could be an
old bucket or a stump of wood. The king/queen
covers their face, counts to 25 and all the players
must then hide. The aim is for the players to get
close enough to the can to kick it. The king/
queen must defend the can (now with eyes
uncovered) and try to get a player out by tagging
him. Once players are out they wait by the can
in 'prison'. The other players then try to free
the prisoners by kicking the can without being
tagged. The game usually involves some high-
speed chases to the can, and a lot of cheering

wink murder

A good game for a wet afternoon, when you've visited every local castle there is and all anyone wants to do is sit in the tent. Rip up a sheet of paper into as many pieces as there are players. On one piece write the word 'murderer'. Fold the pieces and put them into a hat. Each person (sitting in a circle) takes a piece and checks whether they are the murderer, without letting anyone else see. The murderer then winks surreptitiously at each player, who will then 'die'. The murdered one counts to 10 before dying so that others can't guess who the murderer is. High drama and histrionics are fully permitted from the dying player at this point. The aim of the game is for the murderer to wink each player out without anyone guessing who the murderer is.

sports day

This works best with a large group of people, but even if you are in a small group it's still a lot of fun. If you want you can mark out a start and finish line with a biodegradable line of flour, but you could just do it with things you have lying around on site, like a skipping rope, a spare guy rope or an anorak. Use your imagination when choosing the sort of heats that you want to have: fiercely competitive running races are a good place to start, but you could quickly graduate to the three-legged race, hopping race, running-backwards race, egg-and-spoon race and the favourite wheelbarrow race. You could race as teams or individually. Close your sports day with a grand presentation of prizes, maybe in the form of chocolates and sweets.

witch's ring

Mark out a small circle on the ground using flour or a rope (or mark the sand with a stick). Choose one player to be the 'witch'. She (or he) crouches in the circle while the other players walk around it. The witch then slowly rises and, on reaching full height, shouts 'Here I come!' She then dashes out and tries to catch another player. Anyone she catches is turned into something of her choice, for example, a dog or a toad and the player has to freeze in that pose. The whole thing is then repeated until all the players have been caught by the witch and she is surrounded by a field full of strange-looking people contorted into silly shapes. Great fun and loads of hilarity!

devon yurt

Get back to nature without giving up your creature comforts. Yurt life on the edge of Dartmoor comes with a sleigh bed under the stars, a wood-fired bath with a view and a ride-on tractor for budding farmers.

Once you've admitted to the camping fraternity that you're really more of a yurter, at Devon Yurt you need to decide whether you're a Great Links or a Little Links type. While Dartmoor views unfurl from the oak doorframes of both, and each hogs a prime spot on Devon's edge of the Tamar Valley, the characters of these stylish yurts are quite different.

With its enclosed garden and proximity to the shower house (we're talking slate-floored, glass-fronted wetroom overlooking rolling moors), Little Links is well suited to families with little kids. Hens and geese cluck and gabble over the fence, there's a barbecue-cum-campfire area and – perhaps the most important detail for romance-starved parents – the wood-fired bath awaits just footsteps from the yurt.

Great Links shares the same facilities, but attracts slightly more adventurous yurters. In an elevated meadow a short walk from the farmhouse, here you are rewarded with more space, more seclusion and a sleigh bed from which you merely have to plump your pillows to watch the sunrise. Getting so beautifully far away from it all comes with a downside: the walk to the amenities in pitch darkness. But fret not, there's a long-drop loo with a throne-style chair much suited to regal yurters.

Whichever yurt suits you, it's the little things that make this place special: the fire ready-prepared, freshly laid eggs for breakfast, the veg and herb garden and home-baked rainy-day cakes. After all, how many campsites have you stayed in where rain is something you actually look forward to?

Devon Yurt, Borough Farm, Kelly, Lifton, Devon PL16 0HJ; 01822 870366; www.devonyurt.co.uk

THE UPSIDE Rolling Dartmoor views from the yurts, the shower and the bath. Cosy canvas lodgings decked out with proper beds and wood-burners.

THE DOWNSIDE Really very little, unless you count a noisy cow on the farm next door.

WHO'S IN? Small groups – yes. Tents, campervans, caravans, dogs – no.

THE FACILITIES Two yurts (Little Links sleeps up to 2 adults and 2 children; Great Links sleeps up to 2 adults and 4 children) decked out with double beds, roll-out futons, table and chairs, cutlery, crockery, coolboxes and tea lights. As well as outdoor seating, a Belfast sink and a campfire/barbecue area for each yurt, gas stoves and lanterns are provided. A separate bath tent houses a wood-fired bath tub and the shower house has a wetroom-style shower (solar-powered), toilet, laundry facilities and books, games, maps and local information.

ONSITE FUN Farm animals include hens, sheep, geese and ponies, plus there's a ride-on tractor for kids. There are blackberries to pick in season and a range of indoor games for rainy days.

OFFSITE FUN While nearby Dartmoor is one of the biggest attractions (www.dartmoor-npa.gov.uk), there's much more than walking and wild swimming on the doorstep. Go horse riding over the moors with Cholwell Riding Stables at Mary Tavy (01822 810526; www.cholwellridingstables.co.uk), or swing through the Tamar Valley woodland on a high ropes course (01822 833409; www.treesurfers.co.uk). At the latter there are also 25 miles of family-friendly cycle trails (bike hire available), and freewheeling fans have also got the disused

railway track of the Tarka Trail nearby (www.sustrans.org.uk). Families can also make the most of the natural environment at Lydford Gorge (www.nationaltrust.org.uk), where a walk to the waterfall (accessible buggy route) is complete with all the National Trust trimmings, including a café and picnic area.

IF IT RAINS Take cover at Barn Climbing in Milton Abbot (01822 870521; www.barnclimbingwall.co.uk) with indoor climbing walls surrounding a huge boulder and excellent instructors. There's plenty of indoor fun to be had at Trethorne Leisure Farm near Launceston, with all sorts of activities from a soft play area and slides to trampolines and an assault course (01566 86324; www.trethorneleisure.com).

FOOD AND DRINK Fresh seasonal produce including vegetables, fruit, salad and free-range eggs are available on site, and you can help yourself to herbs from the kitchen garden. Beyond Julia's excellent home-baked cakes and elderflower cordial, Lifton Farm Shop is the place to go for the very best local goodies and a mean all-day breakfast (01566 784605; www.liftonstrawberryfields.co.uk). For eating out with kids in tow, a couple of the best pubs in the area include the Dartmoor Inn at Lydford (01822 820221; www.dartmoorinn.com) and the Blacksmiths Arms at Lamerton (01822 612962; www.blacksmithsarmstavistock.co.uk).

NANNY STATE ALERT Ensure you use one of the fireguards supplied for the wood-burners if you have young children with you.

GETTING THERE Exit the A30 at Lifton and continue through the village, past the Arundell Arms on your left, and over a bridge at the bottom of the hill. Turn right, signposted 'Chillaton/industrial estate', and follow this road up the hill for a couple of miles to the crossroads signposted to Kelly. Borough Farm is situated about 50 metres further along, on the left-hand side.

PUBLIC TRANSPORT You can get a bus from Exeter to Lifton, but if you want to explore Dartmoor and all its surroundings then this isn't the place to be without your own vehicle.

OPEN April–late September.

THE DAMAGE £135–£165 per night Friday and Saturday, £595–£795 per week (only weekly bookings taken in peak season), midweek breaks from £295 for 3 nights.

runnage farm

Recharge your fading batteries by plugging into some serious countryside relaxation. You'll find a sprinkling of campfire magic plus a hearty dose of camping by the river in the very heart of wildest Dartmoor.

Heading into Dartmoor feels a bit like travelling back through time and tales, perhaps ending up somewhere between the pages of Arthur Conan Doyle's *The Hound of the Baskervilles*. Much of the land here has successfully spurned modernity's advances, and its middle-of-nowhereness and descending mists give it an air of mystery and adventure; it's bound to stir up even the most sluggish of imaginations.

Runnage Farm is right in the midst of this rolling moorland. Extending over 220 acres, it has been worked by the Coaker family since 1843, long before Baker Street's finest sleuth arrived to solve his famous case. The Coakers are keen to emphasise that running the farm is their priority, but they are happy to offer a small, wild campsite along with a few mod cons. There are no pitches or hook-ups, just two fields next to the river, where campers are free to do as they please. Kids can enjoy running around in this magical wilderness, playing Pooh Sticks in the river, looking at the horses and splashing about in the stream before settling down to toast marshmallows over the campfire.

Any grown-ups who were feeling slightly frazzled can unwind to the tranquil sounds of rural peace and calming, flowing water.

As a certain pipe-smoking detective would say: 'It's elementary, my dear camper'.

Runnage Farm, Postbridge, Yelverton, Devon PL20 6TN; 01822 880222; www.runnagecampingbarns.co.uk

THE UPSIDE Wild-style camping with fires and tasty meats.
THE DOWNSIDE Without a car it's difficult to reach.
WHO'S IN? Tents, dogs on leads (max. 2 per group), campfires – yes. Booking in advance essential. Campervans, caravans, groups without prior arrangement – no.
THE FACILITIES Pitch where you like in the riverside fields; also 3 converted bunk barns (see website for prices). Four clean loos and 2 showers (water supply is from a local spring – please spend no longer than 5 minutes showering); drying room.
ONSITE FUN Splashing along the Walla Brook stream that splits the camping fields, playing hide-and-seek in the forest.
OFFSITE FUN Choose from pony trekking, letterboxing, rock climbing or cycling on Dartmoor. For littler kids, try the Miniature Pony Centre (www.miniatureponycentre.com).
IF IT RAINS For shops galore and 'all-weather' skating, head to Trago Mills (www.trago.co.uk) near Newton Abbot.
FOOD AND DRINK Runnage Farm's meat is perfect for barbecuing (let them know what you need in advance). The Old Inn at Widecombe (01364 621207) provides a choice-full menu and does half-portions from the adults' menu for kids.
NANNY STATE ALERT Please be aware of tractor traffic, fields marked 'keep out' and the river. Don't fuss the farm dogs.
GETTING THERE Take the A382 to Moretonhampstead, where you can get on the B3212 to Postbridge. On entering Postbridge there's a sharp left for Widecombe, take this and Runnage Farm is a mile down this road, on the left.
PUBLIC TRANSPORT Train to Exeter/Plymouth then Transmoor bus no. 82 to Postbridge and just over a mile's walk.
OPEN All year, but weather dependent; call ahead to book.
THE DAMAGE Adult £5 per night; child £3.50; dog £2.

The rolling wilds of Dartmoor

highfield farm

Highfield is certainly not the only campsite set on an organic farm, but how many come with their own half-mile nature trail, riverside woods, pond and (in season) cardoons? We're guessing just one.

On the outskirts of Topsham, a small, pleasingly old-fashioned town on the River Exe, sits unassuming Highfield Farm. While not as high as its name would suggest (it's a modest 15 metres above sea level) it still manages to lord it over the countryside to the east.

So, pitch up in the farm's large, flat camping field and you'll enjoy a vista of the vale that stretches all the way to the far Blackdown Hills. Slide into the much smaller field, where campervans and caravans hang out, and you're favoured with a rather more modest view of Woodbury Common and a water tower.

The half-mile circular trail down to the River Clyst is the jewel in the crown of this 118-acre mixed organic farm. There are plans to put in a jetty, so some day you'll be able to row or paddle here. In the meantime, down by the river there's a wood fit for den making and a dipping pond to get stuck into. A two-acre organic kitchen garden behind the campsite means you don't have to leave the farm to buy raspberries, asparagus, strawberries, squashes and much more besides when in season.

The fields are full of barley or traditional British breeds of cattle such as the beautiful russet Devons. And when you do venture out, a short walk will take you to the River Exe, whose mud flats play host to more birds than you can shake a stork at.

Highfield Farm, Clyst Road, Topsham, Exeter, Devon EX3 0BY; 01392 876388; www.highfieldfarm.org

THE UPSIDE A great ½ mile nature trail that takes in the River Clyst without ever having to leave the farm.
THE DOWNSIDE The distant drone of M5 traffic is a constant. Trains pass fairly close by, too.
WHO'S IN? Tents, campervans, caravans; dogs under close control; fires in the big field; family groups, Duke of Edinburgh, Scouts – yes. Stag and hen parties – no.
THE FACILITIES One small, sheltered strip of grass can accommodate up to 5 campervans or caravans and a handful of tents, while a much larger open field is usually used for tents. An eco-friendly block starring 2 solar-heated showers and recycled rainwater to flush 2 loos should be ready when this book hits the shelves. Free-range eggs and organic fruit and veg grown on the premises are for sale at strikingly reasonable prices. There's a chemical disposal point.
ONSITE FUN The trail around the farm should burn off some pent up energy in small legs. There's an area of woods near the river where kids can build dens, and a pond suitable for pond dipping (bring a net).
OFFSITE FUN The small picturesque town of Topsham is crammed with little independent shops to mooch around. Very close by is the fantastic cycle path that hugs the Exe Estuary from Exmouth right the way around to the outskirts of Exeter and on to Dawlish. The path is very flat, largely off road and perfect for a day's gentle pedalling. Head for either Exmouth (6 miles) or Dawlish (12 miles) for an old-fashioned seaside outing, or treat the family to a boat trip across the Exe (07778 370582; www.topshamtoturfferry.co.uk) from Topsham to the family-run Turf pub (01392 833128; www.turfpub.net)

IF IT RAINS The centre of Exeter is just 4 miles away by road, or a few stops up the railway line, and contains a host of wet-weather bolt-holes, such as the catacombs (free tours 3 times a week; 01392 265203) and the cathedral (01392 255573; www.exeter-cathedral.org.uk). Meanwhile, the city's Crealy Adventure Park (01395 233200; www.crealy.co.uk) offers hair-raising rides, a log flume, water tubes and the altogether more sedate pleasures of a carousel.

FOOD AND DRINK Topsham boasts the best part of a dozen pubs. For families, the Lighter Inn (01392 875439; lighterinn.co.uk) is probably the pick of the bunch — on the quay by the Exe and with a children's menu to boot. On the main drag, Fore Street, there's a cracking sweetshop called Auntie Julie's that you may wish to aim for, or subtly avoid.

NANNY STATE ALERT Look out for the pond and river (though both are quite a way from the campsite). It should also be noted that this is a working farm on which both livestock and heavy machinery reside.

GETTING THERE Leave the M5 at junction 30, taking the A376 signposted to Topsham. Turn right almost immediately onto Sandygate (which becomes Clyst Road). After about 2 miles look out for a telephone box and then take the left-hand turning into the farm.

PUBLIC TRANSPORT Topsham railway station is just around the corner, and bus no. 57 (www.stagecoachbus.com) between Exeter and Exmouth stops very close to the site.

OPEN All year (weather dependent).

THE DAMAGE Tent plus 2 adults £10 per night; £12 for a caravan with a hook-up. £1 for each extra person.

coombe view farm

Branscombe would make the perfect setting for a *Famous Five* story. A picturesque, uppy-downy village perched on the Jurassic Coast of East Devon, it feels more rural than seaside – a truly unspoiled corner.

With walks aplenty and overlooking a pebbled shore, this is the kind of place where Julian, Dick, Ann, George and Timmy the dog could get seriously stuck into some mischievous adventures.

Shaped like an upright horseshoe, with the beach at the very bottom, Branscombe village has two ends and at one of them you'll find Coombe View Farm Caravan and Camping Site.

This relaxed site consists of a sloping field with lovely views over a patchwork of greens and, to your left, you can see the sea. The green expanse in the middle of the field is left free for games, while a few static and touring caravans linger around its edges and there are a couple of picnic tables. It's an understated, quiet place that emanates a rural vibe, with inquisitive ponies stretching long necks over the fence to have a nose at their *neigh*bours.

Campers are more than welcome to explore the surrounding land when they are not on the beach. Kids can play games, create Enid Blyton-style escapades and collect wood for campfires in the fields that aren't occupied by animals.

Things to do nearby include: days at pebbly Branscombe Beach and trips to Sidmouth to pet donkeys and enjoy the picturesque countryside around the Donkey Sanctuary; a day at Pecorama to marvel at their toy trains; or heading underground at Beer Quarry Caves.

And when the sun goes down, the village's Mason's Arms pub is just the spot for lashings of ginger beer beside the roaring log fire.

Coombe View Farm Caravan and Camping Site, Branscombe, Seaton, Devon EX12 3BT; 01297 680218; www.branscombe-camping.co.uk

THE UPSIDE Stunning rural, campfire-permitting location, with a beach within easy reach.

THE DOWNSIDE There are quite strict rules on, for example, excessive cycling speeds and hanging out your washing.

WHO'S IN? Tents, campervans, caravans, dogs, awnings/gazebos – yes. Large groups – by arrangement. Campfires allowed in designated spots (ask owners where).

THE FACILITIES Nine toilets; 4 showers – all very basic, but with a good supply of hot water to wash away salty waves and ice-creamy fingers. There's also an outside tap and CDP.

ONSITE FUN There's plenty of room for kids to run about and play, and the centre of the main field is the perfect size for a makeshift cricket pitch to keep budding Alastair Cooks happy.

OFFSITE FUN Long, pebbly and part of the acclaimed, fossil-filled Jurassic Coast, Branscombe Beach is perfect for stone-skimming and swimming in its clean waters.

IF IT RAINS Step 300 years back in time to Branscombe's National-Trust-restored old Forge, Manor Mill and Old Bakery.

FOOD AND DRINK Branscombe's Mason's Arms pub (masonsarms.co.uk) has a log-fire atmosphere and good food.

NANNY STATE ALERT Horses in the neighbouring fields have a tendency to bite (there are warning signs on the fence).

GETTING THERE Take the A3052 past Sidmouth towards Seaton. Take the third signed right-hand turn to Branscombe; Coombe View Farm is ½ mile down the track, on the right.

PUBLIC TRANSPORT Train to Poole/Exeter, then bus no. X53 to Beer Cross, then a 2-or-so-mile-walk.

OPEN Mid March–mid October.

THE DAMAGE Family of 4 £22–£30 per night. Dogs £2.

caffyns farm

'Yes' is a word you'll hear a lot at this spacious spot with coastal views, and access to beaches and Exmoor walks aplenty. If you say 'Can I...?' they aim to answer in the affirmative – and it shows. Happy campers? Yes indeedy.

After a successful reign as the camping hosts at Cloud Farm (p78), Colin and Jill Harman have upped sticks and moved to another breathtaking location; this time with sea views, open fields and endless space on the North Devon coast.

When they moved to Caffyns Farm, the Harmans brought with them their trove of cool campsite know-how, and have been busy setting up a relaxed, rule-free, pitch-wherever-you-fancy site. A campfire culture is encouraged and made even more magical as you're surrounded by expansive countryside and views out over the Bristol Channel (stretching to as far as Wales on a clear day).

Campers are free to wander over any of the 150 acres of farmland, which is some of the flattest in this undulating area of Exmoor – all the better for pitching. So far there are four camping fields edged by protective hedgerows, but there are plans to open up more; a couple of which will be adorned by a yurt or two for a glamping option… And this is just a fraction of what the Harmans have in store for Caffyns Farm.

Even if it takes a while for their dream site to be completed, this campsite is a cracker as it is. The location is beautiful and the laidback vibe ensures friendly, relaxed campers. It's an irresistible spot for kids who are hooked on riding and beach days, too, with pony trekking right from the farm's own stables and walks down to the stunning beach down at Lee Bay for days spent bodyboarding, sandcastle-building and rockpooling.

Caffyns Farm, Lynton, Devon EX35 6JW; 01598 753967; www.doonevalleyholidays.co.uk

THE UPSIDE Lots of space in gorgeous surroundings plus a beach within reach, ponies to ride and campfires to build.
THE DOWNSIDE You'll need a car to get here.
WHO'S IN? Everyone plus dogs. If you're in a group it's worth phoning ahead. Campfires rule okay.
THE FACILITIES A collection of fields for you to pitch where you like and make a campfire when you like – just grab some stones from the boxes scattered around the fields and buy a bag of logs from the little shop (which stocks all sorts: gas and camping equipment, basics, local produce and even some games) and you'll be all fired up. Most campers tend to pitch around the outside of the fields to use the hedges as shelter from any sea breezes and keep the middle free for games. Water taps are dotted about the fields. At the time of writing there were temporary loos (3) and showers (3) by the farmhouse, along with a washing-up sink under shelter. These are clean and the water is hot, but plans are afoot to complete a facilities block with 8 showers, 16 loos and more washing-up sinks by the camping field nearest the farm and to move the 3 temporary toilets into other fields. There are bins and recycling banks near the entrance. When the Harmans have finished creating their vision there should be a sheltered games room, tea room and yurts, too: watch this space.
ONSITE FUN There are 30 friendly ponies here, so you can go off trekking to your heart's content (£25 per hour; age 5 plus). An indoor riding school is in the pipeline, too. Otherwise just enjoy all the space and splash about in the little streams.
OFFSITE FUN Walk directly from the farm down the steep coastal pathways to Lee Abbey and on down to the private beach (better to drive if you have very little children as the

Lee Bay

terrain's not buggy-friendly). The beach has big, grey rocks for playing giant stepping-stones (and Who's the King of the Castle?) with little pools in between for fish-spotting. The waves are high enough for bodyboarding but low enough for swimming. Take a trip on the cliff railway, between Lynton and Lynmouth (01598 753486; www.cliffrailwaylynton.co.uk), and gape at the scenery before stopping for ice cream at the Cliff Top Cafaurant at the top. Hire mountain bikes from the farm and head off to explore Exmoor.

IF IT RAINS The BIG Sheep near Bideford (01237 472366; www.thebigsheep.co.uk) has indoor activities to get stuck into, such as EWEtopia play zone, a sheep show and lamb feeding, so you'll *bah*ly notice it's raining. Watermouth Castle near Ilfracombe (01271 867474; www.watermouthcastle.com) has dungeon labyrinths to explore.

FOOD AND DRINK Jill's cakes are to die for. Really. And if the tea room and garden she and Colin plan to set up next to the shop haven't yet been finished by the time you read this, then hopefully she's still supplying the County Gate Visitor Centre (on the A39 just at the Devon/Somerset border) so you can have a slice of Dorset apple cake, carrot cake, Victoria sponge, a cream tea... the list goes on. They also serve lunches, snacks and hot drinks there and have plenty of helpful info about Exmoor. Two-and-a-half miles away, down steep and winding roads, is the Hunters Inn (01598 763230; www.thehuntersinn.net) – a great family pub with gastro grub and peacocks on the lawn.

NANNY STATE ALERT There are a couple of little streams (not near the camping fields) on the farm as well as machinery to be aware of. Please don't feed the horses.

GETTING THERE You'll find detailed directions for various options on the Caffyns Farm website, but the most straightforward route is to take the A39 coastal road westbound all the way to Barbrook. Continue along the road for a further mile and you'll see a sign for Caffyns Cross; turn right here and go up the lane, ignoring the first campsite turning on the right and carrying on until you see the Caffyns Farm sign to turn right down the long driveway to the farm.

OPEN All year.

THE DAMAGE At present it's £5 per adult per night; £3.50 per child (aged 5–15), under-5s free. Dogs are free. No advance bookings – just show up – though it's best for groups to call ahead.

cloud farm

Pitch the tent anywhere you fancy at this intimate riverside site snuggled tightly into a stunning Exmoor valley. And if you've not yet read *Lorna Doone,* take it with you; there's no need to imagine the setting – you're right in the midst of it.

Sitting pretty in its own self-contained hamlet surrounded by the purple haze of the famed Doone Valley, Cloud Farm's campsite occupies a prize riverside setting alongside Badgworthy Water.

Since our last visit, a couple more fields have been opened, expanding the narrow strip of campsite along the greenery by the water to allow more space for all who visit this popular site. Further work has been done to level some of the fields for flatter pitching, and there are plans to open more showers, too. James is an attentive host and can be seen in the wood-smoke-filled evenings (yes, you can have real campfires here) wandering among the campers to check that all's well.

Unsurprisingly, he has few complaints. Kids spend hours in the river, spotting fish, skimming stones and even managing a little doggy-paddle in the deeper pools. Parents are happy to just lounge about on the banks in the summer sunshine and marvel at the valley's walls of gold and green flecked with unmistakeable Exmoor heather. It's a little like sitting in a kaleidoscopic colour cocoon and, as there's no mobile signal here, you really can feel like you've escaped modern urban life.

Meanwhile, the walking opportunities are fabulous; one rambler's treat is to follow the river all the way along the valley, past the stone monument dedicated to *Lorna Doone* author RD Blackmore, and on to the ruins of a medieval village, which lie resplendent in the afternoon sun.

Cloud Farm, Oare, nr Brendon, Lynton, Devon EX35 6NU; 01598 741278; www.cloudfarmcamping.com

THE UPSIDE Pitch-where-you-like riverside camping – with campfires – in a beautiful Exmoor valley.

THE DOWNSIDE This site is popular, so be prepared to wait for facilities at peak times.

WHO'S IN? Couples, families, groups and well-behaved dogs in tents, campervans or caravans – yes.

THE FACILITIES The site is essentially comprised of narrow fields running alongside the river, as well as a couple of other fields set on higher ground. Campfires are allowed and bags of logs cost £5 (or special offer of 2 bags plus all the kindling and firelighters for £10). There are 4 water taps, mostly around the central hub of buildings that make up the facilities blocks, shop and café. The washing-up room has 4 sinks as well as a washing machine and dryer. At the time of writing there were 10 showers and 9 loos, with a further 2 of each in the pipeline. The showers are powered by a generator and so can only be used in the mornings and evenings. Campers can charge phones in the onsite café, which serves hot drinks, cream teas and has breakfast, lunch and dinner menus if you fancy a break from the washing-up. The shop sells all sorts – from food and camping accessories to water pistols and dog toys.

ONSITE FUN It's all about the river: swim in it, paddle in it, sit and sunbathe by it, build dams in it or fish in it (£5 for a day). You can also head off on walks directly from the site; ask James for details of some of his favourite routes. Look out for some of the area's wildlife, too; kingfishers and otters have been spied hanging out here in recent years. Kids delight in buying up all the water pistols and water bombs from the shop on hot days, so take care as you walk through the site.

OFFSITE FUN You've all of Exmoor to explore – by bike, on horseback (Brendon Manor Riding Stables; 01598 741246) or on foot, and the North Devon coast, with its swimmer- and surfer-friendly beaches, is an easy drive away. Dunster Castle (01643 823004), near Minehead, is also nice for a day out, and Exmoor Zoo (01598 763352; www.exmoorzoo.co.uk), half-an-hour's drive away, has plenty of animals to meet, some of which the kids can handle and help to feed.

IF IT RAINS The Milky Way adventure park (01237 431255; www.themilkyway.co.uk) boasts Devon's largest rollercoaster, but also a bird of prey centre with an indoor falconry area, Toddler Town and Fantasy Farm, as well as other delights to keep children amused. The Mill's activity centre (03336 006001; www.rockandrapidadventures.co.uk) has an indoor climbing wall and café, as well as outdoor climbing if the weather perks up. You could take the West Somerset Railway (01643 704996; www.west-somerset-railway.co.uk) on a picturesque 20-mile trip from Bishops Lydeard to Minehead; snacks such as home-baked cakes and local apple juice (and cider) are available on board.

FOOD AND DRINK The onsite café does cream teas, full English breakfasts and burgers and chips (you can order takeaway, too). At the end of Cloud Farm's lane, take a left for the Buttery Riverside Bar & Café (01598 741106; www.thebutterymalmsmead.co.uk) for an excellent pizza. The best local pub, which is relatively child-friendly, is the Staghunters Inn in Brendon (01598 741222; www.staghunters.com); while the food is pretty standard, it's a fine place for lunch with the kids. Porlock Weir's Bottom Ship Inn (01643 863288; www.thebottomship.co.uk) has stirring Channel views to admire while you're sipping from a pint of locally brewed Exmoor Ale or a glass of cider.

NANNY STATE ALERT The river is delightful but could, of course, be dangerous for small children unaccompanied.

GETTING THERE From the A39 Porlock to Lynton Road, take the road to Doone Valley and Malmstead, which will be signposted. At Oare Church turn right for Cloud Farm and you will come to the signposted site further up the lane on the left.

OPEN All year.

THE DAMAGE £8 per adult, per night; child aged 3–5 £3, 6–12 £4, 13–15 £5, under-3s free; £2 per dog; £3 for an extra-large tent. Electric hook-up £4.

somerset yurts

Remember that old tale about the Town Mouse and the Country Mouse? Well, there's no need to choose between town and countryside here; you're just 10 minutes away from both. Absolutely squeaking marvellous.

You need only flick through the guestbook in the bunting-strewn communal Dutch barn at Somerset Yurts for a taste of this site's restorative powers. The book overflows with enthused messages about the four cosy yurts whose sunny doors welcome campers into their warm embrace. One couple even got engaged during their stay here, so it's not just a spot for families to unwind, but a romantic getaway for two as well.

Children's gleeful smiles match Mum and Dad's as they open the red, orange, blue or green door into their snug Mongolian sanctuary, where they can get to grips with lighting the wood-burning stove before picking herbs from the pot outside ready for a barbecued dinner on the wooden deck.

The neighbouring fields are home to the farm's dairy herd, tended by Mark and Emma, who set up the yurt site and are forever adding little touches to the place, upping its glam ante each year. They meet and greet their guests on arrival, and any kids are welcome to join Mark for evening milking time before heading back to huddle around the large communal firepit in the corner of the yurt field.

It may feel as though you're in your own remote hideaway here, situated as you are in the countryside calm just a short drive from the natural beauty of the Quantock Hills, but in fact you're only 10 minutes away from the many trappings of Taunton town. So come and help yourself to the best of both worlds and leave your own mark in the guestbook – if, that is, there are any blank pages left.

Somerset Yurts, Hill Farm, West Monkton, Taunton, Somerset TA2 8LP; 07811 350176; www.somersetyurts.co.uk

THE UPSIDE Lovely eco-friendly yurts; easy to reach.

THE DOWNSIDE In August there can be a few pesky flies hanging about the barn, though there's spray provided.

WHO'S IN? Families, couples, groups (if booking the entire site) – yes. Pets, tents, caravans, campervans – no.

THE FACILITIES There are 4 fully equipped yurts in total (sleeping up to 4 adults, or a family of 5). The communal barn houses 4 sparklingly clean power showers and 4 loos. Its living area has a kitchen, eating area, maps, info and games to borrow. There's a huge communal firepit in the corner of the field.

ONSITE FUN A whole field in which to run around or cycle your socks off. Watch Mark milk his herd of dairy cows in the evenings. Kids love using the hay bales beneath the outer barn's roof as an improv theatre.

OFFSITE FUN Look no further than the welcome pack in your yurt to discover a whole heap of things to do.

IF IT RAINS Taunton is reached in no time by car and has a cinema as well as plenty of shops for a sheltered day.

FOOD AND DRINK No visit to Somerset is complete without a sip of cider or apple juice; luckily you're close to Sheppy's cider farm (www.sheppyscider.com). PYO fruit and veg at nearby Thurloxton Fruit Growers (01823 413413).

NANNY STATE ALERT It is a working farm; machinery to be aware of and an electric fence between cow field and yurt field.

GETTING THERE Full instructions on the website.

PUBLIC TRANSPORT Train to Taunton, from where Mark/Emma will pick you up if pre-arranged or a 15-minute taxi ride.

OPEN All year.

THE DAMAGE Yurt £60–£120 per night (depending on stay length/season). Book for a weekend/midweek break/full week.

Firepit
Wood ↓

rocks east

A cave, a moss-covered dell, complete with grotto and woodman on the edge of the 100-acre forest. All you Enid Blyton fans will be ecstatic to finally find the enchanted wood incarnate and, possibly, a magic faraway tree as well.

Most campers return to Rocks East for two reasons: the golden opportunity to sit around an open fire, and to have the run of 100 acres of ancient woodland. And wondrous woodland it is, too.

Rocks East has a very distinct culture. On one level it is very much a traditional, basic campsite. It does accept caravans, but canvas is king. All campers may roam free in the forest (day visitors pay a nominal fee) and the useful illustrated information boards educating novices about flora and fauna in the area are a great resource for adults and kids alike. But this is juxtaposed with what can only be described as bizarre. In the midst of all this natural beauty is a trail guarded over by garish garden-gnome-type sculptures leering out of the undergrowth, including a woodman and two large Easter Island sculptures carved from cedar wood. There's even a teddy bear house. You may be forgiven for thinking you're stuck in some strange land at the top of Enid Blyton's 'magic faraway tree'.

There are no serried ranks among which you have to pitch your tent at the campsite. You can pretty well choose your spot (with the exception of very busy weekends), which creates a chilled, informal vibe. Back in the wood, you may even think that you've mistakenly checked into a full-on adventure weekend. Don't panic, as the outdoor amphitheatre is sometimes used by outward-bound-type groups. Although, if you wanted to stage your own version of *Peter Rabbit* we're sure no one would mind at all.

Rocks East Woodland, Ashwicke, nr Bath SN14 8AP; 01225 852518; www.rockseast.org.uk

THE UPSIDE Traditional camping with open fires. One hundred acres of woodland to explore.

THE DOWNSIDE Being an educational trust, it's very popular with groups, especially at weekends, so it's advisable to book in advance. No cycling allowed.

WHO'S IN? Tents, campervans, activities-based groups – yes. Dogs – by arrangement. Noisy groups, caravans – no.

THE FACILITIES Two camping fields at the edge of the forest, sheltered by trees. Log-cabin camp HQ sits in the middle, providing basic, but clean, facilities. This translates as 1 dishwashing sink; 1 shower, 2 loos and 2 hand basins for ladies, with free hot water; the same for gents – so be prepared for a wait. A twee shop provides basic provisions and snacks such as cans of fizzy drinks and sweets, watched over by a dusty selection of woodland taxidermy. There's firewood for sale by the treeload, as well as a choice of hand-whittled wooden items, from walking sticks to bird houses.

ONSITE FUN Chilling by an open campfire while the kids roam free. Enjoying everything the forest has to offer, from the badger's hide to a serene nature walk, or even a surreal encounter with carved wooden animals on the Sculpture Trail.

OFFSITE FUN Cycling or wandering around the country lanes in this area of outstanding natural beauty. If you're cycling, the nearby villages of Marshfield, Colerne and Ford are all good destinations for those not requiring *Tour de France*-esque distances.

IF IT RAINS Bath is only 20 minutes away, with its stack of family fun: the Roman Baths, the Royal Victoria Park and Botanical Gardens, and the award-winning young people's Egg Theatre (visitbath.co.uk).

FOOD AND DRINK The Fox and Hounds at Colerne (01225 744847; www.foxandhoundscolerne.co.uk) is within cycling and walking distance and offers decent children's meals (food from the adult menu, but at smaller prices – we like). The White Hart at Ford (01249 782213: www.whitehartfordpub.co.uk) has the bonus of a riverside setting and does a mean Sunday roast. For lovely local shops selling local produce for local people (oh, and to a few tourists, too) pop into Marshfield, about 5 minutes' drive away. The Marshfield Central Stores (01225 891260) has a divine deli selling fresh bread and cakes from the Marshfield bakery, and Marshfield ice cream – all made in, yep you've guessed it... But if supermarkets are more your bag, there's a Sainsbury's in Chippenham, about 6 miles away, and a Morrison's on the way into Bath.

NANNY STATE ALERT The eerie taxidermy room may cause one or two nightmares.

GETTING THERE Leave the M4 at junction 18 and head towards Bath on the A46. At Pennsylvania roundabout, turn left towards Chippenham on the A420. From the A420, take a right turn into Marshfield and then right again along St Martin's Lane. Follow signs for Ashwicke and Colerne. Continue out of Marshfield, for about 3 miles. The entrance is on the right, clearly marked 'Rocks East Woodland'. From Batheaston, take the road to Colerne/Bannerdown, up the hill and along the Fosseway. Turn left at the signpost for Marshfield/Ashwicke. The entrance is 300 metres on the left.

PUBLIC TRANSPORT Either take the train to Chippenham, then a taxi to the site, or the train to Bath Spa then the First Bus (08456 064446) no. 228 from Bath to Hunter's Hall, alighting at the Ashwicke turn. From here it is a 300-metre walk to the site.

OPEN 1 April–31 October.

THE DAMAGE Prices vary according to season and tent size. High season averages out at about £21 per unit (up to 2 adults and 2 children) per night. There are extra charges for awnings, gazebos and additional people. If your family fancies a stay in a basic yurt, there is one available for £40 a night.

eweleaze farm

A private beach on Dorset's Jurassic Coast is just for starters; locally sourced organic produce is the main course, with marshmallows melted over a roaring campfire for pud. All digested with the help of stunning sea views. Yum!

The setting at Eweleaze Farm is superb, with panoramic sea views from many of its expansive 80 acres, but it's the refreshing outlook of the proprietor that really makes this place special. It's a laidback approach that allows campers to enjoy the true freedom of camping – to roam free and choose a pitch anywhere across seven green fields, to forage for firewood (in the designated areas) and build a roaring blaze or to haul straw bales from the barn and plonk them in front of the fire for authentic countryside seating.

This anti-Nanny-State style is a winner with liberal-minded families, who gather here in August, often forming little nylon communes of two or three family groups. For kids, it's straight down to the beach for swimming, paddling, snorkelling or sandcastling, or perhaps a game of cricket or football in all this lovely space.

For parents, the backdrop of the Jurassic Coast may be entertainment enough, although the South West Coast Path runs adjacent to the site and is a worthwhile excursion if you can drag yourself away from the campsite, as is Weymouth's Sandworld.

Eweleaze Farm's greatest asset is undoubtedly the space – not just the physical kind, but the head space too – to relax, to unwind and to be a family. And, these days, you don't have to wait for August, as the owners have opened up another site just across the road for July camping (Northdown Farm; www.northdown.eu). They even put on a shuttle bus to ferry campers to the private beach. Magic.

Eweleaze Farm, Osmington Hill, Osmington, Dorset DT3 6ED; 01305 833690; www.eweleaze.co.uk

THE UPSIDE Great views, a private beach and campfires.
THE DOWNSIDE It's only open for a short spell.
WHO'S IN? Everyone plus dogs; advance booking essential.
THE FACILITIES Around 250 pitches on 7 fields; 24 showers in total, including 4 outdoor solar-powered ones. A mixture of compost loos and conventional flush toilets are scattered about the fields – 45 in total; straw bales available for campfire seating; firewood available. A few fields are car-free.
ONSITE FUN Paddling and swimming at the beach, snorkelling in the rockpools, feeding the chickens, scoffing tasty pizza (see Food and Drink) and building a fire.
OFFSITE FUN The South West Coast Path follows this stunning coastline in both directions from the campsite; an easy 2-mile family walk eastwards takes you to the Smuggler's Inn (see p90). Nearby Weymouth is a great spot for sailing; courses are available (08453 373214; sail-laser.com).
IF IT RAINS It's only 5 miles to Dorchester, where there's a heap on offer to keep the kids amused. Pick of the crop is the Dinosaur Museum (www.thedinosaurmuseum.com) featuring life-size dinos and lots of hands-on, interactive exhibits.
FOOD AND DRINK The onsite organic farm shop (8am–9pm) sells meat (some frozen), vegetables and other essentials; a wood-fired pizza van and food stalls are popular (12–9pm). Daily fresh bread from the bakery; brekkies available 8–11am.
NANNY STATE ALERT No lifeguard on the beach.
GETTING THERE Eweleaze Farm is down a dirt track just off the A353, by the speed limit sign just outside Osmington.
OPEN August. Northdown Farm is open in July, though.
THE DAMAGE Adult £7/£14 (per weeknight/weekend night); child £3.50/£7; under-3s and dogs free. Vehicle £10.

rosewall

Pristine, perfect Rosewall is *Cool Camping*. The horse riding, fishing lakes and top-notch site facilities make for an easy family break, and the Dorset views are pretty fantastic too: hills to one side and, on the other, just the big, blue sea.

Dorset's cliff-and-beach coast has all the credentials for that perfect summer holiday. If the sun's shining, everyone's out paddling, playing and rockpooling. If it rains, the region is well prepared, with aquariums, museums and soft-play centres.

With demanding tourists descending here in ever-greater numbers, it's no surprise that many of the campsites have progressed up the evolutionary chain. One such place is Rosewall, which started life as a dairy farm's field and has now developed into a highly polished, lovingly manicured camping ground with awards and accolades to prove it.

Gradual, almost imperceptible, changes have occurred over the years; the grass has been thoughtfully tended, the amenities upgraded and the facilities expanded. The result is a highly evolved operation offering a comfortable, easy, hassle-free family holiday with options to ride horses and fish the neighbouring lakes (access via the riding stables). If evolutionary pioneer Charles Darwin had been a camper, this is where he would have most probably stayed.

Such manicured perfection won't suit all Cool Campers, but the cracking views and coastal location will. Anyway, those seeking a more traditional, rough-and-ready campsite will be around the corner at Eweleaze Farm (see p88). But for those looking for an easy holiday, Rosewall is, as Darwin would say, the natural selection

Rosewall Camping, Riding and Lakes, East Farm Dairy, Osmington Mills, Weymouth, Dorset DT3 6HA; 01305 832248; www.weymouthcamping.com

THE UPSIDE Sea views, horse riding and coast access.
THE DOWNSIDE Rough-and-ready campers may not like the carefully coiffured nature of this site.
WHO'S IN? Tents, campervans, dogs – yes. Charity/family groups if pre-arranged. Large/single-sex groups, caravans – no. No campfires or Chinese lanterns; barbecues off ground okay.
THE FACILITIES A 13-acre site with space for 225 tents and 2 pristine amenity blocks (1 with disabled facilities); 2 laundry rooms and a play area. The onsite shop is well stocked.
ONSITE FUN For younger children there's a play park with swings, slide, springies, a play tower and a bird's-nest swing. The riding stables are near the entrance to the campsite and lessons and rides can be booked at the stables or on 01305 833578.
OFFSITE FUN There is a small rocky beach at the end of the lane. For swimming, head to the shingle beach at Ringstead Bay, about 10 minutes' drive. Monkey World Ape Rescue Centre (www.monkeyworld.co.uk) is a 20-minute drive away.
IF IT RAINS The Tank Museum (www.tankmuseum.org) at Bovington is fun and informative for kids.
FOOD AND DRINK The Smuggler's Inn (01305 833125) is a cute country pub with good-value food, just down the road.
NANNY STATE ALERT There are lakes at a nearby site.
GETTING THERE At Osmington, turn left onto Mills Road signposted 'Osmington Mills', then look out for campsite signs. Rosewall is the second campsite; turn right after the stables.
PUBLIC TRANSPORT Train to Weymouth, then a bus (no. X53/108) to Osmington village. Then walk up Mills Lane.
OPEN April–end October.
THE DAMAGE Family of 4 costs up to £31 per night. Pets £3.

campfire cooking

Cooking over a campfire is one of the greatest joys of camping.
Check out our easy recipes to get the kids involved.

Campfire cooking with children is great, but it creates its own special challenges. You might have fond dreams of sourcing some locally caught fish to chef up with a bit of lemon and garlic, but it's quite likely that your children will be clamouring for good old burgers and marshmallows – again. If you're not careful you can spend an entire holiday eating Pringles for breakfast, Kit Kats for lunch and a portion of chips, if you're lucky, for supper.

Of course, that's also part of the fun of camping: it skewers domestic routine, which is precisely why children love it so very, very much.

What follows is by no means a definitive list of the kind of food you might want to cook with kids while camping (no, if you want that, then beg, borrow or steal a copy of the *Cool Camping Cookbook* for some proper tasty, grown-up-friendly fare).

Instead, the following recipes are guaranteed to bring great big smiles to your children's faces, even in the most inclement weather conditions. Forget all about the calories and the fact that you haven't clapped eyes on your toothbrush for the past week. That doesn't matter. Seeing your children having a great time is actually what it's all in aid of.

garlicky herb bread

Cream 150g of butter until it's nice and soft.
Chop up a handful of fresh herbs. Parsley and
chives are good choices, but at a push you could
use tarragon or coriander instead. Add the herbs
and two crushed cloves of garlic to the butter
and mix it all together thoroughly. Add salt and
pepper, too, if you like. Prepare thick slices of
bread by toasting them on a grill over your fire
or dry-frying them in a pan. When one side is
toasted, spread with a generous knife-full of your
butter mixture and return to the grill or pan so
that the butter melts through.

orange eggs

Slice the top off an orange, putting the 'lid' on
one side, and then carefully scoop out the flesh,
while keeping the skin intact. If you have made
any holes in the skin, plug them up with a bit of
pith. Put a dab of butter inside each orange, and
a pinch of salt and pepper, if you like. Carefully
crack an egg into each orange, replace the 'lid',
then wrap the whole thing in foil. Put the parcels
onto some glowing coals in your fire. Allow
them to cook for about 10–15 minutes before
unwrapping them to eat. You can also use this
method for other recipes – it's a real winner
using a pre-bought muffin mix.

campfire baked apples

Cut the top off a large cooking apple, then make
an incision into its centre and remove as much
core as you can – down to about halfway is fine.
Mix a small handful of raisins with some brown
sugar, cinnamon and nutmeg, if you have it. You
can even chop up some pieces of ginger very
finely, or add a pinch of powdered ginger, but
remember that younger children sometimes find
fresh ginger a bit too hot. Put a blob of butter
into the hole where the core was, then stuff the
rest of it with the spicy raisin mix. Blackberries
(or any berries you happen to have) can also work
well as a stuffing. Put another blob of butter on
the top, then wrap the stuffed apple in foil and
cook on the fire for about 20 minutes.

chocolate banana treats

Carefully slice a banana open along one long side, leaving the two ends sealed. Break up some milk or plain chocolate (Dairy Milk works really well, as does flaked Flake and ripped Ripple). Make small incisions along the centre of the banana and wedge a bit of chocolate inside each incision. Push the remaining pieces of chocolate inside the skin of the banana, then wrap the whole lot in foil. Put the parcels onto the fire for 5–10 minutes, depending on the heat of your coals. When you unwrap your banana it should be soft and gooey, and the chocolate melted into a delicious mess.

frankfurter sausage rolls

Add a pinch of salt to 600g of self-raising flour and mix with enough water to form a basic dough. It shouldn't be too wet, but if it is just add a bit more flour. Knead until smooth, then leave to chill out for a bit while you go and find some long, greenish sticks. Scrape the loose skin or bark from the sticks then spear thick Frankfurter sausages onto the end of each stick and push three-quarters of the way down. Roll out sections of dough so that they are relatively thin, then wrap them carefully around your 'dogs'. Cook the dough over some glowing coals. Don't try and cook over flames as the dogs will just burn. When the dough is cooked through, your dogs should be nice and sizzling, too. Slather with ketchup and mustard and eat immediately.

s'mores

For this British version of a classic American campfire treat, take two digestive biscuits and lay pieces of a favourite chocolate bar (Mars, Snickers, plain chocolate – anything goes – cut into slivers) on top of one. Toast a marshmallow (or two) to gooey perfection on the campfire or barbecue. Place the melted marshmallow(s) on top of the chocolate pieces, before squishing the second digestive biscuit on top to form a deliciously gooey sandwich. This is probably the best creation known to man, and kids absolutely love making as many as they can. Once you've done one, do s'more.

stoneywish

A peaceful meadow, adjacent to a nature reserve, sheltered by the folds of the South Downs. Who could wish for more?

Michael Alford had a wish. He had a wish to transform the East Sussex dairy farm that had been in his family for generations into a unique and diverse naturescape, showcasing beautiful wetlands, native woodlands, wide-open meadows and wilderness areas where nature could run its own course. He had a wish to nurture the landscape back to life, fill it with flowering colour, handsome foliage and a flourishing population of animal life.

Michael realised his wish in the form of Stoneywish Nature Reserve: 50 acres of countryside 'as it used to be'; an area so natural that it attracts a wide range of wildlife, including green woodpeckers, herons, goldcrests and thousands of butterflies. There's also a 19th-century-style homestead, complete with free-range sheep, pigs, goats and chickens, so even if the animals of the wild variety prove elusive, there's opportunity aplenty for the kids to get to know this friendly lot.

Camping takes place on the outer edge of the reserve, in a large, flat meadow surrounded by mature hedgerows. There are no camping facilities at all yet, other than a tap with drinking water, although campers are welcome to use the toilets at the reserve's visitor centre. But who has time for a shower when there are bugs to hunt and giant carp to feed? And if you're concerned this might be a nature overload for Junior, fear not — urban relief is only 20 minutes' drive from here, where Brighton's beach-bustle will be an instant change of pace.

Stoneywish Nature Reserve, Spatham Lane, Ditchling, East Sussex BN6 8XH; 01273 843498; www.grasshoppers-uk.com

THE UPSIDE Simple, basic camping with nature-reserve fun right next door.

THE DOWNSIDE There is an additional charge for access to the reserve (adult/child £4.50/£3.50; under-3s free), which is open daily during school holidays, but only from Friday to Monday during term times.

WHO'S IN? Tents, campervans, caravans, groups who book in advance, dogs – all get a yes. (Dogs are not allowed into the reserve). Campfires are permitted so long as they don't damage the grass, so either bring your own firepit or use one of the designated spots.

THE FACILITIES This is easy – a tap. That's it. You can use the toilets/washbasins at the visitor centre, which is in the small car park just beside the camping field. The centre also acts as reception and sells gifts and cold drinks but no camping gear or supplies (the nearest shops are in Ditchling). Please note that there are no facilities at all for rubbish disposal – so come prepared to take away and dispose of your own rubbish and recycling.

ONSITE FUN Strictly speaking, there's nothing (except lots of space) on the campsite itself, but head into the nature reserve for a world of fun. Wildlife spotting, bug hunting, a stone circle to look at and play around, a small farm... not to mention the slightly random attraction of the Emett Hut, a tribute to local cartoonist and inventor Rowland Emett, who was responsible for many of the elaborate inventions that appear in the film *Chitty Chitty Bang Bang*.

OFFSITE FUN The South Downs National Park is a step away from Stoneywish, offering a host of walks, views and pubs. The website (www.southdowns.gov.uk) is a great

resource for downloading walks and cycle routes. If you have older kids in need of an adrenaline fix, then take your pick from zorbing (08456 434360; www.orb360.co.uk) or hot air ballooning (08454 564202; www.horizonballooning.co.uk).

IF IT RAINS The regency resort of Brighton is 10 miles south of the campsite, with a princely pot of attractions (www.visitbrighton.com). You might favour the cultural surroundings of the opulent Royal Pavilion, but the kids are more likely to push for the Pier, where the arcades, rides, doughnuts and candyfloss may just cause excitement overload. Or sugar overload, at least.

FOOD AND DRINK The Bull at Ditchling (01273 843147; www.thebullditchling.com) proves to be a local winner, with inventive fare at the upper end of the pub-food price spectrum. It's a cosy, stylish place; families are welcome and there's a large garden with a kids' play area.

NANNY STATE ALERT A quiet B-road runs directly alongside one edge of the campsite and is accessible by a stile.

GETTING THERE Stoneywish is located 5 miles south of Haywards Heath, and just east of Ditchling. Driving east from Ditchling on the B2116, take the left turn onto Spatham Lane on the outskirts of town. Stoneywish can be found ¼ mile along the road, on the left.

OPEN March–October.

THE DAMAGE A flat rate of £4.50 per person, per night. Under-1s are free. Dogs free.

wapsbourne manor farm

With smoky campfires, old rope-swings and free camping for musicians every Saturday night, this is not a site for the Nanny-State obsessed. But go with the flow and this rural wonderland is the perfect outdoor adventure playground.

Wapsbourne Manor Farm, or 'Wowo', as it's affectionately known by regular customers, is a rare and beautiful thing – a fantastic campsite within two hours' drive of London. It's also the least ruled-and-regulated site you could possibly find in this sue-or-be-sued compensation culture. Campfires are allowed, and to facilitate this a firewood delivery man comes around at dusk on his little tractor; camping's equivalent of room service and an evening turn-down all in one.

Children's entertainment is strictly of the old school variety: climbing trees, swinging on tyres, rolling around in ditches, making camps in the undergrowth. In fact, the entire 150-acre site is a huge, natural adventure playground.

The 40 pitches in the camping fields come with plenty of surrounding space for game playing and the eight premium woodland spots in Tipi Trail offer a fairy-tale-like setting for hide-and-seek.

There's usually always some communal fun going on during summer weekend evenings too: soup suppers; pizza making; plenty of mingling, and even a little singing, around the campfire.

This magical place always seems to have something new to discover; another field hidden behind the thicket, a secret pathway, a yurt nestled among the trees. With the evening air scented with campfire smoke, the soft murmur of sociability and the odd sing-song soundtrack, Wowo just oozes rustic back-to-basics appeal.

Leave the rules at home. Let the kids roam free.

Wapsbourne Manor Farm, Sheffield Park, East Sussex TN22 3QT; 01825 723414; www.wowo.co.uk

THE UPSIDE A cracking, chilled-out atmosphere and 'to-your-tent' firewood delivery.
THE DOWNSIDE A crowd of statics at reception is the only downer, but they're an insignificant feature of this huge site.
WHO'S IN? Tents, campervans, dogs – yes. Caravans, motorhomes, groups of unsupervised under-18s – no.
THE FACILITIES There are 40 pitches spread across the fields and a further 8 in the Tipi Trail woodland, near the 4 yurts. Each pitch comes with a trivet for campfires and a picnic table. There are 4 compost loos scattered about the site – set to be upgraded and styled at time of writing. The main toilets and hot showers are in the camping barn (2 hot showers and 2 loos each for guys and gals) plus Portakabins near reception with 2 hot showers and 2 loos each. These are undergoing an upgrade – with a new unit set to replace them very soon. There's also a new family facility with 2 showers and a loo (suitable for disabled users, too). Near reception is a laundry room with washing machine (£2 per wash) and tumble dryer (£1 per cycle) and at reception you can recharge your phone. In the camping barn there are new fridges and freezers. A recent and very welcome addition is the bread-baking clay oven (bread baked on Friday and Saturday nights) and large communal tent where campers can settle down to a bowl of steaming homemade soup and freshly baked bread on Saturday evenings. You can even order breakfast on the weekends – delicious bread accompanied by Wowo jams and eggs.
ONSITE FUN Making camps, splashing in the streams, hiding in the woods, getting muddy, climbing trees and spending far longer than is healthy swinging on the rope swings. Young campers can take part in Wowo-run activities and workshops

including outdoor shelter building, wild Apache and night bushcraft, as well as educational nature and wildlife walks (see website for details). Inside the barn, a piano and table tennis table await, plus balls to borrow and indoor games to play.

OFFSITE FUN Go for a wander around the beautiful National Trust landscaped gardens at Sheffield Park (01825 790231), just up the road. Kids can run about, feed the swans and ducks by the lake and enjoy the children's trail.

IF IT RAINS With a station right next door to Wowo, the Bluebell Railway (01825 720800; www.bluebell-railway.co.uk) has a big collection of steam locomotives – perfect for a *Thomas the Tank Engine*-inspired day out.

FOOD AND DRINK Wowo's reception sells home-produced eggs, veg and herbs and locally sourced organic goodies – including ice cream. Pizza workshops (£2.50 per child) are held most Saturdays, where you can make and bake your own pizza in the clay oven. Avoid the overpriced tea rooms at Sheffield Park (though do call in to pick up some delicious organic cider and apple champagne from the Vineyard & Nursery tucked behind the walled garden). Instead, head a bit further up the A275 to the Elephant Café Bar at Trading Boundaries (www.tradingboundaries.com). The family-friendly Sloop Inn (01444 831219) is a 40-minute walk away through shady woodland and serves up hearty food and local ales. For foodies, there are 2 excellent gastropubs; the Coach and Horses (01825 740369;) at Danehill and the Griffin Inn (01825 722890) at Fletching.

NANNY STATE ALERT If you're concerned about health and safety, best not come here.

GETTING THERE Follow the Bluebell Railway signs along the A22. Pass the railway on the right and Wowo is the second entrance on the right.

PUBLIC TRANSPORT The nearest station is at Haywards Heath, from where a taxi costs about £15. If the Bluebell Railway is running its trains from East Grinstead, it's only a 10-minute walk to the farm from the terminus.

OPEN Standard camping March–October; Tipi Trail and yurts all year.

THE DAMAGE Tent: adult £10 per night; child (4–16 years) £5, under-4s free. Minimum 2-night/3-night stays on weekends/Bank Holiday weekends. Car £5 per night. Dog £4.50. Tipi Trail pitches cost £10 extra per night. Yurts £112–£250 per 2-night stay. Musicians free by arrangement only. Book early.

safari britain

Visiting this site is like being dropped into the middle of a Bloomsbury-set house party. If you want even more glamour, you can take a trip down the road to Glyndebourne for some operatic high culture. But do remember to wear your dressing gown.

It is said that Lydia Lopokova, the eccentric and colourful Russian ballerina of the twenties and thirties, danced naked along the chalk hill behind the site at Safari Britain for her husband John Maynard Keynes. She was one of the many Bloomsbury eccentrics who gathered at Charleston. She also went to the opera down the road at Glyndebourne wearing her dressing gown.

Perhaps she set a precedent, because an atmosphere of bohemia pervades this site. Everything that you want, and probably a lot more besides, is on site, including pre-erected bell tents and two glorious yurts, which sit in a sunny bowl of the Sussex Downs. You are surrounded by 300-year-old oak trees, a chalk track peeling across the fields and the sea the other side.

The kitchen looks like a vintage photo shoot; shelves stocked with old French enamel, copper cooking pots and a gigantic frying pan big enough to cook a fry-up on the open fire for the whole party. There's a gorgeous yurt at the centre of the camp, furnished like a Moroccan souk with sofas, sheep and cow skins, cushions, a wood-burning stove and painted bookshelves: unlike plenty of yurts, it's genuinely comfortable.

Children will love the optional activities, including foraging, bow-and-arrow making and falconry, or they could easily spend an afternoon building dens, climbing trees and exploring – miles away from the nearest house or road – while you stretch out with the Sunday papers.

Safari Britain Campsite, Firle, Sussex; 07780 871996; www.safaribritain.com.

THE UPSIDE You need only bring food and drink.
THE DOWNSIDE All good things have to come to an end.
WHO'S IN? Families, couples, school groups, hen and stag parties, organisational work teams, tents – yes. Pets, cars, caravans, campervans – no.
THE FACILITIES The site sleeps a maximum of 20 people in up to 11 bell tents, each of which has mattresses, pillows and cotton covers. For £20 extra you can hire a duvet. There's a well-equipped, large kitchen yurt as well as the communal yurt; you can also cook on the huge central firepit or barbecue outside, where there are tables, benches and a circle of log seats. All the crockery, pots and pans that you could dream of have been provided. There's an eco-loo in a little hut with binoculars for checking out the fabulous view, and another up the hill, where you can watch the moon at night. Take your open-air shower under a leafy canopy in a wooden enclosure. Everything bar food and drink is provided.
ONSITE FUN In the yurt there are bookshelves full of maps as well as reading and reference books. There's a guitar, board games, kites, rounders bats and balls for plenty of campsite fun and games. Activities can be arranged depending on the age of your party, and most of them are led by local people: you can try plant foraging for supper, or even find out how to cook rabbits, squirrels or snails. Or you could learn fire making, den building and even spear throwing. A falconer brings in birds of prey, who will alight on your arm with some food enticements, and you can have a landscape drawing lesson, study local wildlife or go on a birdsong walk.
OFFSITE FUN You can walk from the camp in almost any direction for a good distance without seeing a car or crossing

a tarmac track, and the South Downs National Trail is just above the campsite, with great views over the Channel. At the Seven Sisters Country Park the museum has bike and canoe hire. Firle House (01273 858307; www.firle.com) is a 20-minute walk away, with great gardens to romp around in. This is free-spirited Bloomsbury country, and Charleston house (01323 811265; www.charleston.org.uk) is just next door; the cottage garden is particularly sweet. At Wilmington church, try brass rubbing and admire the stained-glass windows of local butterflies. Local swimming places are good; try Tide Mills near Seaford or between the chalk cliffs at Hope Gap.

IF IT RAINS Drusillas Park zoo (www.drusillas.co.uk) near Alfriston is a 10-minute drive away and has a big playground and train. Five minutes away by car you will find Middle Farm (01323 811411; www.middlefarm.com), which has an open farm area where children can visit animals and see milking in action. There's also a hay play barn and nature trail. Lewes is a pretty downland town with a castle, a big indoor play centre – Monkey Business – and a swimming pool at the leisure centre.

FOOD AND DRINK A 20-minute walk away is the Ram Inn (www.raminn.co.uk), and further afield, in Alciston, is the Rose Cottage Inn (www.therosecottageinn.co.uk). The village shop in Firle is good for basics, but Middle Farm's shop has masses of excellent local produce. For grown-ups, the cider house is an essential stop, on the pretext of buying apple juice for the kids.

NANNY STATE ALERT Ponies sometimes wander up to the camp, even though it is fenced.

GETTING THERE Follow the A27 east, past Lewes. Seven miles beyond Lewes, and shortly after the entrance to Charleston Farmhouse (on the right), you'll arrive at Selmeston. Immediately after the Barley Mow pub take the turning right to Bo Peep Lane. Follow the road for 1 mile until you reach a cluster of buildings on your left. Turn right opposite Bo Peep B&B onto the old chalk coach road. After a short distance, Old Shepherd's Cottage is on the right, followed by an old Sussex barn. Parking is just beyond the barn in the large clearing. Safari Britain folk will pick you up and transport you to the site.

PUBLIC TRANSPORT Jump on a train to Lewes, from there it's a 10-minute taxi ride to the campsite.

OPEN April–October.

THE DAMAGE Adult £90 per night; child £40. Prices for exclusive bookings of the whole site start from £1,100.

cobbs hill farm

Who doesn't love animals? Furry ones, shaggy ones, stinky ones. This cute collection of pet-able lovelies will enthral the kids for simply seconds – before they dash off to the big field to join the beasts of the two-legged, home-counties variety (or, Mum and Dad).

Hip and Hop are lion-head rabbits. They scamper around all day, sniffing and scratching and occasionally saying hello to visiting children. They're furry and cute, and when you're used to rabbits of the standard, domestic variety, these hairy munchkins are a wonder to behold. They would also, undoubtedly, taste great on a barbecue…

But the animals aren't here to be cooked, they're here to entertain the kids. Not in a performing-circus kind of way, more in a 'look, there's a lion-head rabbit' kind of way. Which is a nice diversion when the kids have started screaming at each other like hyenas. Animals aside, Cobbs Hill Farm is made for kids.

Much of the site is reserved for caravans, but the dedicated camping field has level pitches and some hook-ups. A large rally field is opened for small groups to camp in. It's safe and well ordered and, however many tents are lined up in the camping area in high season, there are always two fields empty and open for playtime.

A decent adventure playground has a ropey-climbing thing, a spaceshippy roundabout thing and a swinging tyre thing, all made with sturdy wood and good craftsmanship. And those foamy soft-landing areas will help to minimise the bruise-count. As for the animals, there are also horses, goats and guinea pigs to get acquainted with. None of which are much good for the barbecue.

Cobbs Hill Farm, Watermill Lane, Bexhill-on-Sea, East Sussex TN39 5JA; 01424 213460; www.cobbshillfarm.co.uk

THE UPSIDE Playgrounds plus animals equals happy kids.
THE DOWNSIDE No views, no campfires, a bit strict; annoying coin-operated shower system (20p).
WHO'S IN? Tents, caravans, campervans, families, dogs – yes. Small groups – by arrangement. Large groups – no.
THE FACILITIES The toilet and shower block has just 4 showers. There are also 2 family rooms. Hairdryers, shaver points and laundry facilities (£2) are all available. A small shop at reception sells basics, camping gas and ice creams.
ONSITE FUN Animals and a playground; the large, dedicated children's play area often has football goals.
OFFSITE FUN Bexhill (3 miles away) is an old-fashioned seaside resort with a pebbly beach and De La Warr Pavilion.
IF IT RAINS Bexhill Leisure Pool (01424 731508) has a wave machine, a long twisty slide and a café in which to relax afterwards. Hastings is only 5 miles away and has a cinema, Smugglers' Adventure Caves (01424 422964) and a castle.
FOOD AND DRINK There are plenty of family-friendly pubs and restaurants in Battle; go via Catsfield village if you need to stock up on delicious fruit and veg – the farm shop at Great Park Farm Nursery offers high-quality produce plus a range of biscuits, cakes, chutneys and preserves. There's a café there, too.
NANNY STATE ALERT Kids shouldn't stray beyond the obvious campsite boundaries.
GETTING THERE From the A271 at Ninfield, take the A269 southbound. Look out for a left turn onto Watermill Lane. The site is about 1 mile down Watermill Lane, on the left.
OPEN Easter/April–late October.
THE DAMAGE Tent plus 2 adults and car £13–£18 per night; child under-5 £1, over 5s £2. Dog 50p. Gates close at 11.30pm.

nethergong nurseries

Damson picking, riverside strolls and resident barn owls mean that camping at Nethergong is an absolute hoot.

'Nethergong' is a great name – memorable, expressive and with a playful undertone. It could be a fictional place in a child's story, *The Chronicles of Nethergong*, perhaps. So it's a relief to find that Nethergong Nurseries is the perfect kids' playground: full of secret paths that promise adventure and nooks and crannies in which to hide.

The first of three camping areas is a shady area with English broadleaf trees all planted neatly in rows. Pick your way through some dense woods and thicket and you'll come to an open field for eight tents, with two extra pitches by Pimlico Pond in the far corner. This natural eco-system, with frogs and tadpoles, is just above ankle height, so great for paddling and pond dipping. Beyond that is the area known as Puddle Dock (named after a long-gone port, from when this area marked the extremity of mainland England) where semi-private pitches cut into the field's shrubby borders.

The ridge that marks the site's northern border is the elevated riverbank path running alongside the Little Stour river, a fantastic overgrown throughway for kids to explore and find plums and damsons to pick off the trees. From here you can also see the barn owl nesting boxes across the far side of the field – look out for them in the evening and you might just spy the odd flurry of feather flapping. Keep eyes peeled, too, for herons and egrets – is that the wind or are they talking to one another? This may not quite be the magical kingdom of Narnia, but it's not all that far off.

Nethergong Nurseries, Nethergong Hill, Upstreet, Canterbury, Kent CT3 4DN; 01227 860268 (evenings and weekends) or 07901 368417; www.nethergongnurseries.co.uk

THE UPSIDE Simple camping in a green, peaceful setting with lots of space.

THE DOWNSIDE There is a minor road running alongside the wooded part of the campsite so, if you want to avoid traffic noise, camp in one of the fields further away.

WHO'S IN? Tents, well-behaved small groups – yes. Large groups, caravans, motorhomes – no. Dogs by prior arrangement only and must be kept on a lead.

THE FACILITIES A total of 26 acres for up to 25 tents – so do the maths... Yes, lots of space! The facilities are located in a small wooden stable block by the entrance and reception, where there are 2 electric showers and 4 loos, although there will be an additional 2 of each, plus a small provisions shop, by the time you read this. You'll also find the CDP, water tap and rubbish/recycling facilities there, as well as a fridge-freezer and washing machine for campers. Campfires are allowed. Logs are £3.50 a bag plus 50p for kindling. The main business at Nethergong is a veg box scheme, where veg from the onsite polytunnel and from other local farmers is delivered locally; tasty veg is also available for campers to buy Thursday–Sunday, so don't bother bringing your own if you're coming for the weekend.

ONSITE FUN Paddling pond, kids' play area including goals, picking plums and damsons off the trees, walking along the riverbank, sheltering in the polytunnel when it rains, if owner Christine is kind enough to let you.

OFFSITE FUN Animal magic abounds: the Stodmarsh Nature Reserve (01233 812525) is 5 minutes' walk from Nethergong and a 10-minute drive away are both Howletts

Wild Animal Park (08448 424647; www.aspinallfoundation. org), which boasts big animals including tigers, gorillas and elephants, and Wingham Wildlife Park (01227 720836; www.winghamwildlifepark.co.uk), where you can hang out with penguins and meerkats. Howletts also has a cool 'treetop challenge' course with rope ladders, walkways, cargo nets and zip wires for the over-4s. This area also has an abundance of Blue Flag beaches: Whitstable, Ramsgate, Margate and Broadstairs are all within a 20-minute drive.

IF IT RAINS No need to huddle in the polytunnel – there's plenty to do around here on a rainy day. In addition to the animal parks (see above), you could explore the boutique shops and tasty cafés and restaurants in Whitstable, head to Dover to see the castle and South Foreland Lighthouse (01304 852463; www.nationaltrust.org.uk), a 30-minute drive, or go for a chug on the Dymchurch miniature railway (01797 362353; www.rhdr.org.uk), 45 minutes away.

FOOD AND DRINK Christine can supply you with printed directions to 3 decent pubs within walking distance, including the delightful, ivy-covered Grove Ferry (01227 860302), a picturesque pub with good-sized garden that includes a kids' playground; it's about 10 minutes' walk. Boat trips also leave from here (www.groveferryrivertrips.co.uk for advance bookings). For something a bit special, book in advance for JoJos in Tankerton, Whitstable (01227 274591; www.jojosrestaurant.co.uk) for fine tapas, sea views and a BYO policy in a relaxed, kid-tolerant environment.

NANNY STATE ALERT Although Pimlico Pond is fine for paddling, the river and the dyke are not suitable for swimming. They aren't fenced off, so make sure you keep an eye on your children.

GETTING THERE Head south on the M2 and continue onto the A299, passing Whitstable and Herne Bay. At the A28 roundabout at St Nicholas at Wade, turn right and follow the A28 to Upstreet. Turn right, onto Nethergong Hill, and look out for the campsite, a short way up on the right.

PUBLIC TRANSPORT Bus nos. 8, 8A and 9 run from Canterbury to Margate, Ramsgate and Broadstairs and stop 500 metres from the site, on the A28.

OPEN April–October.

THE DAMAGE £15 per tent per night, throughout the season. Book via christine@nethergongnurseries.co.uk.

swiss farm

If you happen to be in Henley, but want a good reason to avoid the Regatta, here's your excuse. At Swiss Farm you'll find landscaped camping at the foot of the Chilterns, complete with lake and swimming pool. Perhaps you could hold your own regatta!

At first glance, Swiss Farm seems a little on the commercial side and a bit too large-scale to feature in our book. But first impressions can be deceptive, and once you've spied the spacious fields and adventure playground, the outdoor swimming pool and the still waters of the willow-fringed fishing lake, your reservations will soon evaporate.

Just outside the quintessentially English town of Henley-on-Thames, Swiss Farm is a popular and accessible campsite. Families often club together for communal footie or cricket matches in the flat field by the playground, and the delighted cries of goal scorers and top batsmen provide a common soundtrack.

The campsite makes a great accommodation option during the festivities of the summer's Royal Regatta, an annual event launched way back in 1839. In those days it was all about the rowing races, watched by moustachioed, straw-boater-wearing Victorian gents, who stood on the riverbanks clapping genteelly. Nowadays the crowd is a fair bit more raucous and the races seem to play second fiddle to days of riverside fun and frolics in the July sunshine.

At quieter times of the year, Swiss Farm is simply a great place to come and relax by the lake, a base from which to explore Oxfordshire's countryside, hills and interesting towns. And in the evenings it's a place to enjoy family barbecues in the dusky evening glow.

Swiss Farm Touring & Camping, Marlow Road, Henley-on-Thames, Oxfordshire RG9 2HY; 01491 573419; www.swissfarmcamping.co.uk

THE UPSIDE Full of fun for kids – swimming pool, indoor games and play area – all an oar's length from Henley.
THE DOWNSIDE Caravans. So many caravans. It can also get pretty crowded and pricey in summer, especially when the Royal Regatta is on (first week of July).
WHO'S IN? Tents, campervans, caravans – yes. Dogs (on leads) – only during low season. Single-sex/young groups – no.
THE FACILITIES Two large refurbished facilities blocks have toilets, hot showers (inc. family/disabled rooms), hairdryers and baby-changing cubicles. Laundry, wi-fi and hook-ups.
ONSITE FUN Kids can splash about in the open-air swimming pool while parents watch from outside the updated onsite bar. There's a playground in a spacious, rabbit-inhabited field and a lake for fishing (half day £2/£3 per child/adult).
OFFSITE FUN Odds Farm Park (www.oddsfarm.co.uk) is 25 minutes away, with bottle feeding and other farmyard fun.
IF IT RAINS Henley's River and Rowing Museum is full of boats, as well as a fantastic Wind in the Willows gallery.
FOOD AND DRINK Visit Gabriel Machin butchers (Market Place; 01491 574377) for a smokin' barbecue back at the site.
NANNY STATE ALERT The lake and pool are easily accessible, so keeping an eye on youngsters is a must.
GETTING THERE The campsite is on Marlow Road, just outside Henley-on-Thames, on the left.
PUBLIC TRANSPORT Take a train to Henley then walk through the town onto Marlow Road (20 minutes). The bus stop for the High Wycombe–Reading service is outside the site.
OPEN 1 March–November (ring ahead for November).
THE DAMAGE Family of 4 £15–£22. Peak times higher.

britchcombe farm

A mysterious white chalk horse gallops across the emerald-green hills of the ancient Ridgeway above Britchcombe Farm. We don't know why it's there, but we know we want to go to see it.

Historians still debate the significance of the wonderful white horses that are to be seen galloping across the South Downs of England – you'll see them cut into the soft chalk.

Were they religious sites? Fertility symbols? Hunting grounds? Or was making them just Neolithic man's idea of passing the time on a Sunday afternoon? No one knows. But what we do know is that Britchcombe Farm is a magical place to camp, and its proximity to the White Horse must have something to do with it.

The site is owned by the impressive Marcella Seymour, who teaches the uninitiated how to light the perfect campfire (yes, these are allowed here!) and is often up at the crack of dawn taking her sheep to market. When she's not doing that, she's busy either making cream teas for the snug tea shop in the barn or very kindly drying out campers' wet kit in her kitchen. It has to be said, she's nothing less than a national treasure.

If you choose to visit the site on a May morning you're more than likely to bump into a bunch of Maypole-dancing druids. Whatever our ancient cousins were up to here, you won't find much better mystical credentials than that.

Britchcombe Farm, Uffington, Faringdon, Oxfordshire SN7 7QJ; 01367 821022 or 01367 820667

THE UPSIDE Fantastic views across Wiltshire, Berkshire and Oxfordshire beneath the ancient chalk hill of the Ridgeway; lighting a fire is an added bonus.
THE DOWNSIDE Very popular on mystical evenings such as the solstices, so book in advance.
WHO'S IN? Tents, a limited number of campervans and caravans, considerate groups (quiet time from 11pm must be respected), dogs (on leads) – yes. Fires are allowed on site in designated spots (please keep a bucket of water on hand – just in case), and logs and paper (£5) are delivered at dusk.
THE FACILITIES Five camping fields of almost 30 acres dotted on either side of the road, with 2 family fields. There are a few hook-ups in the caravan field near the farmhouse. The 5 showers, 3 toilets and washing-up sinks are also beside the farmhouse, but there are several portaloos in each camping field. Although there are no clothes-washing facilities, Marcella has been known to dry out wet kit in her kitchen. There are also 3 tipis and a yurt, each sleeping 4 people and furnished with a double mattress and 2 singles, plus blankets, cushions, sheepskins and cooking equipment. Bring your own bedding.
ONSITE FUN There's nothing specific for children here, but it is popular with families, and there's usually an impromptu football match going on in one of the family fields.
OFFSITE FUN White Horse Hill is just above the site, and footpaths lead from the farm to the Ridgeway, which is riddled with hill forts and long barrows (burial chambers). Nearby is Dragon Hill (see www.berkshirehistory.com), where St George is supposed to have slain his dragon, and a half-hour walk away is Wayland's Smithy, an impressively

spooky Neolithic burial chamber. The little museum of Tom Brown's School (www.museum.uffington.net) in the village is open Saturday afternoons, and at other times for groups. The dreaming spires of Oxford are only 45 minutes away; the Pitt Rivers Museum (01865 270927; www.prm.ox.ac.uk) has totem poles, voodoo dolls and famously grizzly shrunken heads. Back near the site, Farmer Gow's (01793 780555; farmergows.co.uk) is popular with younger children. In spring you can feed farm animals, including lambs and piglets.

IF IT RAINS There's a swimming pool at Wantage Leisure Centre (01235 766201; www.soll-leisure.co.uk), and a bigger one at Oasis (01793 445401) in Swindon with slides and a wave machine. Didcot Railway Centre (01235 817200; www.didcotrailwaycentre.org.uk) has old engines. Bourton-on-the-Water (www.bourtoninfo.com) has a model village, Birdland (01451 820480; www.birdland.co.uk) and a maze.

FOOD AND DRINK Marcella does cream teas on Saturdays, Sundays and Bank Holiday Mondays, spring–October. The White Horse at Woolstone (01367 820726; www.whitehorsewoolstone.co.uk) does very good food. If you find yourself hooked on ley lines and other mystical magic, try the Barge Inn (01672 851705) at Pewsey. The standing stones at Avebury and Silbury Hill are very close, and the pub is a mine of knowledge on crop circles. If you're in Oxford, go to the fish stall in the covered market, with live lobsters and crabs in tanks, and sometimes a dead shark on display, too.

NANNY STATE ALERT Watch the road between the farm and the family fields; it's small, but cars can speed along it.

GETTING THERE Come through Wantage on the B4507, following a signpost for 'Wayland's Smithy'. Stay on that road for nearly 6 miles and the farm is the first on the left-hand side on a bend.

PUBLIC TRANSPORT Not really recommended, but you can take a train to Oxford or Didcot Parkway. There are regular buses from both stations to Wantage, where you can take a taxi to the site or an irregular bus to Uffington and the site is a mile's walk from there.

OPEN All year.

THE DAMAGE Book in advance (£10 deposit) £7 per adult per night; child 5–14 years £3.50, under-5s free. The 3 tipis and 1 yurt cost £60 for 1 night, £90 for 2 nights, £115 for 3 nights, plus per adult/child camping fees.

cotswold farm park

Err, hello! Camping with children next to the most popular farm park in the country, with an adventure playground, bouncy 'pillows' and baby animals to cuddle and feed – what's not to like?

Being able to pitch a tent in the Cotswolds is an extremely rare occurrence, so it's somewhat apt that you can here – at a rare breeds farm. This place is a huge hit with families, as you're next to the popular Cotswold Farm Park, also known as Adam's Farm on the BBC's *Countryfile*.

You're surrounded by the sights, snorts and smells of all creatures great and small; from Highland cattle and Gloucester Old Spot pigs to chickens and donkeys. Most campers take advantage of the one-off entrance fee for unlimited visits to the farm park. Kids love the adventure playground and the Touch Barn, where you can cuddle such cuties as newborn chicks, rabbits and ducklings.

And then there are the views. You're camping in a flat field on top of a Cotswold ridge, with stunning vistas in every direction. And, because all the land surrounding you is farmed by the park, you have access to the most amazing footpaths. The Wildlife Walk is a two-mile wander from the campsite gate into a beautiful valley and back up again. Even the locals can't believe how lovely it is. Many campers use the site as a basecamp for exploring the Cotswolds and its variety of attractions, from the chocolate-box stone cottages of villages like Stanway and Guiting Power, to the 'bright lights' of the spa town of Cheltenham, now more famed for its shops and eateries than its water.

And the bonus? When all the tour buses and daytrippers have left, you and the animals are still there. Albeit you're in a tent and they're in a stable.

Cotswold Farm Park, Bemborough Farm, Guiting Power, Gloucestershire GL54 5UG; 01451 850307; www.cotswoldfarmpark.co.uk

THE UPSIDE Animal-tastic site nestled on top of the Cotswolds... gold dust in this neck of the woods.

THE DOWNSIDE You might be woken up early by all manner of farm animals 'saying' good morning.

WHO'S IN? Tents, campervans, caravans, groups, dogs (on leads, and not allowed into the farm park) – yes. Barbecues allowed, but no campfires.

THE FACILITIES There are 40 pitches, 16 with hook-ups. The facilities are fairly basic, but very clean. They offer men's and ladies' toilet blocks, with free showers and 2 washing-up sinks in a separate shelter. Baby-changing and disabled facilities are across the yard. An onsite shop offers barbecue packs including home-grown/reared and local produce; iceblock freezing; camping gas; and so on.

ONSITE FUN There's plenty of room in the field to play outdoor games. But the big attraction is being able to spend all day next-door at the Farm Park. There's an undercover sand pit, a fun maze involving questions about the farm's rare breeds and a safari allowing kids to get out and about among the farm's residents. The adventure playground has a zip wire, bouncing pillows, swings, a maze... you name it. And depending on the month you visit, animal lovers get the chance to cuddle newborn chicks and feed the lambs.

OFFSITE FUN The main attractions are right on your 'farm-step'. You're surrounded by 1,600 acres of farmland, with access to wonderful walks. A one-off entry fee gives you unlimited access to Farm Park. You're also in the heart of the Cotswolds, so the famous Cotswold Way footpath is never far from you.

IF IT RAINS The Wild Rock indoor climbing wall (01285 721090; www.wildrockclimbing.co.uk), about 7 miles away, is a perfect antidote to wet weather. In nearby Bourton-on-the-Water (a 10-minute drive away), there's a leisure centre with an indoor swimming pool (01451 824024) plus a jacuzzi and sauna for weary parents.

FOOD AND DRINK Adam's Kitchen at the Farm Park offers a hearty cooked breakfast and food throughout the day. Local pubs serving food are the Plough Inn (01386 584215; www.theploughinnatford.co.uk) at Ford and the Halfway House (01451 850344) at Kineton. Bourton-on-the-Water (4 miles) has facilities including a small supermarket and bakery. For home-grown veg visit Pauline's honesty box stall on the side of the road in Taddington (2 miles away), while Winchcombe (6 miles) boasts the Michelin-starred Restaurant 5 North Street (01242 604566; www.5northstreetrestaurant.co.uk).

NANNY STATE ALERT This is a working farm. Kids should be aware to check for vehicles when crossing from the camping field to the Farm Park entrance.

GETTING THERE From Stow-on-the-Wold or Bourton-on-the-Water (both on the A429), follow the camping signs.

OPEN March–October.

THE DAMAGE From £13 per night for a tent pitch in low season to £19 with electric hook-up in high season.

viaduct barn

What do you get if you mix Cubs and Brownies nostalgia with some of *The Railway Children* antics? An unspoilt site in Frampton Mansell, that's what. Camping in a secret valley with a Scouts-style hut, by a viaduct – it's good old-fashioned fun. Dib dib dib!

You might think it odd to suggest that one of the most beautiful, unspoilt campsites is right next to a mainline train track to London. Strange as it might sound, though, apart from the times when you need to cross it, and the odd toot every hour or so, its existence won't hamper your stay. But it could enhance it. Phoning the Gloucester depot to ask if you can cross the tracks is really exciting – and will prevent the need to re-enact the classic shout of 'Get off the line Bobby!'

The site, which you book out in its entirety, is nestled into the edge of Gloucestershire's Golden Valley, flanked by trees and meadows, with unimpeded views. And thanks to the dormitory-size wooden 'hut' and covered outdoor living area, the kids are able to make themselves at home immediately, giving you time to pitch the tent, light the fire and stick on the kettle.

At the bottom of the valley is the disused Thames and Severn Canal, offering opportunities aplenty for wildlife spotting, pond dipping and generally splashing about. A network of footpaths is also accessible from here, so you really could ditch the car for your entire stay.

Enjoying this unique camping experience is all about slow cooking in the bread oven, kicking back in the hammock, huddling around the campfire on hay bales and then falling asleep to the smells of wood smoke and the sounds of owls hooting.

This isn't glamping, but shabby-chic camping. And it's brilliant.

Viaduct Barn, Frampton Mansell, Gloucestershire GL6 8JQ; 01285 760190; www.gairdin.co.uk

THE UPSIDE Your own private site (booked out to your group – from 1 tent to about 6) in a green green valley, with a rustic wooden shack for inclement weather days.

THE DOWNSIDE If you forget to close the loo door, you might get lots of waves from the 8.15 from Paddington.

WHO'S IN? Groups, families, couples, dogs – yes. Caravans, campervans – no (due to access). Campfires – yes.

THE FACILITIES The campsite sprawls over 2 acres of woodland with natural glades mown in, taking about 5 small tents and 1 large one. The shack/hut houses a wood-burner, a claw-foot bath (no showers), a selection of camping mats (if the kids want to sleep inside), cutlery, crockery and a gas stove – all very rustic. There's a compost loo tucked away in a leafy glade. Outside the shack is a tin roof offering shelter from any rain, a campfire with a trivet, kettle and hay-bale seats. Light the wood-boiler for hot water for the sink and bath. For cooking, there's also a pizza/bread oven.

ONSITE FUN It's easy to while away your time here. Swinging in the hammock, climbing trees, jumping on hay bales and messing about by the canal. There are also birdspotting and trainspotting opportunities galore.

OFFSITE FUN There's a small playground by the local village hall. Minchinhampton Common, 3 miles away, is a lovely place for a walk; a huge, open space on the top of hills full of wild flowers with skylarks flitting above. If you're camping from May to September, pre-book tickets for Giffords Circus (08454 597469; www.giffordscircus.com) – the most beautiful, traditional and mesmerising spectacle for all the family that tours around Gloucestershire in the summer – remember to take a picnic.

IF IT RAINS The Corinium Museum in nearby Cirencester (01285 656611; www.coriniummuseum.cotswold.gov.uk) has one of the most impressive Roman collections in the country. Gloucester's GL1 leisure centre (01452 396666) has heated indoor pools and other sports facilities.

FOOD AND DRINK There's no need for food miles in this neck of the woods; there are numerous high-quality local producers. Owner Colin sells free-range eggs and prime Dexter beef (when available). The Stancombe Beech farm shop (01452 771077) at Bisley, 2 miles away, stocks local meat, honey and seasonal fruit and veg. Kim's Shop at Oakridge Lynch (01285 760239; www.kims-shop.co.uk) also offers local goodness, including fresh bread. The Crown Inn (01285 760601; www.thecrowninn-cotswolds.co.uk), a few minutes' walk away, over the train tracks and up the lane, makes a fine local. For lovers of real ale, the Stroud Brewery is based in Thrupp (01453 887122; www.stroudbrewery.co.uk). The Stroud farmers' market (www.fresh-n-local.co.uk) – voted the best in the country – is on every Saturday. And for the best local ice cream, Winstones (www.winstonesicecream.co.uk) is made on Rodborough Common, about 3 miles away.

NANNY STATE ALERT It is next to a mainline train track, so do brief your kids and take good care.

GETTING THERE Turn off the A419 to Frampton Mansell. Take a left at the Crown Inn and drive down the lane into the valley, with the viaduct on your right. Drive underneath it and Viaduct Barn is the second entrance on your right. Leave your car in the yard. It's a 7-minute walk up the track, so if you have loads of stuff, Colin will taxi you in his 1960s Land Rover.

PUBLIC TRANSPORT Catch a mainline train to Kemble or Stroud. Colin will collect you from Kemble for £20, or free of charge if you're staying for a week. If you're biking from Stroud, you can take the canal towpath for about 6 miles, or, from equidistant Kemble, travel along quiet country lanes.

OPEN All year.

THE DAMAGE For exclusive use of the campsite, it's £12 per adult per night and £8 per child, with a £50 per night minimum – all firewood included.

dome garden

Think *Grand Designs* meets camping. Where else can you and the family inhabit an uber-chic geodesic dome (with en suite) on the edge of the ancient Forest of Dean, while a chap called Jonny cooks you Eggs Benedict for breakfast?

Ten geodesic domes have sprung up in the garden of a former dilapidated Forestry Commission lodge, now ultra-modern wooden home-cum-breakfast-bar-hangout. And as the years go by, like the ancient trees in the forest surrounding the garden, this place is blooming into something magnificent.

Owner Jonny and his family were dedicated tipi-campers, until one winter they made a snow dome that could sleep 10 people. When it melted, they decided to invest in some permanent structures, and the Dome Garden was born.

The garden already has a supremely sociable vibe, with kids making friends on the rope swings, in the tree house or running out into the forest. The ever-growing willow tunnels and clever landscape gardening allow plenty of space for privacy, but by night-time, once the pizza oven is lit and everyone's making their own creations, even hermit-like campers will find it hard not to join in.

Yes, this is glamping on a grand scale. But if you're no fan of the outdoors and open fires, do not apply. Wood is used for cooking or heating, from simple stick-heaters – yes, you feed a tiny fire sticks beneath a kettle – to the garden's log-fuelled central firepit. There are so many innovative yet simple touches here that you'll be hard-pushed to find anywhere else like it. Lime-green AstroTurf carpets your dome, kids sleep in hanging pods and there's an ambient light… just see what colour your dome glows after dark. Kevin McCloud would say that this place is, indeed, a work of grand design.

The Dome Garden, Mile End, Coleford, Gloucestershire GL16 7EN; 07974 685818; www.domegarden.co.uk

THE UPSIDE A glamping experience like no other. With one of the UK's best woodlands through the garden gate.
THE DOWNSIDE Having to leave your *Elle Decoration* lifestyle to go home.
WHO'S IN Families, couples, groups – yes. Dogs, tents, caravans, campervans – no.
THE FACILITIES Domes sleep from 2 to 8 people in pristine, ultra comfy beds with fresh linen. The en suite wetrooms have a flushing loo, a shower or bath and washbasin; the water is heated when you light a tiny wood-boiler. Each dome has a kettle and wood-burner. One dome has full disabled facilities. There are 'natural food safes', a freezer and a communal outdoor washing-up area. If you've forgotten anything, the chances are they'll have it for you to borrow, from sterilisers and high chairs to cots and chargers – and they'll all be modern and clean and lovely. Each dome has its own chimenea and stick stove for outdoor cooking, and at night the huge communal firepit provides a great focal point.
ONSITE FUN Rope swings aplenty, a tree house, feeding and wandering about with the chickens. And the forest is just beyond the fence, through a little gate, for when you feel the need to leave your dome bubble and build dens galore.
OFFSITE FUN The Forest of Dean is at your dome-step, so there are numerous outdoor options. A 12-mile, circular cycle track runs past the garden gate, as does the new Verderer's Trail (7½ miles of off-road track). The Forestry Commission's Beechenhurst Lodge (01594 833057; www.forestry.gov.uk) has an outdoor adventure playground for young kids and is the starting point for the free Sculpture Trail. The Motiva climbing wall (01594 861762; www.motiva.co.uk) is also

based here, and anyone weighing over 20 kilos (approximately aged 6 and above) can have a go at reaching the dizzy heights; £6 for 20 minutes.

IF IT RAINS Head underground to the Clearwell Caves in Coleford (01594 832535; www.clearwellcaves.com) to seek out stalactites and see where eerie episodes of *Merlin* and *Dr Who* were filmed. Half- or full-day kayaking and canoeing on the River Wye (well if it's wet anyway...) is available with Forest Adventure (01594 835116; www.forestadventure.co.uk).

FOOD AND DRINK The Dome Garden has its very own suitably cool bar that serves snacks, as well as a pizza oven; you can eat Jonny's home-cooked breakfasts if you don't want to make your own. Coleford has 3 butchers selling locally sourced meat, and the Crusty Loaf bakery (01594 832360) makes a delicious range of breads that include ancient recipes twice a week. The Severn & Wye Smokery at St Briavels (01452 760190; severnandwye.co.uk) serves delicious locally caught fish and fish-and-chips; peek through a window to watch it being prepared. Three Choirs Vineyard (01531 890233; www.three-choirs-vineyards.co.uk) at Newent produces award-winning English wine. The Tudor Farmhouse Hotel at Clearwell (01594 833046; www.tudorfarmhousehotel.co.uk) offers a decent kids' menu and, if you want a truly local pint, the Royal Forest Inn is at the end of the Dome Garden's track, on the main road.

NANNY STATE ALERT If you leave your dome unzipped, there's a possibility of chicken poo on your pristine AstroTurf – perish the thought!

GETTING THERE Detailed directions are sent with your booking form. Don't follow your satnav once you get to Coleford; it won't recognise the forestry track as a road and will direct you to the wrong side of the forest.

PUBLIC TRANSPORT Take the train to Lydney, then CDS Taxis in Coleford know where to go (01594 834834; www.cdstaxis.co.uk).

OPEN All year.

THE DAMAGE Best to book via the website. A dome for 4 adults or 5 people (including kids) costs from £345 for 4 midweek nights in low season to £945 for a week in peak season. Optional breakfast £7.50 per head; pizza evening £9.50, with discounts for kids.

tresseck

There's plenty of watery fun to please all ages at this no-frills site in a lush green meadow on the banks of the River Wye. Imagine bangers 'n' beans sizzling while you crack open a beer at the end of an action-packed day canoeing down the river.

Once discovered, always a fan, it seems, since this site has plenty of campers who come back again and again. They love the 'no delusions of grandeur' vibe. It's a field by some water. But what water.

Whether it's messing about in boats, splashing, paddling or just admiring this great expanse of river (and the array of wildlife and floating or capsizing vessels on it), the Wye will quickly have you hooked, like one of the local salmon on a fisherman's rod. Everyone rubs along nicely here – from couples holed up in cosy two-man ridges, to groups of families in their domes, to the ever-present canoeists making the most of the landing site by the tiny beach.

Human traffic eases off during the day as campers paddle, wander or drive off to follow their respective pursuits. But by four-ish most are back in the fold again, relishing the relaxed environment. Watery tales are swapped and blistered fingers patched up. With a family-friendly pub by the gate (thenewharpinn.co.uk) and the opportunity to make a campfire – Ruth, who owns Tresseck, visits daily at 8am and 5pm and can sell you firewood (£5 per bag; please don't scavenge for wood) – what's not to like?

Whatever time you choose to climb into your sleeping bag, you can be assured that you'll fall asleep to the crackle of open fires, the swishing of water in the reeds, the cough of a sheep and laughter from the pub garden. Quite a lullaby!

Tresseck Campsite, Hoarwithy, Herefordshire HR2 6QJ; 01432 840235; www.tresseckcampsite.co.uk

THE UPSIDE A horizontally laidback atmosphere, with fires.
THE DOWNSIDE There's a music ban, due to neighbours threatening to close the site, so it's vital to respect this.
WHO'S IN? Tents only. Well-behaved dogs, family/activities-based groups – yes. Single-sex groups – only if you're quiet.
THE FACILITIES There are 6 cold taps, several portaloos, but no showers or electricity. Fishing permitted (ask on booking).
ONSITE FUN Paddling, wild swimming and fishing. The camp field is a ball-tastic throwing and kicking space (extended since the first edition of *Cool Camping: Kids*). Landing spot for canoeists (£1.50 to launch your canoe here; free for campers).
OFFSITE FUN This is picture-postcard territory; wander around the paths. Canoeing to Ross-on-Wye takes about 3½ hours, so arrange a pick-up with one of the helpful local companies (www.herefordcanoehire.com; www.wye-pursuits.co.uk). Get lost in the Symonds Yat maze (www.mazes.co.uk).
IF IT RAINS Goodrich Castle (01600 890538) is a stunning ruin just west of Ross, with roll-downable grassy banks and towers to climb. The Forest of Dean's Puzzlewood (01594 833187) has an indoor wood puzzle maze and animals to pet.
FOOD AND DRINK The New Harp Inn is on your doorstep.
NANNY STATE ALERT The Wye is a fast-moving river.
GETTING THERE From Ross-on-Wye take the A49 north. Take the second right, for Hoarwithy. After 4 miles you'll find yourself by the New Harp Inn; the site is to the right of it.
PUBLIC TRANSPORT Train to Hereford, then taxi or irregular bus no. 30 for Ross; alight outside the New Harp Inn.
OPEN Easter–end September.
THE DAMAGE Adult £5.50 per night; child £2; DoE/Scouts £3. Car £1 flat fee. Book via bookings@tresseckcampsite.co.uk.

wriggles brook

Who doesn't wish they had childhood memories of living in a painted gypsy caravan, snuggling under the covers to the warmth of a tiny wood-burner? So, it's not quite life on the open road (there's no horse), but this is the stuff of which dreams are made.

The lane to Wriggles Brook is one of those narrow affairs with grass growing up the middle, so by the time you arrive, you'll already be enjoying a slower pace of life. The garden where the gypsy caravans reside is flanked by greenery and freshness; cows grazing on the bank, trees offering dappled shade, a luscious veg patch – and a babbling brook that can just about be touched when swinging over it in the comfy hammock.

It's the two pristinely preserved painted wagons that are the initial pull. Owner John-Paul found them on eBay and has restored them both to a high spec. The open-lot wagon, with its canvas doors, is about 100 years old, and the bow-top, with wooden stable-doors, is even older. Kids love sitting on the tiny steps at the front, pretending to 'giddy-up' the horses. And what better way for parents to relax than by stoking up an open fire and quaffing a glass or few of vino under the (extremely clear) Herefordshire night skies?

And another pull, once you're actually here, is that it's foodie heaven. The wagons are offered on a B&B basis; from dawn until a very civilised 11am, breakfast is brought to your very own Garden of Eden. What kids (and parents for that matter) don't want to start the day with pancakes, before chowing down on free-range bacon from pigs that eat scrummy meals that are comprised of the likes of honey, chocolate and yogurt?

Wriggles Brook offers the diet of dreams as well as a dream-like holiday for your kids.

Wriggles Brook Gypsy Wagons, 2 Brookside Cottages, Hoarwithy, Herefordshire HR2 6QJ; 01432 840575; www.wrigglesbrook.co.uk

THE UPSIDE A very pretty spot, run by the most hospitable people who cook divine breakfasts and optional dinners, too.

THE DOWNSIDE None to write home about, although the garden isn't big enough for boisterous ball games.

WHO'S IN? There are just 2 wagons, each sleeping 2. Well-behaved dogs – by prior arrangement only.

THE FACILITIES Two wagons each sleeping 2, so a family of 4 have exclusive use. All bed linen and towels are provided, as are eco-toiletries. The washroom houses an eco-loo, washbasin, shower, fridge and even a hairdryer. The conservatory has tables and chairs, plus a selection of guidebooks. Inside the wagons is a Queenie stove (wood-burner), as well as tea-making facilities. Both caravans have a firepit and barbecue outside. The most amazing breakfast is included, too.

ONSITE FUN Swinging about in the hammocks or tree swings, paddling – or even fishing for minnows or bits of pottery – in the stream. Cooking on open fires and dashing from one wagon to the next, bagseying the best bed.

OFFSITE FUN It's lovely to wander up the country lane into Hoarwithy and watch the river flow by. Really no trip to the Wye Valley is complete without messing about in boats, and Hoarwithy is a perfect place to start – or finish – a day or few hours of kayaking (01432 873020; www.herefordcanoehire.com). Budding ornithologists will like the International Centre for Birds of Prey at Newent (01531 820286; www.icbp.org).

IF IT RAINS Youngsters will love what's on offer at Perrygrove Railway at nearby Coleford (01594 834991; www.perrygrove.co.uk) – from steam train rides to treetop

fun and an indoor adventure playground. The Cathedral City of Hereford is within 9 miles, with the historic Mappa Mundi (01432 374200; www.herefordcathedral.org).

FOOD AND DRINK As well as gypsy wagons, Wriggles Brook is about food. If they don't grow it, they'll source it locally and prepare it in the most delicious way. Though after one of Jane and John-Paul's famous breakfasts (meat-eaters, veggies and vegans all catered for), you may not need food for a while. And if you don't want to do any DIY catering, they can package up a gourmet picnic hamper for you and cook dinner that you can eat alfresco under the vine in the quirky conservatory or inside your wagon. For a great family-friendly pub, the Cottage of Content (01432 840242; www.cottageofcontent.co.uk) is in neighbouring Carey. Meanwhile, the market town of Ross-on-Wye has a butcher, traditional greengrocer and delicious Truffles Deli (01989 762336).

NANNY STATE ALERT If you're worried about your kids falling into the brook, this may not be the place for you.

GETTING THERE Travelling north on the A49 towards Much Birch, take the right turn to Hoarwithy just past Llandinabo village. Then take the second left and next available right, down along a narrow country lane into the valley. You'll see the gypsy caravans on your right before arriving at Brookside Cottages, where you check in.

PUBLIC TRANSPORT The nearest train station is in Hereford. As Wriggles Brook is on the outskirts of Hoarwithy, it's best to book a taxi to the site, for roughly £20.

OPEN All year.

THE DAMAGE Weekend nights are £90 and weeknights £70 per gypsy wagon (for 2 people sharing), breakfast included.

yellow wood

Sleeping in a tent – pah! That's just for wimps! Tarpaulins are the order of the day at these sites. You get the run of a real bush camp, made all the more exciting by the sites' secret locations in ancient woodlands. Just don't forget to bring your Swiss Army knife.

Tucked away in secret locations along the Welsh Borders, Yellow Wood Bush Camps are a number of small sites, mainly nestling in woodland, close to Hay-on-Wye and surrounded by footpaths, more trees and a stunning backdrop of mountains.

If you've ever camped in the States or Down Under, you'll already get what bush-camping is all about. And this was the intention of the folk behind Yellow Wood when they first set up the sites over five years ago. This organisation rewrites the camping rulebook. You won't find a shop that'll freeze your cool blocks or top-up your camping gas here. Certainly not. Yellow Wood is all about appreciating and learning how to work in harmony with your surroundings and getting down and dirty with nature. Party central this ain't. There's a quiet policy from 11pm until 7am – so campers (as well as all the little furry fellas you'll no doubt be sharing the woods with, perched up in trees or tucked down burrows) can fully appreciate their natural surroundings. Families who've stayed before have made signs for some of the pitches, so if you're feeling adventurous you could opt for Wolf's Retreat – or dream up your own name.

Yellow Wood Bush Camps provide the ultimate back-to-nature experience – and like those who've been to one of these secret sites before you, you'll be completely hooked.

Yellow Wood Bush Camps, nr Hay-on-Wye, Herefordshire/Powys; 07800 767519; www.yellowwood.co.uk

THE UPSIDE Cooking on open fires. Creating your own camp, then sleeping under the stars in a hammock or on a groundsheet under a tarpaulin.

THE DOWNSIDE Pets generally not allowed, but you can make friends with a fox, wild rabbit or perhaps just a spider.

WHO'S IN? Tents only. Groups – yes. Dogs – by arrangement at less busy times of year.

THE FACILITIES There are specific pitches tucked about the sites, but these are rotated, so you won't be camping on top of anyone else. The pitch size varies to suit groups of 6, 4 and 2 people. Compost loos (whistle if you hear anyone coming) and bush urinals. If your family dome tent is dull, hire a tarpaulin or even a bell tent. For a refreshing start to the day, try the bush shower (watering cans) dash – though if you're feeling precious, warm up the water first. Firewood is from managed resources, and costs £5 per bag; charcoal £6 per bag. Don't even think about burning fallen branches – every twig is part of the delicate ecosystem.

ONSITE FUN Once you've experienced the excitement of rigging up your camp in the trees, there's cooking on open fires, tree clambering and nature walking. Take part in one of the bushcraft course optional extras to learn how to identify edible plants and light fires in all weathers without matches. Adapt, or make your own, bush furniture – draining boards or chairs – from twigs lashed together with binder-twine. Love the sounds of a wood in full swing: leaves falling, twigs snapping, birds twittering.

OFFSITE FUN The camps are near to nature reserves and the River Wye is close by for river walks, swimming spots and canoeing opportunities. Several local companies offer drop-

offs and pick-ups. Wye Valley Canoes (01497 847213; www.wyevalleycanoes.co.uk) are particularly amenable. Hire bikes from local company Drover Holidays (01497 821134; www.droverholidays.co.uk). Llangorse Activity Centre (www.activityuk.com) has horse riding, rope climbing and a Sky Trek experience. The Brecon Beacons National Park (www.visit-brecon-beacons.co.uk) is within reach and offers most outdoor pursuits, from hiking to caving and kayaking.

IF IT RAINS If rain has you running for the nearest centrally heated leisure centre, Yellow Wood isn't for you. There are tarpaulins by the car-parking spaces, so if you arrive in the rain there's a chance to get your act together before pitching. Tree cover is usually nature's umbrella – and snuggling by a fire is the best way to dry out. If you do decide to duck indoors, you're not all that far from cultural Hay-on-Wye or Hereford, which has a cinema.

FOOD AND DRINK The Yellow Wood folk can point you in the direction of good local pubs that are child-friendly, depending on which camp you stay at. Head for Hay-on-Wye for a Co-op, greengrocers, bakers and cafés.

NANNY STATE ALERT This is the great outdoors. Sometimes poisonous wild fungi spring up, so point out such things to your kids.

GETTING THERE Locations are top secret (to avoid overloading the delicate landscape), so you will be given directions on booking.

PUBLIC TRANSPORT Catch the train to Hereford or bus to Brecon. Then bus nos. 39/39a towards Hay-on-Wye (Yellow Wood people should be able to help you with exactly where to alight once you've booked).

OPEN All year.

THE DAMAGE Adult £5.50 per 24 hours; child (under-16) £3.50. Firewood £5/bag (kindling £1.50). If you arrive by bike or on foot you'll get 10 per cent discount. Booking is essential, via info@yellowwood.co.uk.

astro clear view

Forget the Milkybar Kid, here it's all about the Milky Way. At Astro Clear View Campsite, light pollution is never an issue. Kids love hunting for wildlife – from badgers to owls – and they can even spot the Great Bear.

What campers love about this site is its remoteness, space and views. The 'campsite' sits on a long strip of mown ground at the top of a hay meadow, with a backdrop of the Welsh Black Mountains – better than a 50-inch plasma screen any day. In fact, the campsite is that simple: a long strip of nice tidy grass, flanked by woodland.

The vibe here is a peaceful, back-to-nature one, so the site will never be allowed to get too busy. But no one minds the sounds of kids and families enjoying themselves; rolling around on the ground, racing down the hill or chatting to the donkeys.

The great outdoors possibilities here are endless. In early summer, the hay meadow harbours hundreds of thousands of brightly coloured butterflies. Once harvested, it becomes the world's biggest football pitch. Wander into the wood to go badger spotting at dusk, and at night, if it's stargazing you want, dark skies (there's no light pollution) are illuminated with twinkling stars and glowing planets from other galaxies.

And while you get to grips with the evening's gastro feast (if you've got the handle of this place, it should consist of locally bought meat, veg and the compulsory cider), the kids can go pond dipping at the bottom of the field. Later, you can doze off to owls hooting in the trees and then wake to the cooing of wood pigeons.

What campers also love about this site is its lack of people, so *shhh* – don't tell anyone.

Astro Clear View Campsite, Oaklands, Kerrys Gate, Abbeydore, Herefordshire HR2 0AH; 01981 240882; www.astroclearviewcampsite.co.uk

THE UPSIDE Back-to-nature, basic camping at its best in Herefordshire's Golden Valley.

THE DOWNSIDE None really, unless you crave a shower.

WHO'S IN? Families, couples, groups (even large ones) – yes. Dogs – yes (on leads when near farm animals and must be cleaned up after). Caravans and campervans won't make it into the field, but can park in the yard below. No open fires, but chimeneas/barbecues off the ground are okay.

THE FACILITIES This is a refreshingly basic site, with a single portaloo, barrels of drinking water and a tap and bucket for washing-up. There are no marked sites – pitch where you want. If you fancy rigging up a bush shower, we're sure owners Ann and Eric wouldn't mind, but why not just bask in the scent of *eau de woodsmoke*? The chimenea can be loaded up from the bottomless woodpile, and there's a big barrel to use for barbecuing. A fridge-freezer in the farm garage can be used.

ONSITE FUN Space and fresh air for running around and stretching out. Friendly donkeys nose over the fence from the nearby smallholding. From midsummer, the meadow in front is harvested to make a playing space that's quadruple the size of an Olympic football pitch. A large pond at the bottom of the field is a haven for frogspawn in spring, and the woods behind have a labyrinth of footpaths for exploring and games.

OFFSITE FUN This is 'the great outdoors' at its best, but if walking in a stunning landscape doesn't excite the older kids, the Ultimate Activity Company in Hereford (01432 360057; www.ultimate-activitycompany.co.uk) should do the trick, as it offers the lot: from kayaking and mountain biking to rock climbing and paintballing.

IF IT RAINS The campsite is more or less equidistant from mooch-aroundable towns Abergavenny, Hereford and Hay-on-Wye (www.hay-on-wye.co.uk/tourism). The Baker Street Cinema in Abergavenny (01873 857839; www.abergavennycinema.co.uk) is an old-style picture house showing all the latest films. If it's books you want, then Hay has them all – and, for a more 21st-century approach, Hereford has a leisure centre with a swimming pool and other indoor sports such as trampolining and table tennis (www.haloleisure.co.uk).

FOOD AND DRINK As you're in Herefordshire, cider is the tipple to try. One of the best places to taste the local brew is Gwatkin (01981 550258; www.gwatkincider.co.uk) – only a 15-minute walk away. Kids can opt for local apple juice and, before meandering back to the site, you can pick up home-produced beef, ham and sausages from the farm shop there – foodie heaven. For your basics, head to the quintessentially Herefordian Lock's Garage (www.locksgarage.co.uk) at Allensmore, where you can also get great-quality local produce, from fresh veg to ice cream.

NANNY STATE ALERT Non-swimmers should be supervised near the pond.

GETTING THERE Ask Ann for directions, as the farm is on an unnamed road. The farmhouse is called Oaklands; there are no signs for Astro Clear View campsite, which you access by driving in through the farmyard (next to Oaklands) and taking a left into the field, following it up the hedge (on the right) for 100 metres or so, before arriving at the campsite. If it's very boggy, Eric will load all your gear into the four-by-four scrambler and bump you and the kids up the hill – better than any fairground ride.

PUBLIC TRANSPORT Catch a train to Hereford or Abergavenny. There's only a bus to Kerrys Gate once a week, so a taxi is the best option (Abbey Cars – 01981 570301). If you prearrange it, the lovely Ann is also happy to pick you up, if you're stuck.

OPEN All year.

THE DAMAGE A very simple £5 per head, per night, with firewood included.

residential camps

Your kids will love a bit of independence in the summer hols –
learning a few new skills, making pals and having fun together.

Going off to camp used to conjure up images of an all-American ideal of vacations, with high-kicking girls waving pom-poms like cheerleaders, and the slightly confusing idea that John Travolta or Patrick Swayze might be standing in the wings somewhere, teaching dancing to the older teenagers.

But that was probably a long, long time ago, like the seventies or something, and since then residential camps for children and teenagers have been growing in popularity in Britain, too. Longer working hours mean that fewer of us actually get to spend the whole summer with our children, and the question of how you're going to entertain them for six weeks can be an emotional and logistical nightmare for working parents.

Some of the very big, chain camps do have a depressingly corporate and soulless feel to them, but what follows is a selection of the crème de la crème of residential camps for children. So even if you have to keep your nose to the grindstone, you can be safe in the knowledge that your children are, at least, having a fantastic time messing about in boats or learning how to survive in the wilderness, without you.

The Borrowdale Summer Camp

A stellar camp for robust children and young teenagers who are up for a challenge. Children learn proper skills like foraging, fly-fishing, first aid and mountaineering, and at the end of the week they all go off for a two-day survival expedition with Jocky. Jocky's wife Kate cooks, and there's hot chocolate and marshmallows round the campfire every evening. They've been known to set up a cinema tent and a yurt for indoor fun, too. These guys are the real McCoy.

Escape Adventures Ltd, Barclays Bank Chambers, Market Square, Keswick, Cumbria A12 5BJ; 01768 774596; www.keswickoutdoors.com; from £425 per week.

The House!

If you think there's no chance of your world-weary teenagers agreeing to go to residential camp, then The House! might be all the persuading they need. Run by Camp Beaumont, this is a camp with edge, set on the Norfolk coast at a stylish manor house. The youngish staff ('reps') help with teen activities including urban art, quad biking, fencing and circus skills, ensuring teenagers are kept interested and don't try to sneak off to carry out their own illicit activities. There's plenty of time for socialising, too, with parties on the beach, casino nights and masked balls, so everyone's guaranteed to make lots of new friends, too.

Overstrand Hall, 48 Cromer Road, Overstrand, Norfolk NR27 0JJ; 01603 660333; www.campbeaumont.co.uk; from £489 per week.

Over the Wall

This special camp, for children affected by serious illness or disability, allows them to take part in activities they might participate in at a conventional camp, such as archery, climbing, riding, fishing or canoeing. Offering respite for parents, it also gives sick children a chance to have fun in an environment with other kids facing the same sort of challenges. Over the Wall is run by volunteers and open to 8–17-year-olds, and onsite medics make sure that the children are well cared for. This organisation is truly inspirational; they even run camps for the siblings of sick children, to give them a break.

36 Basepoint Business Centre, Harts Farm Way, Havant, Hampshire PO9 1HS; 02392 477110; www.otw.org.uk; free, including travel.

Wickedly Wonderful

If you dream of your children spending the summer taking part in old-fashioned fun such as sailing, riding, crabbing, scavenger hunts, picnics and making bonfires, then Wickedly Wonderful is the sort of living Boden catalogue that you're dreaming of. The children, aged 6–13, camp in their own tents in the grounds of a big house near Chichester. They put up and prepare the tents themselves and then share them with a friend. There's no end of fun, with talent contests, jelly fights and picnics galore, all run by some lovely girls who are happy to give the kids a bit of a cuddle if they get a little homesick.

nr Chichester, West Sussex; 07941 231168; www.wickedlywonderful.com; from £495 for 5 days/4 nights.

WildWise

An organisation run by outdoor survival experts, WildWise offers a host of courses for everyone – involving all kinds of natural fun. On the Wild Ones four-day camping trip to Dartmoor, 8–12-year-olds learn survival skills such as fire making (even when it's raining), food foraging, bushcraft and wildlife observation. Meals are cooked over a campfire and washed down with storytelling, while there are creative opportunities for sculpture and poetry. All in all the camp equips youngsters with some pretty essential life-skills, such as team work and problem-solving, as well as leaving them with a renewed sense of self-confidence and appreciation for the great outdoors.

Dartington Space, Dartington Hall, Totnes, Devon TQ9 6EN 01803 868269; www.wildwise.co.uk; from £250 for 5 days.

The Venture Centre

This camp has been in the Reed family for 30-odd years and they certainly know their stuff when it comes to keeping kids happy. Originally entirely based around water activities – sailing, kayaking, rafting, canoeing, power boating – they have more recently branched out to include activities such as mountain biking, gorge walking, archery and general survival, with emphasis still firmly on outdoor activities. Each camp is for about 30 children, sleeping in small dormitories, and runs for five days. There are numerous repeat bookings, with some children returning five or six years in a row.

Lewaigue Farm, Maughold, Isle of Man IM7 1AW; 01624 814240; www.adventure-centre.co.uk; £220 for 5 days.

pencelli castle

A highly colourful past (lots of blood), thankfully long gone, has been replaced by a harmonious and equally colourful present (lots of flowers) at Pencelli Castle. And everything's so clean and orderly; the loos might well be even cleaner than your own.

Arriving at Pencelli Castle you are greeted with a truly psychedelic display of flowers beside the play area. Not for nothing have the Rees family owners won the Wales in Bloom category year after year.

This is a place that is just packed full of history, though the more gory bits are now consigned to the file labelled 'historical interest'. Thankfully the bloody battles that were fought here up until the 1300s are now a thing of the distant past. The castle was around until the late 1550s, when it was pulled to bits and taken to be used for local building material. But there are shadowy reminders all over the site that point to its former grandeur, like bits of the old walls, or the house, which was part of the chapel until 1583.

Everything about this site says child-friendly, all the way from the spanking-clean loos to the generous play area to the well-clipped camping fields. The Meadow is tents-only and has plenty of space in which to spread out. A shop at reception stocks basic provisions as well as ice creams and locally pressed apple juices, and you can order bread for the next day (before 2pm).

The Reeses run the place like clockwork, and their attention to the finer details is what makes it work so well: there's a much-appreciated bike- and boot-wash, and the camping fields are kept well drained to reduce the amount of tarmac on site.

Paying quiet consideration to a camper's every need is what this dedicated family does so very well, and the reason why staying here is so very nice.

Pencelli Castle Caravan and Camping Park, Pencelli, Brecon, Powys LD3 7LX; 01874 665451; www.pencelli-castle.com

THE UPSIDE Manicured, easy camping with a playground.
THE DOWNSIDE The loos are quite a walk if you're staying in the nicest camping field – the Meadow.
WHO'S IN? Tents, camper/caravans – yes. Dogs, groups – no.
THE FACILITIES When the soundtrack to *The Phantom of the Opera* is piped into a campsite's washblock, you can be assured of its class. And not only are the loos/showers musical, but they are kept sparklingly clean with 2 separate family/disabled rooms, all heated. There's also a laundry, info room, microwave, 4 fridge-freezers, drinks machine and washing-up facilities.
ONSITE FUN There's a good play area with a grass pitch. A nature trail around the site includes a red deer enclosure and vintage farm machinery. The canal running alongside the site means you can launch a canoe directly from the Meadow.
OFFSITE FUN Take a boat trip down the Brecon and Monmouthshire Canal. There is pony trekking at Cantref (www.cantref.com), plus a play farm with pig racing.
IF IT RAINS Climbing at Llangorse (www.activityuk.com).
FOOD AND DRINK Just up the road is the Royal Oak pub – with a beer garden overlooking the canal – but the best food is found in the White Swan (01874 665276) in Llanfrynach.
NANNY STATE ALERT The canal running alongside the site.
GETTING THERE From Abergavenny, take the A40 towards Brecon; 6 miles from Brecon turn left to Talybont. In the village turn right; the site's a couple of miles further, on the right.
PUBLIC TRANSPORT Train to Abergavenny then bus no. X43 towards Brecon/Cardiff. The bus stops very near to the site.
OPEN All year, except 3–29 December.
THE DAMAGE Adult £6.50–£11.50 per night; child £5–£6.50, under-5s free. Hook-up £3.60. Deposit of £25 on booking.

erwlon

If you're a bit of a camping novice, then Erwlon will help you get your tent legs. In fact, this site might turn you into such a happy camper that you'll be striking out on a wild walk into the mountains before you can say 'tent peg'.

There is an element of camping that is all about surprises. The surprise, for example, of finding yourself eating crisps for breakfast. Or realising you haven't had a bath for a week. Or waking up to a priceless view of a Welsh valley. And because camping can sometimes be a bit unpredictable (the moody weather, for instance) it can be rather soothing to arrive at a campsite that does exactly what it says on the tin. And that's precisely what Erwlon does.

There are no frills and no surprises to be had here, but it's a friendly, well-maintained and attractive little site in the bosom of Wales's loveliest countryside which, among other treasures, boasts more castles than you can shake a stick at. The site is made up of two fields of over 100 pitches – most have hook-ups and are dedicated to caravans, but there are 20 grassy ones without.

The Rees family has been running the site since the 1950s and brothers Peter and Huw are now the third generation in a row to be involved. Along with warden Richard, they lovingly tend the site and keep the facilities in tip-top condition.

Open year-round, it's a popular site with walkers who want to explore this gorgeous pocket of land on the edge of the Brecon Beacons. Clean, award-winning facilities, a lovely location just a mile from Llandovery town and a friendly welcome: like we said, Erwlon does exactly what it says on the tin.

Erwlon Caravan and Camping Park, Brecon Road, Llandovery, Carmarthenshire SA20 0RD; 01550 721021; www.erwlon.co.uk

THE UPSIDE Spanking-clean, heated facilities in a quiet little site snuggled up to the Brecon Beacons.
THE DOWNSIDE Space can get a little tight during busy times; it's very caravanny. You can hear some traffic noise, too.
WHO'S IN? Tents, campervans, caravans, dogs (on leads) – yes. Family groups – yes. Single-sex groups – no.
THE FACILITIES Five family rooms in the spotless washblock. There are laundry and dishwashing facilities, plus a drying room and fridge-freezer. Wi-fi (buy a card at reception). Handy baby changing facilities as well as a dog-walking area.
ONSITE FUN There's a play area with swings, climbing frames and a fireman's pole for under-12s. Children are welcome to go (with parents) to watch the cows being milked.
OFFSITE FUN Big Pit Mine (www.museumwales.ac.uk), Showcaves at Dan-yr-Ogof (www.showcaves.co.uk) or Dolaucothi Gold Mines (01558 650177) for underground fun.
IF IT RAINS Cantref (see p150) for horses. Check out the dungeons at Carreg Cennen (www.carregcennencastle.com).
FOOD AND DRINK Llandovery's Penygawse Victorian Tea Rooms (penygawse.co.uk). Beneath the tinkling chandeliers you can enjoy lunches, cream teas and the best coffee in Wales.
NANNY STATE ALERT There's a thick hedge along the edge of the site, but be aware of the road beside it – it's quite fast.
GETTING THERE The site is just off the A40, 1 mile east of Llandovery, on the road towards Brecon, on the right-hand side.
PUBLIC TRANSPORT Train to Llandovery then a 10-minute walk, or take the bus that stops at the supermarket (2 minutes).
OPEN All year.
THE DAMAGE Family of 4 £16–£23 per night.

tir bach farm

We sincerely hope you don't get lost in the snaking lanes that twist and turn their way towards the mellow spot that is Tir Bach Farm. But we promise that, once you've finally found this farmland site, you'll be reluctant to leave.

Most people have dreams. Some people dream about winning the lottery or writing a bestselling novel. Living in Bristol, Ashley and Roze had a dream about moving to Wales to farm a smallholding and run a cute little family-friendly campsite. It takes all sorts.

They heard about Tir Bach Farm, which, appropriately, means 'small land'. And as soon as they visited this special little patch of Wales, and met the farmer, they realised that their dream was right in front of them. All that was several years ago. They now have not only a campsite comprised of 20 tiered tent pitches and two comfy yurts, but also a grand collection of animals in their care: cows, breeding sows, kune kune pigs and goats, as well as geese, ducks, turkeys and the odd chicken scratching around the farmyard. There's plenty of fun and exploring for children to do on site, as well as a new and highly exciting option of taking part in one of the survival courses run by Roze's son Luke, in which accompanied kids can learn how to build shelters, carve wooden spoons and such like; and there are enough local beaches and castles to keep you and your gang amused for several weeks.

One of the nicest things is that, at the end of a day out, you can return to the whispering stillness of Tir Bach Farm. It's a mellow spot, because Roze and Ashley are mellow people.

We think that you'll like it here so much that you might just start dreaming of moving to the Welsh countryside, too.

Tir Bach Farm Campsite, Llanycefn, Clunderwen, Pembrokeshire SA66 7XT; 01437 532362; www.tirbachfarm.co.uk

THE UPSIDE A pretty spot run by a seriously special couple. With climbing frames and farmyard animals (including 2 super-cute Shetland ponies called Cadog and Carreg) to amuse the kids, in countryside dotted with castles.

THE DOWNSIDE It's not easy to get to without a car.

WHO'S IN? Campers, glampers, dogs (on leads), campervans (NB there aren't any hook-ups) – yes. Groups must book in advance and pre-pay (maximum of 2 pitches can be booked together). Caravans – no. Communal fires – yes.

THE FACILITIES The lilac-painted shower block in the old milking parlour is spot-on, with 4 showers, including 2 big ones for washing kids. There's also a washing-up area with 2 big sinks, clothes-washing (£4–£5) and drying facilities (£1 for 30 minutes), a shared fridge-freezer and electricity sockets (20p for 4 minutes), book shop/swap, info leaflets and posters of all the farm's animals with their name tags. The adjacent barn, with its own nesting swallows, makes a top hangout during inclement weather, coming equipped with a barbecue, chimenea, punch bag, table tennis, football table and children's painting wall. Round the corner you'll find the pool room, too. There's a communal firepit at the bottom of the field. The yurts (sleeping 6 and 4) have fixed kitchens plus utensils, a wood-burning stove, gas hob and water, but bring your own bedding. Balconies look out to the Preseli Hills.

ONSITE FUN Children love the swings, slides, basketball court, badminton net and football area. Expect plenty of animal action. The farm's surrounded by mountains and 12 acres of ancient woodland with paths ripe for exploration and a small river, complete with a fallen tree-trunk-bridge.

OFFSITE FUN Castell Henllys Iron Age Fort at Preseli Hills (www.pembrokeshirecoast.org.uk) is a 20-minute drive, with roundhouses constructed on original foundations. Scolton Manor (01437 731328) is just outside Haverfordwest. Llys-y-Fran reservoir (01437 532273) is great for fishing, boating, cycling and walking, and there's a café and play area. St David's is 45 minutes away, with plenty of history to keep everyone amused. The nearest beach is at Newport; kayaking and sailing at Cardigan Bay. There are other beaches less than an hour away, including Newgale (for watersports), Dinas Head (cute little sandy beaches) and Newport Sands (big sandy beaches).

IF IT RAINS There's a heated swimming pool at Fishguard (01437 775504). You could easily spend a day touring the local castles, including Carew (01646 651782), Pembroke (01646 684585) and Llawhaden (01443 336000).

FOOD AND DRINK The Old Post Office (01437 532205) in Rosebush is good for homemade grub, including vegetarian and vegan options. Also try the traditional Welsh pub Tafarn Sinc (01437 532214) – good for meat-eaters. The Bont Inn at Llanglydwen (01994 419575) does Sunday lunches. At Nevern there's the 16th-century Trewern Arms (01239 820395), which does decent food. For groceries try Bethesda farm shop and café (01437 563124), which sells fab local meat, veg and bread.

NANNY STATE ALERT There's a small river in the woodland at the bottom of the site. Stand well back as cows are milked.

GETTING THERE Turn right off the A40 onto the A478 and go through Llandissilio. Look out for the Bush Inn at the end of Llandissilio on the right-hand side. A mile further on look out for a left-hand turning signposted 'Llanycefn'. Follow until you come to a 5-road junction. Take the third lane off this junction, keeping the yellow house to your right. Next look for a sign for 'Tir Bach' on a telegraph pole. Follow this lane. Tir Bach's drive is opposite the thatched cottage – Penrhos Cottage.

PUBLIC TRANSPORT Pretty limited. The best option is to take a train to nearby Clynderwen then hop in a taxi for the next 6 miles.

OPEN Easter–end September.

THE DAMAGE Adult £7–£8 per night; child £3.50–£4, under-2s free. Dogs are free. Yurt prices range from £110 for a low-season weekend in the Carved Yurt (sleeping 4) to £560 for a week in the Painted Yurt (sleeping 6) in high season. Weekly stays only in high season.

dale hill farm

Fresh sea air, French cricket, flat lilos, frizzled sausages and spilled milk in the cool bag. This is bargain-bucket camping, with a million-dollar view. High above Milford Haven Estuary, you have a 180-degree vista before you. All for just a few squid.

Overlooking the mouth of the Pembrokeshire Heritage Coast is a simple field where you and your kids (and, of course, anyone else who fancies it) can pitch your trusty canvas home-from-home and enjoy the simple pleasures of life – think of your kids roaming free in a lovely big field.

The farmers run a very relaxed ship and seem somewhat perplexed by campers' fascination with this field. After all, it is only a large field, backed by a rocky outcrop with a few grazing sheep, and swallows zipping overhead in May and June – oh – and did we mention the view?

In high season it's a wetsuit-drying Mecca, littered with surfboards and dinghies, smoking barbecues, impromptu ball games and kids ducking in and out of the guy ropes. Sheer magic.

Beware though; this site should really come with a warning – camping at Dale Hill Farm could induce a certain smugness. You could become smug because you are on the closest campsite to coveted Dale, with its surfy, yachty gang. Smug because you know that there's a shortcut from the back of the site to surftastic West Dale. And, finally, smug because you know that you have a field 'with a view' (unless, of course, the sea mist has rolled in).

Dale Hill Farm, Dale, Haverfordwest, Pembrokeshire SA62 3QX; 01646 636359

THE UPSIDE Stunning views; space by the bucket-load.
THE DOWNSIDE Smugness may get the better of you.
WHO'S IN? Tents, campervans, caravans, dogs (on leads), groups – yes. No campfires, but barbecues off the ground okay.
THE FACILITIES One huge field, where you can pitch wherever you want. It's best to set up your camp around the edge, so that everyone can roam free in the middle. The farmers are very chilled about what you can do here. One year, by request, they cut the grass into a cricket pitch. There's a functional but clean amenities block just outside the field gate in the farmyard. It's no oil painting, but offers 2 metered showers (£1 for 20 minutes and 20p about 4 minutes), 2 loos and a washing-up room with a fridge-freezer. Queuing is unavoidable in high season, unfortunately. The field has large recycling bins.
ONSITE FUN Batting, balling and bicycling, tag and just hooning about the field.
OFFSITE FUN Crabbing on the pontoon is a compulsory pleasure (apparently it's bacon that gets them clinging on). Take a trip to the offshore island nature reserves of Skomer and Skokholm from the quay (01646 603110; www.dale-sailing.co.uk). Don't forget you're in the heart of the Pembrokeshire Heritage Coast, with its array of stunning beaches and cliff walks (www.visitpembrokeshire.co.uk). The area is popular with divers, too (07545 967180; www.divepembrokeshire.com).
IF IT RAINS Wander across to the stunning bay of West Dale for some surfing/bodyboarding. The local surf shop (01646 636642; www.surfdale.co.uk) offers lessons (and hires out all the latest gear) for surfing, windsurfing, kayaking,

catamarans – if it floats they'll sort it. Folly Farm (01834 812731; www.folly-farm.co.uk) is one of those well-organised family-fun-day-type venues. Don't let this put you off, as it's actually perfect for a really soggy day, with animals to stroke, a tour of the farm on a covered tractor-train, adventure playgrounds and a huge traditional funfair to round off the experience.

FOOD AND DRINK Dale's popular Griffin Inn (01646 636227) has kids coming out of its ears in high season – and is a great place for pub grub, or just to watch the comings and goings in the estuary. For teas, sandwiches and breakfasts, the café on the quay is good enough. There's a small shop in Dale for basics and hypermarkets in Haverfordwest. There are hopes to start a small farm shop selling bread and milk-type basics.

NANNY STATE ALERT The only rule here is no kite flying due to the overhead cables. This is a working farm, so be aware of vehicles and machinery.

GETTING THERE As you enter the outskirts of Dale (on the B4327) you'll see ponds and marshland on your left. Go over the humpbacked bridge and shortly after take the right-hand turn by the postbox. Drive up the hill for about a mile and you'll come into Dale Hill's farmyard with the shower block in front of you.

PUBLIC TRANSPORT The nearest train station is at Milford Haven. From here you can take the Puffin Shuttle Bus (nos. 315 and 400), the coastal service between Haverfordwest and St David's, that stops at Dale, and then walk to the site.

OPEN June–October, but worth ringing if you fancy visiting earlier in the year.

THE DAMAGE A flat fee per night of £10 per tent/campervan/caravan.

trehenlliw farm

Beauty and the Beast? This back-to-basics site, where you're left to your own devices, is surely Beauty on a Budget, all set against a stunning backdrop of marshland and examples of North Pembrokeshire's finest mountains.

The buildings at Trehenlliw are those of a working farm, so might not be as spick as span as the ones you'll see at other campsites, but this all seems to add to the character of the place. It's definitely a function-over-form kinda hangout – and that's precisely what all the regulars love about it.

The large, flat camping field is cocooned within the 115 acres of farmland, which is mainly used for breeding sheep and suckler cows. There isn't a set number of pitches here. Once the area around the perimeter of the field is full, that's it, until someone moves off. There are no streetlights to pollute the night sky, so the strip of moor immediately behind the campsite is a wonderful place to watch for wildlife after dark, including fox cubs and barn owls.

The well-known local landmarks of mountains Carnllidi and Penberi frame the serenest of sunsets and also let you know that surf and sand central, aka Whitesands Bay, is only a mile or so away – so if everyone's clamouring for sand and sea, this is a good place to aim for.

St David's is only a quick 15-minute stroll away, though it can get pretty hectic during the summer months. And the flag-down shuttle bus service around the peninsula passes the site three times a day – hop off it where you fancy and enjoy a coastal roam back. So you'll find that Trehenlliw is not too far from the madding crowd, but far enough away to let you breathe easy in high season.

Trehenlliw Farm, St David's, Haverfordwest, Pembrokeshire SA62 6PH; 01437 721601; sue@trehenlliw.fsnet.co.uk

THE UPSIDE No rules. Secluded, but with a beach in reach.
THE DOWNSIDE Tricky, because we like that it's basic.
WHO'S IN? Tents, campervans, caravans (pre-book a hook-up), dogs (on leads), small campfires – yes. Activities-based, religious, family groups – yes. Young/single-sex groups – no.
THE FACILITIES Male and female toilet blocks plus 2 unisex showers behind the farm buildings. The outdoor washing-up sink and water tap are at the entrance to the field. There are 5 electric hook-ups (please don't cook using the electricity; the supply is weak, so it can trip the farm's supply) available for campervans and caravans, and a CDP behind the nearby trees.
ONSITE FUN Space in the field for games. With permission from owner Sue, kids can walk down the track to the woods.
OFFSITE FUN There are beaches galore around here. Learn to surf with the Ma Simes dudes (www.masimes.co.uk) at Whitesands, just a 5-minute drive away. See also p167.
IF IT RAINS St David's has galleries, shops and a cathedral.
FOOD AND DRINK The tiny City Hall has a country market every Thursday morning. Cwtch (01437 720491) serves modern classics in cool, friendly surroundings (with colouring-in bits to keep kids amused while they're waiting).
NANNY STATE ALERT Take care as this is a working farm.
GETTING THERE Coming out of St David's on Nun Street (A487), take a left at the rugby club onto the B4583. Pass the left turn to Whitesands and shortly after you'll see a drive on the left with a 'Camping' sign. This is Trehenlliw Farm.
PUBLIC TRANSPORT Train to Haverfordwest then the bus to St David's, from where it's a 15-minute walk.
OPEN Mid-April–end October.
THE DAMAGE About £10 for a family/£12 with hook-up.

celtic camping

Knock-out sea views, the warmest of welcomes, a beach within reach, direct access onto the Pembrokeshire Coast Path: all just four miles from Britain's tiniest city, St David's. Celtic Camping showcases the best of Wales from its enviable cliff-top eyrie.

This campsite will have you dancing a little jig of joy as soon as you've stepped foot on its delightful ground. Nuzzling the shores of the Irish Sea, the gaping National Trust land on which the farm and campsite reside offers spectacular views along the coast in either direction, as well as direct access to the Pembrokeshire Coast Path and a sheltered little pebbled swimming cove.

Owner Ian is a softly spoken guy who greets campers with warmth and ease. He and his wife Judy opened the site back in 1992 with just a tiny green corner of grass (our favourite) for campers. Since then he's added a flat 'family' terrace with hook-ups that is situated even closer to the coast; and later a third field – huge, undulating and guarded by a magnificent army of hawthorn bushes – was cleared for family groups camping. And the farm's evolution didn't stop there; its outbuildings have also been transformed into an impressive facilities block and a scattering of cosy bunkhouses.

Testament to the site's allure are the tales of grumpy teenagers who arrive in a sulk at the lack of mobile-phone signal but who, after a week spent taking part in outdoor activities, sitting around campfires and cooking over barbecues, become tearful when it comes to going home. One or two *Cool Camping* authors can confess to having felt the same when it came to packing up their tents…

Celtic Camping, Pwll Caerog Farm, Berea, St David's, Pembrokeshire SA62 6DG; 01348 837405; www.celtic-camping.co.uk

THE UPSIDE A beautiful campsite on the beautiful Pembrokeshire coast.

THE DOWNSIDE It can get pretty darn windy in exposed areas; best pitch near any hedge cover.

WHO'S IN? Tents, campervans, caravans, well-behaved dogs – yes. Any type of group welcome – Celtic Camping offers stag and hen weekends with barbecues and outdoor/sea activities. Fires are allowed off the ground; firepits can be borrowed.

THE FACILITIES Endless. There are 3 camping fields, each offering something to suit everyone: the flat family field has hook-ups while the third field has plenty of space for groups. There are 3 cosy bunkhouses, all with cooking equipment and linen provided, and further dorms in the main barn. Another barn was being converted into a facilities block at time of going to print. This is in addition to the 2 washblocks there now – the main one in the barn (which has row upon row of picnic benches inside at which to cook and eat if the weather's inclement plus 2 washing-up sinks) has super-hot showers and rows of loos; the other block is fairly rudimentary, but close to the family field and has a couple of showers and loos. There's a drying room, and there are rooms available for families and people with disabilities. Water taps can be found by the main entrance and there are large bins and recycling skips by the third field.

ONSITE FUN Sign up to a survival course, on which you'll be trained in how to chop logs and make fire (hugely popular with lads and their dads), go down to the field by the pond to build rafts and catch a rabbit for your supper. There are ponies and pigs on the farm. The pebble beach is a 10-minute

walk away – just off the coast path. It's only small but has rockpools and is good for swimming.

OFFSITE FUN What do you fancy doing today? Rambling along the Pembrokeshire Coast Path towards the famous Blue Lagoon? A spot of horse riding, perhaps? Or how about something a little different? Pembrokeshire Sheepdogs (01437 721677; www.sheepdogtraining.co.uk), just down the road, do sheepdog demonstrations with their working dogs, who shepherd ducks as well as sheep. There's a pleasant farm walk to be done there, too. The Strumble Shuttle bus (no. 404) drops off and picks up outside the gates; you can hop on and off at any point of its journey around the peninsula.

IF IT RAINS Just get wetter with TYF Adventure (01437 721611; www.tyf.com) in St David's. They offer all sorts – from coasteering (they invented it) and surfing to sea kayaking and climbing. Voyages of Discovery (01437 721911; www.ramseyisland.co.uk) do RIB rides to the North Pembrokeshire Islands and whale- and dolphin-watching. On site, take a look at the graffiti wall in the Stage Room adjacent to the barn.

FOOD AND DRINK You can pre-order brekkies (which feature the farm's home-produced sausages and bacon), packed lunches and evening meals (when available). Amble along the coastal path to Porthgain harbour's famous Sloop Inn (01348 831449; www.sloop.co.uk). As well as your standard meal times they offer an hour of bacon sarnies at 11am and an afternoon menu from 3–5pm, so you'll never go hungry.

NANNY STATE ALERT Farm machinery and the onsite pond (although this is ringed by a fence) to be mindful of; and you're on a cliff-top.

GETTING THERE Take the A487 into St David's and head north out of the city on Nun Street. Take the first left (before the rugby club) and continue along the road for 3½ miles, passing Pembrokeshire Sheepdogs and the nursery. Celtic Camping is on the left, down a track.

PUBLIC TRANSPORT Take a train to Haverfordwest and from the bus station hop on the Puffin Shuttle (no. 400) to St David's, then the Strumble Shuttle (no. 404), which will drop you off near the site on request.

OPEN All year.

THE DAMAGE Tent: adult £8 per night; teenager £6; child (2–12 years) £4, under-2s free. Electric hook-up £4. Bunkhouse bed: £16 per person per night. Campfires are £2 and a starter kit will cost £10; nets of logs £4 each. Brekkie £6 per head.

naturesbase

Nature versus nurture? There's no need to get into this old debate at Naturesbase; a gorgeous natural environment nurtured to perfection by its caring, sharing owners. So, come and help yourself to a hefty chunk of nurtured nature, and a slice of pizza, too.

As his day job, Gyles teaches sustainability, designs school grounds and leads expeditions around the world; so, as campsite owners go, he's more than equipped to steer the verdant helm of Naturesbase with his green fingers.

One of two Ceredigion-based eco-sites in this book (see also Denmark Farm, p172), the dreamy, clover- and buttercup-carpeted meadows at Naturesbase have just 10 pitches, each in their own little mown spots among the wild grasses and flowers. Two of the pitches are taken up by pre-erected safari tents, which afford campers the added luxury of laziness: just turn up and settle in for the night without so much as touching a tent peg.

The site caters perfectly for children, with a rubber-stamp nature trail to follow, a willow den, animals to feed, a mini football pitch and streams to hop across. And then there are Gyles' campfire nights; everyone sits around the huge firepit near the communal hub for sing-songs and chats after having their fill of homemade pizza. The kids get to help make the pizza before watching it brown and sizzle in the clay oven.

The atmosphere here is unbeatable: tranquil and restorative, but happy and friendly too. There is plenty of space for everyone to enjoy their fair share of nature around here, as well as inviting communal areas in which to chill, sing, play and, of course, scoff your pizzas.

This site couldn't have a more fitting name than 'Naturesbase', really.

Naturesbase Holidays, Tyngwndwn Farm, Cilcennin, Lampeter, Ceredigion SA48 8RJ; 01570 471795 or 07773 817058; www.naturesbase.co.uk

THE UPSIDE A safe natural playground with buttercups galore and all sorts of activities to get stuck into.

THE DOWNSIDE With just 10 pitches this place gets booked up fast, so you have to reserve your pitch in good time.

WHO'S IN? Tents, those who fancy staying in one of the onsite safari tents, well-behaved dogs (on leads; max. 2 per tent), family groups, school groups (Monday–Friday summer term only) – yes. Trailer tents – by arrangement. Campervans, caravans, single-sex groups – no.

THE FACILITIES Leave your car in the designated parking spot and transport your gear to your pitch in one of the colourful wheelbarrows. Each of the 10 pitches has a firepit. Adjacent to the open-all-hours whitewashed, bunting-strewn barn replete with furniture, games, info and a tempting array of home-baked cakes for sale you'll find the onsite honesty shop. It stocks all sorts, from fair trade and homemade produce to basics, hand-drawn postcards and earthy stationery. Opposite the barn is the beautiful wooden amenities block, with the most stunning compost loos we've ever seen – there's one in both the ladies' and the gents', along with 2 hot showers and a conventional flushing loo. There's also a family/disabled wetroom, which comes with baby changing. Just outside are a couple of washing-up sinks, recycling bins and a blackboard with colourful up-and-coming events chalked up.

ONSITE FUN Lots. A tyre swing, outdoor playbarn with 2 football tables, a sandpit and little scooters and tractors to borrow. Kids can accompany Gyles to feed the pigs and chickens at 8.30am before dashing off to the willow den or makeshift footie pitch. There's a rubber-stamp trail to follow,

Wednesday

5.45pm — 6.45pm

Make your own

£3 **PIZZA** £3

in our earth pizza oven.
Bring your own plate, salad,
wine etc and use the tables
in the courtyard or take the
pizza back to your tent.

Then join us for children's
campfire from 7.30pm - 8.30pm

a stream and, of course, all that space to enjoy running about in. They also run weekly pizza nights and communal campfire fun, as well as other outdoorsy educational courses. The stone barn has games for any inclement weather days.

OFFSITE FUN Just half an hour's drive away you'll find the sheltered sands of Llangrannog Beach. It's a beautiful spot with plenty of amenities. The natural wildernesses of the Cambrian Mountains (www.cambrian-mountains.co.uk) are close at hand for hikes and picnics. See also p175.

IF IT RAINS Take the steam train (01970 625819; www.rheidolrailway.co.uk) from Aberystwyth to Devil's Bridge. The scenery is eye-poppingly stunning.

FOOD AND DRINK Cooked breakfasts are available (book the previous day) as are homemade ready-meals that you can heat up in the microwave in the communal barn. Gyles' wife Alison is a fabulous cook and her cakes are temptingly on offer in the honesty shop. For eating out, the seafood at Aberaeron's Harbourmaster (01545 570755; www.harbour-master.com) is hard to beat and, in the other direction, the Talbot Hotel (01974 298208; ytalbot.com) is a proper Welsh pub with hearty meals and afternoon teas.

NANNY STATE ALERT There is a stream to be aware of, an electric fence around the animal enclosures and the odd piece of equipment near the farm (axe for chopping wood).

GETTING THERE From Lampeter head west on the Aberaeron Road (A482). After about 1 mile past Felin Fach take a right (signposted with a brown tourist sign towards Ty Mawr Hotel). Follow the road over the bridge and steeply up the other side, until you reach a junction. Turn right (leaving the Ty Mawr hotel on your right). Continue along and take a left just before the blue village signs of Cilcennin. Follow the road for about a mile, through a group of houses, and Naturesbase is just after the black metal gates on the right.

PUBLIC TRANSPORT Train to Aberystwyth/Carmarthen, and hop on bus no. X40. Alight at the junction for Cilcennin (near Ciliau Aeron), from where it's a mile's walk up a steep hill, or ring Naturesbase for a lift from the bus stop.

OPEN Easter–end of October half term. Full-week bookings only over the summer holidays. Pre-booking only (see website).

THE DAMAGE Tent plus 2 people and a car £20 per night; child (aged 4 and over) £5, under-3s free; dog £2. Safari tent (weekly bookings only) from £395. Discounts for cyclists.

denmark farm

Spy real, live dragonflies dancing over lily-rich ponds as you head out in search of sleepy dragons in the wooded wonderland at this quiet eco site. There's a magical roundhouse hidden amid the trees too: set up your own round table and play knights errant.

'There are dragons in there!' one young camper enthused as we made our way into the dark woodland adjoining the camping meadow at Denmark Farm. Fearing for our safety, this gallant squire grabbed his trusty sword (okay, so it was a long stick) and rushed past us with a chivalrous 'And I'm going to get them'.

Although we didn't encounter any dragons during the visit, their presence is eminently plausible at this Welsh conservation site, situated amid the green humps and bumps of Celtic Ceredigion. You wouldn't blame the mystical creatures for slumbering off the effects of battling with medieval knights in a centuries-long hibernation somewhere within this 40-acre treasure trove of landscape.

Encircling the camping meadow are woods and fields and ponds that have been slowly nursed back to life from the land's former farming days. A commendable job has been carried out by Denmark Farm Conservation Centre in helping nature to restore the site, much to the joy of the local flora and fauna (dragonflies included).

Pathways that lead through the woods beckon you towards fairy-tale adventures, one leading to a magical roundhouse, another to a spikey hide – is it a bird or a hedgehog? – by the long lake. Just be careful where you step; you wouldn't want to awaken any dragons – at least, not unless you have your own little St George to hand.

Denmark Farm Eco Campsite, Betws Bledrws, Lampeter, Ceredigion SA48 8PB; 01570 493358 (weekdays 9am–5pm only); www.denmarkfarm.org.uk

THE UPSIDE Forty acres of natural, imagination-firing space in which to roam.

THE DOWNSIDE If you take a lot of kit, you're not going to love the wheelbarrow trips from car to camping field.

WHO'S IN? Tents, small groups, guide dogs – yes. Campervans, caravans, pets – no. Advance bookings only. Campfires only permitted in fire woks, with prior agreement.

THE FACILITIES Room for just 10 tents/approx. 20 people along the mown section of the meadow, and there's a yurt for hire with a table, benches and stove (bring mattresses and bedding). In the adjacent woodland you'll find the communal kitchen, a neat little wooden hut with a sink (there's a standpipe for cold water in the field), double-ring gas stove, a couple of big saucepans and a kettle. The hut has 3 walls, so you have views out over the meadow while you wash-up. A little further into the woodland is the compost loo – near enough not to be a long trek from your tent, but far enough away for privacy. On booking, campers are provided with detailed notes for their arrival (no staff live on site) and a helpful map. Included is the code to get into the building for use of the showers (1 each in the men's and ladies') and loos (2 each). There's also a wetroom for those with disabilities. These facilities are kept extremely clean. The dorms are also located within this building. There's another compost loo near the wildlife garden. Campfires are not usually permitted – you can hire a fire wok with a bag of charcoal for £10

ONSITE FUN Acres of meadow and woods in which to hunt for dragons. Nature trails are waymarked across the site. The Denmark Farm Conservation Centre also runs courses such

as family bushcraft, mini-beast hunts, woodcraft and other outdoor educational fun – so do check if anything's going on during your stay. A small natural play area is also being developed and should be ready when you read this.

OFFSITE FUN Visit the huge bog at Cors Caron's national nature reserve (01974 298480; www.ccw.gov.uk), about 7 miles away. The wetlands form a sanctuary for many species of birds as well as other wildlife; its resident otters are so at home that they can sometimes be seen during the daytime. A circular walkway provides access to a huge stretch of peaty Welsh bog. See also p171.

IF IT RAINS There are swimming pools in Tregaron and Lampeter; sweetshops and cafes in coastal town Aberaeron; Fantasy Farm Park is a 25-minute drive away (01974 272285; www.fantasyfarmpark.co.uk), with an indoor play area, rodeo and restaurant as well as a menagerie of animals.

FOOD AND DRINK The Organic Fresh Food Company (01570 423099; www.organicfreshfoodcompany.co.uk) is just off the A485 (you'll pass it on your way to the campsite) and has a fantastic array of produce and can deliver to your door. For eating out, the Talbot Hotel in Tregaron (01974 298208; ytalbot.com) can't be beaten.

NANNY STATE ALERT There's a pond and a deep lake in the grounds and some barbed wire around the site.

GETTING THERE From Lampeter, take the A485 out of the town (it's the right-hand fork), signed towards Tregaron. After 2 miles take a left off the A485 (signposted to Denmark Farm) and continue up the lane. Keep going for another couple of miles and you'll see a sign for the farm, which is on the left.

PUBLIC TRANSPORT Not advised. The nearest train station is at Carmarthen, about 30 miles away.

OPEN April–October.

THE DAMAGE Adult £8 per night; child (aged 6–15) £4, under-6s free. Course participants £10 per night (includes use of indoor facilities). Yurt hire £60 per night (bring your own wood for the stove and sleeping equipment for up to 4 people). Groups comprising up to 20 adults and kids (plus any children under 6) can hire out the whole campsite (including use of the yurt) for £200 per night. The site's dorm beds cost £15 per person per night. To book, send an e-mail to info@denmarkfarm.org.uk.

woodhouse farm

Want to 'get back to nature'? If you like the sound of this, then the wild-flower fields of this site are perfect places to make contact with the natural world. And it's nice to be able to sleep in a real tipi, too.

If your children are bookworms then they might well know that Rupert Bear often talks about the flower meadowsweet. So we think Rupert would have been very happy at Woodhouse Farm, a registered nature reserve, with meadowsweet growing in abundance, and the River Marteg happily running alongside it.

It's a pretty harmonious spot, surrounded by rolling upland pastures studded with caramel cattle and white fluffy sheep. And meadowsweet is only for starters: if you pitch your tent there in late spring or summer, the chances are you'll wake up in a field carpeted with wild flowers. Hay rattle, speedwell, forget-me-nots, milkwort, red clover, white celandine, meadow buttercups, harebells and meadow vetch all burst forth in the large camping field down by the river.

Most children love getting up close and personal with bugs, beetles and things that can swim, and so they can get stuck into pond dipping among the bulrushes and giant golden king-cups, while you get stuck into a bottle of Chablis. You can keep an eye on the sunset at the same time.

Before you know it, you'll be trying to bottle up some sort of meadowsweet wine to take home. Do watch out though: Rupert Bear never let on, but it's pretty potent stuff.

Woodhouse Farm, St Harmon, Rhayader, Powys LD6 5LY; 01597 870081; www.campingmidwales.co.uk

THE UPSIDE Heavenly camping in a mellow valley.
THE DOWNSIDE The facilities are limited.
WHO'S IN? Every man and his dog (if his dog is on a lead) on the campsite. No dogs permitted in the bunkhouse or tipi. Campfires are permitted in specified areas down by the river.
THE FACILITIES There's a lawn-like field of 5 pitches with hook-ups; down on the riverside meadow there are no designated pitches, but you're unlikely to be squashed. There's a tipi (sleeping 8) with a central chimenea as well as gas-burner and stove; charcoal's provided, but bring bedding for the airbeds. The bunkhouse sleeps up to 20 (a room for 6 downstairs; upstairs sleeps 14 fairly cosily) and comes with a kitchen that'd make most homes feel jealous; a dining room with dartboard, piano and video/DVD player; a utility room with laundry and games. Duvets can be hired. Facilities for campers are basic at present: a solar shower can be borrowed, and chemical loos are available for hire (£2 per day), but you're advised to bring your own lav tent. But plans are afoot for a toilet and shower for campers' use near the farmhouse.
ONSITE FUN The place is run as a smallholding, with pigs, sheep, ponies, cows, ducks and chickens; children can help at feeding time. The river's good for swimming if the water's not too high. You can fish, as this is one of the best salmon rivers in the country. It's a great place for spotting wildlife, too.
OFFSITE FUN A network of tracks runs off the site for walking, cycling and horse riding, and if you have older children the Glyndwr's Way long-distance path (01597 027382; see www.nationaltrail.co.uk) and Gilfach Farm Nature Reserve (01597 870301; see www.westwales.co.uk) are within walking distance. You can hire ponies at the

Lion Royal Hotel (01597 810202; www.lionroyal.co.uk) in Rhayader. At the Gigrin Farm Red Kite Centre (01597 810243; www.gigrin.co.uk) red kites are fed every afternoon. If you wish to bring your own horse, grazing is available on site.

IF IT RAINS Hereford's just over an hour away; there's plenty to explore around the cathedral, including the Chained Library (01432 374200; www.herefordcathedral.org) and the Mappa Mundi. Rhayader Leisure Centre (01597 810355) has a pool with supervised activities for children during the holidays. Quackers Play Barn (01597 860111) at Newbridge-on-Wye should keep little children amused.

FOOD AND DRINK The Adamses sell their own pork, bacon, lamb and eggs when available; other basic provisions can be bought in for your arrival, if you pre-order. They do home-cooked dinners, packed lunches and breakfasts (you must book the previous day). There's a small health-food shop in Llanidloes beside the Cobbler's tea rooms (07973 782646), and another in Rhayader (the Wild Swan). Also in Rhayader, you can get a mean cream tea at Günter's tea rooms (01597 811060) and sublime fish and chips at Evan's Plaice (01597 810317). Thursday night is curry night at the Crown Inn (01597 811099).

NANNY STATE ALERT The river along the edge of the site can flow very fast and gets quite deep in wet weather. There's also an electric fence running around the small campsite.

GETTING THERE From Rhayader take the A470/A44 towards Llangurig for about 140 metres. Just past the leisure centre, take the turning signed B4518 to St Harmon. Continue, passing through St Harmon and on to Pant-y-Dwr. At the Mid Wales Inn turn right towards Bwylch-y-Sarnau. After a mile turn right just before a garage and continue for about ½ mile. Woodhouse is on the right, signed with a finger post. (Don't use satnav – it'll take you up a tricky single-track lane.)

PUBLIC TRANSPORT The nearest train and bus stations are at Llandrindod Wells, Newtown and Hereford. From Llandrindod there is a twice-daily bus service to Rhayader, then take a taxi.

OPEN Bunkhouse and campsite: all year, but call ahead in winter to check. Tipi: Easter–September.

THE DAMAGE Adult £4 per night; child (5–15 years) £2.50, under-5s free, camping in the riverside field. Pitch in smaller field: £13 for 2 adults, with hook-up (£8 without hook-up). Dog £2; extra vehicle £2. Tipi: £88 for 1 night; £50 per night subsequently. Bunkhouse: £220 per night for exclusive use; £170 for the upstairs dorm.

gwerniago

Is it a pirate castle? Or a soldier's battalion? A fairy glen? Or a princess's tower? Don't tell the kids, but it's actually a rocky outcrop protruding from the camping field that they'll just love playing on. Making this the perfect place to play out a childhood dream.

What makes a perfect campsite? Quiet farmland location? Nearby beach? Friendly owners who like campfires, children and dogs?

Gwerniago Farm has all of the above and a lot more besides. Located in the pretty Dovey Valley, it's a hotchpotch of undulating fields offering a variety of valley views from its various nooks and crannies. A rocky outcrop, woodland and spreading oak form a befitting natural boundary to one side. The Welsh-speaking Jones family has farmed here for three generations now, so camping at Gwerniago gives you a great insight into a farmer's working life. Arrive at tea time and you might see farmer Trevor's sheepdog herding the sheep back out to their field, with Trevor opening gates ahead of them on his quad bike.

Little firepits dot the site and the hustle and bustle of urban life seems a long way away; it'd be all too easy to spend several days here without feeling the need to leave the site at all.

But that might be a shame, as the beach and little harbour at Aberdovey (Aberdyfi) is less than a 15-minute drive north, and there's also Borth to the south. There's even a family-friendly pub in the village, within walking distance down a quiet lane.

You can't really ask for much more than that, now, can you?

Gwerniago Farm Camping, Pennal, Machynlleth, Powys SY20 9JX; 01654 791227; www.gwerniago.co.uk

THE UPSIDE Open space and lush valley; all you have to worry about is getting the kettle on.

THE DOWNSIDE There are a good number of statics about the place and at busy times tents are pitched close together.

WHO'S IN? Tents, campervans, caravans, dogs (on leads), family groups (book in advance) – yes. Campfires too!

THE FACILITIES The undulating field's divided into 3 sections with masses of flat pitches, 3 with hook-ups. There's a brand-new facilities block with 4 loos, 2 showers each for gents and ladies, a family room (with loo and shower) and a room for disabled users (with loo and shower). There are recycling bins, a fridge-freezer and 2 washing-up sinks in the block, and 1 in the field. Internet is also available. The nearest launderette is 3 miles away in Machynlleth. Reception is stocked with brochures on things to do nearby.

ONSITE FUN Natural boundaries and mature trees – one with a rope swing – provide plenty of excitement for children to explore and space to run around in. They can help feed the lambs in season. In the evenings, Trevor takes the farm's ponies out for rides around the site (£3 a ride/£5 for 2 children). Campfires are permitted in designated spots, and in firepits; bags of logs can be purchased from reception (£3 per bag).

OFFSITE FUN The nearest beach is at Aberdovey (01654 767321; www.aberdovey.org.uk). Meanwhile, half an hour away, there are more seaside activities at Borth, and the visitor centre there (01970 871174; www.visit-borth.co.uk) is staffed by friendly ladies. The pebbly beach is great when the weather's nice. It's a good spot for low-key surfing, and in summer there are lifeguards. Down the coast is Newquay,

The Dylife Valley from the mountain road to Machynlleth

with daily cruises to spot dolphins, harbour porpoises and grey Atlantic seals. North of Pennal, CAT (the Centre for Alternative Technology; 01654 705950; www.cat.org.uk) is popular with all ages. Grandma's Garden (01654 702244), with its arboretum, sculpture park, children's enchanted garden and 'sight and light'/'scent and touch' gardens is worth a visit. There's an RSPB reserve at Eglwysfach, where they've filmed ospreys for BBC's *Springwatch*; you can see red kites and peregrine falcons.

IF IT RAINS King Arthur's Labyrinth (01654 761584; www.kingarthurslabyrinth.com) at Corris Craft Centre is 15 minutes away and you can explore the myths of Arthur on a boat trip through the caverns. There's a leisure centre at Machynlleth (01654 703300) with a pool and slide. You can catch the train along the coast to Pwllheli (tourist info: 01758 613000) from the town.

FOOD AND DRINK Try the homity pie at CAT for a meal with a small carbon footprint, and if you're in Machynlleth their Quarry Café does local vegetarian food (01654 702624). There's a nice little coffee shop at Borth called Oriel Tir a Mor Gallery, which has a lovely upstairs room with squashy sofas if the weather is grim. Their cheese omelette makes a delicious lunch after a blustery walk on the beach. Buy dressed crabs a few doors up at Peter George, the butcher, who also does a mean line in homemade sausages.

NANNY STATE ALERT It's a working farm so there are tractors around and sheepdogs who don't like to be fussed.

GETTING THERE Turn right by the clock in Machynlleth; continue along the road before crossing the bridge over the river, then immediately left. Follow that road for about 2 miles. You will see a site sign on the left-hand side. Take that little road and the site is the first farm on the right.

PUBLIC TRANSPORT Take a train to Machynlleth (3 miles away from the site) then you can hop on irregular bus no. 29 (towards Tywyn), which will stop at the bottom of the lane to Gwerniago. Otherwise, take a taxi from the station.

OPEN 1 March–31 October.

THE DAMAGE Prices per night: £14 per couple, £10 per single person (£5 for anybody who's made their way there on foot or by cycle/public transport), £3 per teenager, £2 for children aged 4–12.

treehouse

Yes, you really are staying up in the trees in a little wooden house, but no, it's not a bodged job made from the remnants of a garden fence, or the wood you never got round to throwing on the bonfire. This breaks the mould in tree house design.

From the moment you arrive in the farmyard, which is nestled halfway up a secret valley on the edge of Snowdonia National Park, you know you're onto a winner. The air is so fresh, the sheep-filled meadows so lush and green – and the views... well, they're simply to die for.

The best way to transport your stuff is to load it into one of the carts waiting in the yard and then, depending on which of the tree houses is yours, bump everything along the farm track and across a field or two, heading for the woods. As the site is over 300 acres, you won't be able to see any of your fellow 'tree housers' from your spot and, thanks to the melodic sounds of the mountain stream and the wind in the leaves, it's unlikely you'll hear any of them either.

The one likelihood is that you will be thrilled when you encounter your home. How exciting: actually staying in a tree house, clambering up its handmade wooden spiral staircase, supported by a twisted willow balustrade. The pod-like creation is a beauty unto itself, with trees growing through, and supporting, its structure – all uber-modern on the inside and with a living roof outside.

With no electricity on site, kids love dozing off to candlelight in the cosy wooden bunks and, if it's windy, you'll be dropping off to the creaking of your house as it slowly sways with the trees. Just as well that owls and squirrels aren't jealous types...

Treehouse, Bryn Meurig Farm, Cemmaes, Powys SY20 9PZ; 01654 703700; www.living-room.co

THE UPSIDE Staying in a unique tree house in stunning rural surroundings.
THE DOWNSIDE There are currently only 3 tree houses, so demand is high. Though there are 3 more in the making.
WHO'S IN? Families (up to 2 adults and 2 kids) and couples – yes. Large groups, campervans, tents, campfires, dogs – no.
THE FACILITIES Each tree house has its own bush shower and compost loo, with water heated via a wood-burner that can also be used to cook on. Wood and firelighters are provided. The kitchen space has a 2-ring gas hob and all the crockery, cooking utensils and cutlery that you'll need. Light is generated by solar- and tea-light-lamps and there's an 'eco' coolbox – a marvellous contraption that's basically a plastic bucket with a lid that's set into sand in a terracotta pot and cools via evaporation. No iceblocks needed. There's a double bed, plus 2 bunk beds, all with bedding provided. A small library of books and games is also great for wetter weather.
ONSITE FUN There's heaps of space and freedom here for kids: watch them hurling themselves onto a rope swing, damming the stream and playing hide-and-seek. There are several circular walks within the 300-acre site, and flora and fauna fans will love seeking out unusual species in the ancient woodland.
OFFSITE FUN As well as the Snowdonia National Park and its mountains, there are beaches within a 20-minute drive; north and south of Machynlleth. Aberdovey offers white sand dunes, surfable sea, boats galore and crabbing from the quay (www.aberdovey.org.uk). The Centre for Alternative Technology (01654 705950; www.cat.org.uk) has loads of

interactive displays for kids (and adults) of all ages, and an adventure playground. Enter via the water-powered funicular railway. There's also a good veggie café – perfect for lunch. Further into the valley, the Dolgoch Waterfalls (see www.snowdoniaguide.com) are magnificent if there's been rainfall in the area.

IF IT RAINS Corris has several options. The Corris Railway (www.corris.co.uk) steam train travels through the valley north of Machynlleth. If it's a tourist attraction you've after, take an underground boat ride in an old slate mine at the quirky King Arthur's Labyrinth (01654 761584; www.kingarthurslabyrinth.com).

FOOD AND DRINK Free-range eggs can be bought from the farm. Machynlleth has lots of food shops selling local produce, including a bakery, butcher (01654 702106; www.wil-lloyd.co.uk), the Blasau deli (01654 700410) and a Co-op. The Penrhos Arms (01650 511243; www.penrhosarms.com) is a family-friendly pub just 15 minutes' walk down the valley from the site. The Wynnstay Hotel in Machynlleth (www.wynnstay-hotel.com) has a pizza oven and, a little further on, the Riverside Hotel at Pennal serves freshly prepared, locally sourced food and has a good kids' menu (01654 791285; www.riversidehotel-pennal.co.uk).

NANNY STATE ALERT You are staying up in the trees and have to climb a spiral staircase to get up there, so it's not the best option for families with toddlers.

GETTING THERE From Welshpool follow the signs for the A458 (towards Machynlleth). At Mallwyd village join the A470 (signposted Machynlleth). At Cemmaes village pass the Penrhos Arms (on the left) and take the first left (not signposted). Follow the small country road for about a mile, and turn right, signposted 'Treehouse'. As you enter the farmyard, you'll see another 'Treehouse' sign, where you park.

PUBLIC TRANSPORT Take a train to Machynlleth, and the lovely Treehouse team will collect you – just give them a bit of prior notice.

OPEN All year (except January), but advance booking only.

THE DAMAGE Family of 4 for 2 nights costs from £349.

the green caravan park

Dare to camp deep in rural Shropshire with *The Sopranos*? Fear not; it's unlikely you'll bump into Tony and his crew here – unless they have wings. Rare soprano pipistrelle bats are just some of the residents at this eco-friendly site.

Part-manager Karen Donohue's family has been running this campsite for over two decades, and she has seen many families return year after year. She reckons it's the magnetic effect of the river (especially on the kids) that keeps 'em coming back.

The site has three main camping areas – a rally field, hook-up area and tent field – and sits in the Onny Valley, with the River East Onny running through it. You'll also find a few other little camping nooks and crannies. The 'island' has 11 pitches (restricted to camping couples in busy periods), and there are several 'dingles' – small grassy areas next to the river, surrounded by trees.

Shallow enough for paddling and catching tiddlers (don't worry if you didn't bring a net – the onsite shop will be happy to sell one to you), the river is also great for playing Pooh Sticks from its little bridges. And the local wildlife likes it here, too. There are 40 bird boxes along the river and 59 species of bird have been recorded by campers. Bat boxes, a wild area, recycling facilities and energy-efficient lighting have also helped the site to gain a David Bellamy Gold Conservation award for good environmental practices and commitment to preserving the natural world.

The site has a friendly and relaxed atmosphere, and Karen tries to keep it a fairly rule-free zone, but she does have three: keep to the five-miles-an-hour speed limit, keep your doggy friend on a lead and be sure to clear up after him, too. Well, four if you count the quiet zone from 10pm to 8am.

The Green Caravan Park, Wentnor, Bishop's Castle, Shropshire SY9 5EF; 01588 650605; www.greencaravanpark.co.uk

THE UPSIDE Simple ppp-pleasures by the riverside – Pooh Sticks, paddling and picnicking.
THE DOWNSIDE There are lots of caravans.
WHO'S IN? Tents, campervans, caravans, groups, dogs on leads – yes. No campfires, but barbecues off the ground okay.
THE FACILITIES The fairly large facilities block in the middle of the site has toilets and showers (20p coins). Five washing-up sinks, laundry and info board. The shop is open 9am–6pm at weekends, and subject to demand at other times. A small charge (for charity) is made for freezing icepacks or charging mobiles.
ONSITE FUN A new play area with a wobbly bridge, balance bars, swings and climbing frame (suitable for all ages) keeps kids entertained if they're not in the river or walking the goats.
OFFSITE FUN This is great walking country. The Offa's Dyke Trail runs close by, and the valley lies between the heather-clad Long Mynd and the craggy outcrops of the Stiperstones Ridge.
IF IT RAINS Head into higgledy-piggledy Bishop's Castle.
FOOD AND DRINK The fantastic Inn on the Green (01588 650105; www.theinnonthegreen.net) is next door to the site.
NANNY STATE ALERT Beware of the river.
GETTING THERE From the A49, turn onto the A489 and follow the brown signs onto the A488 to the site. Or, from the A483, turn onto the A498 and again follow the brown signs.
PUBLIC TRANSPORT Limited. However, Shropshire Shuttle Buses (www.shropshirehillsshuttles.co.uk) from Shrewsbury stop outside the Inn on the Green 3 times a day at weekends and Bank Holiday Mondays.
OPEN March–October.
THE DAMAGE A tent with 2 adults and 2 children costs £19 per night. Dogs £1.

bosworth water trust

Grab your buckets and spades, kids – we're off to Warwickshire! Not located in a county immediately associated with a stunning coastline, Bosworth Water Trust, with its small sandy beach by a lake, is quite a find.

If you and your brood fancy an action-packed trip, head for Bosworth Water Trust campsite, on a 50-acre country park with 20 acres of water sports. Probably pretty uniquely for a campsite – particularly in this neck of the woods – it offers kayaking, windsurfing, sailing and canoeing. And you don't need to splash out on any fancy kit: the campsite will hire out everything you need in the way of tackle and togs, and runs sailing, windsurfing and power boating courses.

If you are feeling less adventurous (or energetic), you will find rowing boats and pedalos, and you can fish from dawn to dusk.

A small sandy 'beach' next to the lake's roped-off swimming zone should keep younger bods happy building sandcastles and, in keeping with the seaside theme (if not strictly *Cool Camping*-style) the park has a pirate-ship playground, 12-hole crazy golf and even bungee jumping. There's also plenty of space for everyone to roam free and play.

When you're finally ready for a sit-down, the café has tables overlooking the lake, and as the campsite takes only families and couples aged over 25, the absence of groups means you get a well-earned good night's sleep come shut-eye time.

Just remember to bring along £3 in change to operate the barrier at the country park on arrival. The site will then give you a barrier card once you've checked in, for a £10 refundable deposit. Not that you'll be wanting to go anywhere, what with all the splashing onsite fun to be had here.

Bosworth Water Trust, Far Coton Lane, Wellsborough Road, nr Nuneaton, Warwickshire CV13 6PD; 01455 291876; www.bosworthwatertrust.co.uk

THE UPSIDE A beach in the landlocked Midlands – super!
THE DOWNSIDE The caravan-to-tent ratio is about 50:50. The showers can't always cope with all those wet people.
WHO'S IN? Families and couples over 25, dogs on leads, tents, caravans, campervans – yes. Single-sex groups – no.
THE FACILITIES Pitches with hook-ups, and unmarked tent spaces without in 2 large, flat fields. There are 2 toilet/shower blocks; 1 is on the campsite, the other near the shop that also has a disabled toilet/shower. No campfires.
ONSITE FUN At the pay-and-play Saturday Kids' Club (10am–12.30pm; book a week in advance on 01455 291876) kids aged 8 and over get the chance to try sailing, kayaking and windsurfing. Fishing (£2 for a day ticket). The country park has pirate-ship-theme play equipment and crazy golf.
OFFSITE FUN Twycross Zoo (www.twycrosszoo.org) is about 20 minutes down the road, or visit Bosworth Battlefield Heritage Centre and Country Park (01455 290429).
IF IT RAINS The Battlefield Line Railway runs from nearby Shackerstone station (www.battlefield-line-railway.co.uk).
FOOD AND DRINK On site, there's Café Kouts for brekkies, jackets, sarnies and daily specials. Market Bosworth's Black Horse Inn (01455 290278), with gastro food, is a walk away.
NANNY STATE ALERT Supervise children swimming, as lifeguards may be attending other parts of the lake.
GETTING THERE Half a mile west of Market Bosworth, on the B585, the country park entrance is signed from the road.
PUBLIC TRANSPORT A bus stops 200 metres from the site.
OPEN All year.
THE DAMAGE Tent £10–£26 per night. Book in advance.

the dandelion hideaway

A top camping combo for parents who love their creature comforts and kids who love their creatures: luxury glamping in vintage-chic canvas cottages, with goats, ducks and ponies to meet, eggs to collect and campfires fit for expert marshmallow-toasters.

Ah, the first joy of glamping – no tent to put up. Just park the car, load a wheelbarrow to cart your stuff to your 'cottage', get the wood-burning stove going and pop the kettle on.

John and Sharon Earp have been catering for glampers on their Leicestershire farm for a good few years now and have perfected the combination of comfortable, luxurious camping with all the fun that staying on a working farm can offer.

Five stylish 'country canvas cottages' (which even have en suite bathrooms) are set out across the top of a field within 250 acres of farmland. You can sit back and admire the view across rolling countryside from the comfort of your rocking chair on the front deck of your cottage.

But staying at the Dandelion Hideaway is also a chance to reconnect with nature and find out more about where your food comes from. John's tour of the farm includes an introduction to his goats – there are around 900, with about 680 used for milking at any one time. He'll show you what they eat and how they are cared for before letting you have a go at milking them and a taste of the finished produce.

Once the kids are clued up on goats, they can dash back to the cottage, where they'll find a 'discovery' trunk full of family games, toys and a stash of wildlife books and equipment to help them explore the surrounding countryside.

They'll think it's just dandy here, and we think that you will, too.

The Dandelion Hideaway, Osbaston House Farm, nr Market Bosworth, Osbaston, Leicestershire CV13 0HR; 01455 292888; www.thedandelionhideaway.co.uk

THE UPSIDE Super-glamping with all the fun of the farm thrown in.

THE DOWNSIDE It is a treat, but glamping is always pricey compared with conventional camping.

WHO'S IN? Groups, dogs – yes. Tents, campervans, caravans – no. Fires at the communal firepit.

THE FACILITIES Five vintage-chic canvas cottages sleep up to 6 people in 2 bedrooms (a double and a twin) and a small 'hayloft' that kids can clamber into. Each cottage has proper beds with mattresses and duvets, a sofa, dining table and chairs, wood-burning range, fully equipped kitchen with butler sink and coolbox, hot and cold running water and an en suite bathroom with a roll-top, claw-foot bath and overhead shower. There isn't any electricity; lighting is supplied by tea lights. Outside, you'll find a deck with rocking chairs, barbecue and picnic table to sit and have a sundowner.

ONSITE FUN As well as the tour of the farm to meet the goats, children can also collect eggs from the chicken shed, befriend the ducks and help to groom the ponies. There's a badger sett and Muntjac deer in the woods, and a communal campfire in the evening provides the opportunity to meet your fellow family glampers.

OFFSITE FUN Just a short drive away is Twycross Zoo (08444 741777; www.twycrosszoo.org). The Battlefield Line Railway (01827 880754; www.battlefield-line-railway.co.uk) runs from Shackerstone station to the site of the Battle of Bosworth, at Shenton. There's fishing and water sports as well as a large playground at nearby Bosworth Water Trust (see p190) – a 50-acre country park with 20 acres of lakes.

IF IT RAINS If you aren't escaping city life, a good rainy day out can be had at Leicester's National Space Centre (www.spacecentre.co.uk). Closer to the farm, Bosworth Battlefield Heritage Centre and Country Park (01455 290429; www.bosworthbattlefield.com) includes an indoor visitor centre with a hands-on weapons wall; or Snibston science and technology musuem (www.snibston.com) has lots of indoor interactive galleries exploring the area's industrial heritage. Bosworth and Snibston both have plenty to do outside, too, if the weather brightens up.

FOOD AND DRINK It's fun to try cooking on the wood-burning range; the farm's Old Cow Shed honesty store sells bread, cakes, biscuits, cheeses, jams and pickles as well as local and rare-breed meats. But if you fancy eating out and want to maintain an upmarket theme for your glamping trip, head to Market Bosworth and try Softleys Restaurant (01455 290464; www.softleys.com) with its pristine white tablecloths and delicious gourmet fare.

NANNY STATE ALERT This is a working farm, so there are vehicles moving around. Notices remind you to wash your hands after touching the animals.

GETTING THERE From the A42, take the A511 towards Coalville then turn right onto the A447 and carry on along this road until you reach the Osbaston Tollgate Crossroads. Turn right into Lount Road, and Osbaston Farm is 200 metres on the left. Pass the farm and go through the silver gates. From the M1 heading north, take the A511 towards Coalville. Turn left onto the B585, then right onto the B582 and left onto the A447 and follow the above directions from the Osbaston Tollgate Crossroads.

PUBLIC TRANSPORT Sharon will pick up car-less campers from Nuneaton train station and will even lend them a bike for their stay. Bus no. 159 runs hourly between Coalville and Hinckley, stopping about 10 minutes' walk from the farm.

OPEN April–October and over Christmas and New Year.

THE DAMAGE Prices per cottage (sleeping up to 6 people) range from £239 for a short midweek break in low season to £866 for a week over high season.

cliff house

Cliff-top, woodland site with direct access to the beach. Sounds good? It gets better! It's right bang next door to a bird reserve – so pack your kites, bikes, binoculars and walking boots to make the most of your trip.

If you look at the website before your visit, don't be put off by the emphasis on holiday cottages and caravans. This 30-acre woodland site has lots of prime tent pitches among the trees and on the lawn in front of the house.

A large shop selling everything you could need – fresh and frozen food, fresh bread daily, camping equipment and first aid, and it's licensed – is open all day and during the evenings in high season, and until about 3pm in low season.

If hiding-and-seeking in the woods, pedalling round the figure-of-eight-shaped path through the site or playing ball games isn't enough to keep the kids busy, they can always head off to the playground for climbing, swinging and sliding, or to the indoor family games room for table football and pool. Or go and visit the neighbours: the National Trust's Dunwich Heath Coastal Centre and Beach is right next door, with hides and nature trails.

Steps (rather steep ones) take you down to the stony beach at the bottom of the cliff, where you can fly kites, beachcomb or paddle in the sea, or take the short walk along the beach to the Coastal Centre, for porpoise- and seal-spotting in the Seawatch Room there.

Also on the doorstep (or should that be tentstep?) is the RSPB's Minsmere bird reserve, which has hides and nature trails throughout the heath, woodland, beach and dunes, and organises special events all year. You can try your hand at nest-box-building and join in their birdwatching safaris.

Cliff House Holiday Park, Minsmere Road, Dunwich, Suffolk IP17 3DQ; 01728 648282; www.cliffhouseholidays.co.uk

THE UPSIDE Peaceful wooded site with direct beach access.
THE DOWNSIDE Caravans, statics and holiday lodges. The prices are a little steep on Bank Holiday weekends.
WHO'S IN? Tents, campervans, caravans, groups, dogs – yes.
THE FACILITIES There's a loo/shower block, undercover washing-up areas and a laundry. The playground has climbing frames, swings, football goals and a slide; there's also an indoor games room, as well as a new bar/restaurant.
ONSITE FUN Children love being in the woods, and the site is also good for cycling around. The playground and games room make meeting other kids easy.
OFFSITE FUN Nearby Walberswick is great for crabbing and boat trips. Southwold has a sandy beach, colourful bathing huts and a quirky pier with handmade penny-slot machines.
IF IT RAINS Aldeburgh's attractions are a short drive away.
FOOD AND DRINK The new bar/restaurant on the site has an ever-changing menu, with a specials board and children's meals. They also do takeaway teas and coffees, and breakfasts on weekends. The National Trust tea room along the beach at the old Coastguard Cottages (01728 648501) has splendid views and boasts the best puds on the Suffolk coast.
NANNY STATE ALERT The steps down to the beach are quite steep, so hold on tight to young children.
GETTING THERE Heading north on the A12 from Ipswich, turn right at the sign for Westleton and Dunwich. At Westleton turn left, drive through the village and turn right at the top of the hill, towards Dunwich. Turn right onto Minsmere Road. The campsite is about 1 mile down this road, on the left.
OPEN March–October.
THE DAMAGE A family of 4 in a tent £20.60–£33.80 a night.

clippesby hall

Safe, comfortable, highly organised Clippesby Hall is the first-time family-campers' delight. From the mini-golf to the swimming pool, from the well-stocked shop to the family-friendly pub, it's all here, like a posh holiday camp. Hi de hi, campers!

The idea of holiday camps is inherently a very good one: lots of activities for kids, good-value food, comfortable accommodation and, most importantly, a bar for the grown-ups. But somehow, when you put these elements together, the result can be quite horrible.

But it's all in the execution, and what the guys at Clippesby have managed to do is to craft an exceptionally family-friendly place, with plenty of onsite fun for children, without resorting to the tacky bright-light arcade-culture and cheesy entertainment of the plastic parks.

Instead, you'll find traditional, wholesome activities here, like crazy golf, swimming and tennis on real grass courts. The onsite shop sells local and fair trade produce, and you can get local ales and ciders at the onsite pub, the Muskett Arms.

It's a fairly large site and it does get busy during peak times, but there are half a dozen different camping areas, so it never feels as if you're all lined up like old-men's legs in a knobbly knees contest. And the strict 'no noise from 11pm' rule helps keep night-times peaceful and quiet.

While Clippesby isn't the quietest, peaceful-est of *Cool Camping* campsites, it is quite possibly the family-est. With its flat, sheltered, spacious pitches, it's the easiest, too. What's more, it's all packaged in a neat, refined, country-estate garden setting. *Brideshead Revisited* meets Maplin's, if you like, although it's quite definitely more Emma Thompson than Ruth Madoc.

Clippesby Hall, Hall Lane, Clippesby, Norfolk NR29 3BL; 01493 367800; www.clippesby.com

THE UPSIDE All you need for the family, except the redcoats.
THE DOWNSIDE It can get busy (and noisy) in peak season.
WHO'S IN? Tents, campervans, caravans, dogs on leads – yes. Large groups – no. No campfires, but barbecues are okay.
THE FACILITIES There is a handy café, a small shop and a relaxed family pub, with outdoor terrace, serving good-value family meals. Clean and plentiful loos and showers are found in subtle wood-clad structures; family bathrooms are available.
ONSITE FUN Kids will be in their element here; a small swimming pool, grass tennis courts, BeWILDerwood-style adventure playground, cycle-hire centre, crazy golf, volleyball, archery and football are all available.
OFFSITE FUN Explore the waterways of the Norfolk Broads (www.finewayleisure.co.uk). For animal fun, head to nearby Thrigby Hall Wildlife Gardens (www.thrigbyhall.co.uk).
IF IT RAINS Visit the Seal Sanctuary in Hunstanton (www.sealsanctuary.co.uk), or Great Yarmouth is 10 miles away.
FOOD AND DRINK Morton's Farm shop (01603 712320) in North Burlington sells fresh, home-grown fruit and veg as well as speciality local foods. They also have an onsite coffee shop, picnic area, fishing lakes (£5 for the day) and, most exciting of all, a maize maze to keep youngsters entertained for hours.
NANNY STATE ALERT There is a swimming pool on site.
GETTING THERE From the A47 between Norwich and Great Yarmouth, take the A1064 at Acle. Take the first left at Clippesby onto the B1152 and follow the 'Clippesby Hall' signs.
PUBLIC TRANSPORT Get the train from Norwich to Acle, then grab a taxi for the short ride to the site.
OPEN All year.
THE DAMAGE Family of 4 £18.40–£38.40 nightly. Dog £4.

thecanoeman

Paddling idly down the Norfolk waterways with only the plip-plop of your paddles to accompany you: this is the best way to explore the river and, if you're really fortunate, you might even spotter notter.

Mark 'TheCanoeMan' Wilkinson (you can just call him Mark), did what many of us dream of but never dare to do – he left his well-paid office job and decided to find a way to make his passion pay the bills. Fast-forward a few years and Mark is now at the helm (sorry) of a veritable canoeing empire. Around these parts, he is Raja of the Rivers and Lord of the Broads.

Mark offers tons of river-based activities packages, but his tipi-canoe trails are truly *oar*-inspiring (sorry). The idea being that you set off from one campsite and then canoe down the river and stay in tipis along the way.

Now, let's get one thing straight – this is not glamping. These tipis are basic. It's proper camping, only with more standing room. Having said that, everything you need is provided, albeit in slightly utilitarian tupperware containers. And, in the colder months, the tipis do come equipped with gas fires to keep everybody snug.

There is a wonderful sense of freedom in setting off in your canoe for a day of paddling, knowing you don't have to double back. There are no timetables – it's just your family, the river and all its curious creatures. This gentle mode of transport won't disturb your surroundings, leaving the river birds and mammals to go about their daily business uninhibited. Keep your eyes peeled for kingfishers, moorhens, coots, herons, water voles and, if you're really quiet (and really lucky), otters.

TheCanoeMan Canoe and Tipi Adventures, 10 Norwich Road, Wroxham, Norwich, Norfolk NR12 8RX; 08454 969177; www.thecanoeman.com

THE UPSIDE Canoe, camp, canoe, camp, canoe... You get the idea. A rare chance for a real river adventure, all at your own pace – otter bliss!

THE DOWNSIDE The hours you'll spend trying to explain to your kids that a Canadian canoe just isn't a necessity in Milton Keynes.

WHO'S IN? Groups, couples, families – yes. The oldest paddler to date was 85 and the youngest has to be able to fit into a buoyancy aid (normally 4 years and over). There are a number of portages (river barriers over which your canoe must be carried) en route, but these aren't problematic for most.

THE FACILITIES Mark has a number of camping spots along the river. Exactly where you stay will often be dictated by the length of your trip and the size of your group. Cool Camping took a 3-night trip from the Goat (01692 538600; www.skeytongoatinn.co.uk) in Skeyton to Wroxham, staying in the grounds of the Norfolk Mead Hotel along the way. All tipis have beds/mattresses (no linen provided so bring your own sleeping bags and pillows), cooking utensils, drinking water, firewood, barbecuing facilities and coolboxes, and all luggage is transferred throughout your trail. Each site will definitely have a toilet (chemical or flushing), first-aid kit and fire-safety equipment. If you stay at the Goat, you also get hot showers (50p for 5 minutes; tokens can be bought from the bar at 12–2pm and 6pm–midnight), and Radio 2 is piped in, so you can shower with Simon Mayo, if you so desire.

ONSITE FUN At the Goat there's a children's play area and plenty of space. Otherwise, the tipis and campfires offer endless diversion.

OFFSITE FUN You'll be on the water for the majority of the time, so just enjoy the river and all its wildlife. Pack some food and moor-up for a memorable riverside picnic.

IF IT RAINS You still have to get to your next camping spot, we're afraid. Wear good waterproofs and you'll soon find that the river takes on a special beauty under cloudy skies. Having said that, if it's truly miserable and you've got very little ones, one of TheCanoeMan crew would probably bundle you into the minibus if you asked very nicely and produced some semi-believable tears.

FOOD AND DRINK You'll find a basic welcome food pack, which includes the likes of bread, wine, cheese and tea, inside your tipi. The Goat is a real family pub – the menu is varied, the portions are large and there are plenty of local ales on offer. The nearest shop is Thoroughgoods (01603 737654), 1 mile away at RAF Coltishall. It sells firewood and charcoal, plus all manner of groceries, including fresh meat and vegetables. If you camp in the grounds of the Norfolk Mead Hotel, you'll be able to explore Coltishall, which just so happens to have a fantastic Thai restaurant – Chang Thai (01603 736655; www.leelathaicuisine.co.uk).

NANNY STATE ALERT Canoeing is in water! Make sure each member of the family wears their buoyancy aid at all times and try not to get into a fight with a swan.

GETTING THERE Detailed directions will be sent to you, along with your all-important itinerary, on booking.

PUBLIC TRANSPORT Take a train to Norwich, from where TheCanoeMan crew can provide transport to Horning (£10 additional charge each way), or catch a connecting train on to Wroxham and they'll pick you up from there (£5 additional charge each way).

OPEN March–mid October, or all year if Mark thinks your sleeping bag passes muster.

THE DAMAGE From £99 per night for a midweek adventure for 4–5 people in low season, to £310 per night for a weekend adventure for 7–8 people in high season. Canoe for 3 adults, or 2 adults and 3 children £65. Canoe for 2 adults £50. **Bookings also via info@thecanoeman.com.**

nature's path

With a field full of disappearing cows, broken old objects magically transfigured into new ones and a steam train to rival the Hogwarts' Express going past, all is not what it seems at Nature's Path…

Okay, so the cows don't really disappear – they just come and go as they please via a secret tunnel under the road – but Shane is definitely the greenest campsite owner we've met. Not because he looks like Shrek or anything, it's just that he recycles and repurposes everything. So maybe, in that sense, he's more like a Womble. Tobermory, perhaps…

Nature's Path was originally just that, a path (well, a tractor track) that ran between Yaxham Waters Holiday Park and the picturesque field beside it. Using no small amount of imagination, Shane dreamed up a bijou glamping idyll. With a few yurts or a tipi (all sleeping four – or two adults and three children) to choose from, it just so happens to be the perfect way to introduce your little ones to the joys of sleeping outdoors.

A welcoming and enthusiastic host, Shane will regale you with the tales of provenance for anything and everything at the site. From the South African barbecue that was once a gas canister, to the World War II sand buckets from the roofs of Norwich City Council that now happily serve as ash bins, these items have been given an eco-minded second chance. Even the lofty lengths of wood for the tipi poles were sourced locally and stripped back by Shane and his friends and family.

The good thing about being so close to a large holiday park is that its facilities are at your disposal. There are various farm animals to feed, a play area, and well-stocked ponds to fish. Let your lot loose on this site and they'll just love wombling free.

Nature's Path Tipi and Yurt Holidays (Yaxham Waters Holiday Park), Dereham Road, Yaxham, Norfolk NR19 1RF; 01692 671834; www.naturespathtipis.co.uk

THE UPSIDE An easy way to experience tipi or yurt camping, without the isolation of many glamping spots.
THE DOWNSIDE With the holiday park just beyond the fence, you're pretty much surrounded by caravans and chalets.
WHO'S IN? Groups, dogs – yes. Caravans, campervans – no. Tents – yes, if you're renting the whole site.
THE FACILITIES A new facilities block has a couple of loos and showers each for men/women and disabled facilities. The holiday park's well-stocked farm shop refreezes iceblocks. Shane provides enough wood to start the campfire and briquettes for the indoor stoves. The main gate is locked at 5.30pm and the key requires a £20 deposit.
ONSITE FUN There are 2 well-stocked fishing ponds, a play area and Poppy and Pandora, the pygmy goats, to feed.
OFFSITE FUN Dinosaur Adventure at Weston Park (01603 876310) is a T. rex-cellent day out. See p216 for other options.
IF IT RAINS There's a Hollywood Cinema (01362 691133) in Dereham, as well as tenpin bowling at Strikes (01362 696910).
FOOD AND DRINK The onsite farm shop and café will satisfy most, but there's a Tesco about a mile away in Dereham.
NANNY STATE ALERT The fishing ponds are deep.
GETTING THERE From Dereham, take the A1075 and follow signs for Watton. At the roundabout with the big Tesco, take the exit onto the B1135, signed for Yaxham. Yaxham Waters Holiday Park is about a mile towards Yaxham, on your right
PUBLIC TRANSPORT From Norwich bus station, you can get the no. 4 to Yaxham, and then walk up the road to the site.
OPEN April–October.
THE DAMAGE £360–£575 a week; shorter breaks available.

manor farm

Think back to when you were a child. Remember the excitement of arriving on holiday and being able to glimpse the distant sea for the first time? Nearly all the pitches at Manor Farm have views of the sea. You can't get much more 'holiday' than that.

Your arrival at Manor Farm is just the thing for creating the right atmosphere. To get to the site you have to drive through a farm gate that runs between cobbled and flint barns, and then up a dirt track with hedges brushing your car on either side. The camping fields are at the top of the hill, with the seaside town of Cromer a mere 10 minutes' walk away. And in the distance, like an ironed-out pancake, you'll see the sea.

It's a good view and this feels like a suitably remote spot to pitch your tent, even though you can walk to Cromer. The fact that you reach it via the farm track and there are no roads nearby means you can let the kids run wild without worrying too much about traffic thundering past.

And boy do they have the space to roam around here – this site is seriously sprawling. And while it's pretty, it's far from being twee, so avoiding all the floral-wellie-clad crowds of 'Chelsea-on-Sea' at nearby Brancaster.

Manor Farm is a family-owned working farm, so there are lambs and calves to see if you happen to be visiting at Easter, and ponies to pet all year round. The place feels wild, and yet you have all the advantages of a small seaside town on your doorstep. We can think of few nicer places at which to spend your summer hols.

Manor Farm Caravan and Camping Site, East Runton, Cromer, Norfolk NR27 9PR; 01263 512858; www.manorfarmcaravansite.co.uk

THE UPSIDE Rolling fields with the sea on the horizon, and both a seaside town and the seaside itself within walking distance.

THE DOWNSIDE The rolling fields mean that a few of the pitches are slightly sloped, and the caravan pitches get the best sea views.

WHO'S IN? Tents, caravans, campervans, dogs on leads, families, couples – yes. Single-sex groups, large groups – no. No campfires, but barbecues off the ground are okay.

THE FACILITIES There are 250 standard and serviced pitches, spread across 18 acres. Marlpit and Moll's Meadow are for everyone, while Gurney's Plantation is just for caravans and campervans. Dogs are allowed in Moll's Meadow only. The site feels sprawling, but the facilities are never too far away, with 2 new, timber-clad shower blocks in each field. Both are fully equipped with hairdryers and razor points. There are also 2 laundry rooms with coin-operated washing machines and dryers. Freezers are provided.

ONSITE FUN Children love the space at Manor Farm, and the gently undulating fields are great for running around in. There's a small play area and a field for football and other ball games. Children are also very welcome to look at the farm animals.

OFFSITE FUN The beaches at Cromer and Sheringham are the main local attractions, and you can walk through the site into the village, with its pretty green, swings and slides to the beach at East Runton. The beach is fairly quiet, with good rockpools and nice views to Cromer pier. It's a sweet, old-fashioned village, with a butcher, tea room, fish-and-chip

shop – even an excellent Army Surplus store and a hairdresser – so all essentials are covered if you are suddenly struck with a desire to get a perm. You can catch the North Norfolk Railway, a steam train, in Sheringham going to Weybourne and Holt.

IF IT RAINS The Muckleburgh Collection (01263 588210; www.muckleburgh.co.uk) at Weybourne, with a fearsome array of tanks and fighting planes, is just up the road. There's a shire horse centre in West Runton (01603 736200), Splash Leisure Centre in Sheringham (01263 825675) and Aylsham Fun Barns has furry friends and pony rides (01263 734108). Cromer has a Movieplex (01263 510151) with 4 screens. At Blickling Hall (01263 738030), the headless ghost of Anne Boleyn is supposed to haunt the corridors, but if the supernatural's not for you, you can always explore the estate's beautiful gardens.

FOOD AND DRINK Cromer is packed with fish-and-chip shops and old-fashioned cafés. The Victorian Tea Room (01263 517154) on Meadow Road is one of the best. Mary Jane's is the prime place for fish and chips, but closest to the site is Station House (01263 514000). The Pepperpot Restaurant (01263 837578; www.the-pepperpot.com) in West Runton is fantastic, but more expensive. For local meat try Icarus Hines the butcher (01263 514541; www.icarushines.co.uk), in Cromer, or Arthur's butchers in West Runton; and there's also a farm shop at Groveland Farm in Roughton (01263 833777).

NANNY STATE ALERT Although you are well away from the main road, this is a working farm with farm traffic.

GETTING THERE Take the A149 into the village from Cley and turn right by the brown-and-white site sign saying 'Manor Farm'. Follow the road just into the village and the site is on the left-hand side.

PUBLIC TRANSPORT Catch a train from Norwich to Cromer, then either walk the mile or so to the site, or pick up the Coasthopper bus (01553 776980; www.coasthopper.co.uk) on Cadogan Road and go one stop to the White Horse in East Runton, then walk from there.

OPEN Easter–end September.

THE DAMAGE A standard pitch for a family of 4 costs £15.50–£18.50, a serviced pitch (with hook-up) for a family of 4 costs £20–£22 (depending on season). Dogs £1.

kelling heath

A patchwork quilt of heathland, woodland and wild-flower meadows criss-crossed by cycle tracks and nature walks. And the sea just at the bottom of the hill, too. You could spend a week here without ever wanting to leave the site – except to fetch ice creams.

Set amid 250 acres of woodland and open heathland on the North Norfolk coast, Kelling Heath is in a designated area of outstanding natural beauty. Don't be put off by the slightly imposing complex that greets you on arrival; the rest of the park is lovely and the 300 pitches are arranged sympathetically over several areas, broken up by pine trees and mature woodland for the happiest possible camping.

There is so much to see and enjoy in the area, but the onsite fun is particularly good at Kelling, where the focus is very much on the natural environment with an educational angle. Don't worry though – it's not too much like school, so your kids won't feel cheated out of having a holiday. Acorn Events, for budding naturalists of all ages, sounds like good fun – and it is. Children can take part in various activities like pond dipping, story walks and creative arts. Kelling Heath has a dark sky policy, so come sundown the site is wonderfully inky thanks to the lack of glaring lights normally found in municipal sites, and perfect for enjoying one of the evening bat and nightjar walks. Just don't forget your torch.

The cycling and walking is great; a number of leaflets means heading off by yourselves and learning about the estate along the way couldn't be easier. As well as playing boules, enjoy table tennis, swimming in the outdoor pool and using the tennis courts or adventure play areas. So watching, playing and learning are what it's all about at Kelling Heath. As well as eating lots of ice creams.

Kelling Heath Holiday Park, Weybourne, Holt, Norfolk NR25 7HW; 01263 588181; www.kellingheath.co.uk

THE UPSIDE Big fields amid heathland and lots of onsite fun.
THE DOWNSIDE It's a big old site, and a little commercial.
WHO'S IN? Tents, caravans, campervans, family groups, dogs on leads – yes. Single-sex groups – no. No campfires.
THE FACILITIES There is a token-operated launderette, and each area has its own amenity building, with all facilities. The Village Store sells everyday essentials, fresh produce and gifts, while various eateries cater for all sorts, using local produce.
ONSITE FUN There are several marked trails around the site, including the history trail and an orienteering course. There are also 2 adventure play areas and table tennis tables, plus bike hire, pools and a health club. Acorn Events run seasonal activities to learn about the environment and resident wildlife.
OFFSITE FUN West along the coast is the vast expanse of Holkham Beach. Towards Kelling you will hit the marshy expanses of Morston (perfect for crabbing).
IF IT RAINS Norfolk is heaving with grand piles; the National Trust's Felbrigg Hall (01263 837444) is nice to explore, as is Blickling Hall (01263 738030) with its beautiful grounds.
FOOD AND DRINK The Dun Cow pub in Salthouse (01263 740467) is good and the portions are huge.
NANNY STATE ALERT Watch the open water at the fishing ponds and the steep descents on Cromer Ridge.
GETTING THERE From Holt, turn left into Sandy Lane just before the village of Bodham. The site is down on the left.
PUBLIC TRANSPORT The North Norfolk Railway (www.nnrailway.co.uk) stops at Kelling Heath (by request). The Coasthopper bus service runs from May to July.
OPEN Mid February–2 January.
THE DAMAGE £18–£39 per pitch per night. Dog £3–£5.50.

wild luxury

Seven safari tents are dotted across the Norfolk savannah, but this place is not so much *Born Free* as *Little House on the Prairie*. Now where's Pa Ingalls with his axe?

They say that anyone can love the mountains, but it takes a soul to love the prairie. Well, Norfolk is that prairie, with its majestically flat landscape and never-ending skies. And by the end of your stay at Wild Luxury, you'll feel like a special soul indeed.

Step into your lodge to be engulfed by the earthy scents of pine and cedar wood. From the floor to the furniture to the cabin bed – everything has been hobbitly hewn from natural materials. You even burn wood on your very own range. The seven lodges are completely off grid; there's no electricity, and all the water is stored on site. In fact, for five months of the year there's nothing here but grass and badgers. So in many ways this is wild camping, but there's nothing wild about having your own hot shower and flushing toilet, no siree.

Dragging yourself away from your luxury lodge seems foolhardy, but it's worth it to discover that the whole of North Norfolk is right on your doorstep. Not only are there miles of beautiful coastline to explore, but endless inland diversions involving shire horses, country piles and adventure playgrounds, too.

Back at camp, kids are in their element – there are guinea pigs to cuddle, chickens to chase, and making friends is a doddle. There's plenty of space in front of the lodges for minors to mingle, and evenings spent around the communal campfire are encouraged. So just relax on the deck of your safari lodge, glass of wine in hand, and take a good long look at that breathtaking sunset in the endless expanse of Norfolk sky… It's a bit good, isn't it?

Wild Luxury, Pigeon Wood, Sedgeford, Hunstanton, Norfolk; 08455 441757; www.wildluxury.co.uk

THE UPSIDE Absolutely low-impact luxury, with the perfect suggestion of adventure. And guinea pigs.

THE DOWNSIDE The never-ending farm track is tough if you want to be to-ing and fro-ing, but then that's what makes this place so wonderfully remote… Oh drat, what a quandary.

WHO'S IN? Families, couples, groups, single-sex parties (providing they take over all 5 lodges), dogs on leads – yes. Tents, campervans, caravans – no.

THE FACILITIES Seven luxury safari lodges are set In a fenced-off field in the middle of working farmland. Each lodge can sleep up to 6, with a double bed, bunk beds and a cute double bed in a cupboard… it's better than it sounds, trust us. All linen and towels are rentable. There is a wood-burning range in the kitchen and your day's allocation of firewood is supplied. There's also a double gas hob if you can't wait for the range to heat up before you have your morning brew. All cookware and tableware is provided, and there's a massive coolbox for your fresh food. Indulge in local sausages and bacon from the 'Wild Cooler' or stock up on essentials in the treasure trove that is the honesty pantry. You can even place orders for newspapers and fresh bread the day before.

ONSITE FUN You can hire bikes for all ages, as well as child seats, on booking – just remember to bring your own helmets. No cars are allowed in the field, except for unpacking/packing up, so it's incredibly safe. There are nature walks from the site, and plenty of space for kite flying and family games. Kids will love making friends with the guinea pigs and collecting eggs from the chickens. If none of those appeals, never underestimate the fun to be had in a purple wheelbarrow (you'll find several around the site).

OFFSITE FUN We have never seen such a comprehensive welcome pack as the one you're presented with here, so don't worry for a moment about being stuck for things to do/see/eat/wear/watch/touch/sit on... A selection: North Norfolk is home to beautiful beaches galore – try Brancaster, Holme and Holkham just for starters. Pensthorpe nature reserve and gardens (01328 851465; www.pensthorpe.com) hosts the BBC's *Springwatch* and is home to numerous bird species and other wildlife for a day out with new feathered friends.

IF IT RAINS Majestic Cinema in Kings Lynn (01553 772603; www.majestic-cinema.co.uk) has 3 screens and shows the latest releases, including 3D. Splash Leisure Centre's pool (01263 825675; www.dcleisurecentres.co.uk) in Sheringham has a giant waterslide, children's paddling area, sun terrace and a poolside café.

FOOD AND DRINK It's great fun to cook at camp, either indoors on the range, or barbecue-style on the campfire outside. If you want a night off, there are loads of options just a short drive away. The Rose and Crown (01485 541382; www.roseandcrownsnettisham.co.uk) in Snettisham is a proper local pub, which serves delicious food with a local slant. For something a little upmarket, head to the award-winning Orange Tree (01485 512213; www.theorangetreethornham.co.uk) in Thornham – it's a culinary force to be reckoned with. Don't let the *X Factor*-style flames outside put you off; the service is outstanding, the food is local and innovative and the children's menu is something else!

NANNY STATE ALERT There is no anti-scald feature on the showers, so children should be supervised.

GETTING THERE Pigeon Wood is located well off the main roads near Sedgeford. Precise directions are included in the welcome pack that you'll receive on booking.

PUBLIC TRANSPORT You really need a car here.

OPEN Late March–October.

THE DAMAGE Each lodge sleeps up to 6; prices range from £269 for a 2-night weekend break in low season to £895 for a week in the summer holidays. Dogs £5 each.

high sand creek

Lick your lips as you crawl out of your tent and you will almost be able to taste the sea, which lies just beyond the purple haze of heather-covered tidal marshes. This network of salt-water creeks will make expert crabbers of you all.

A proper British seaside holiday is on offer at High Sand Creek campsite in Stiffkey, on the North Norfolk coast. With miles and miles of marshes just outside your tent, the potential for a real-live adventure is just huge.

The site itself is very pared-down, offering about 80 marked pitches spread over about five plain acres, but that doesn't mean that your opportunities for a top family holiday are limited. The flat, slightly melancholic, beauty of the marshes – shimmering with dusky purple marsh heather – is magnetic. And get ready for sunsets so breathtaking that the whole campsite heads down to the marshes for an unimpeded view.

The site has been in the same family for over four decades and is much loved by families of campers, who return year after year with multiple generations tacked on to augment their numbers. This stretch of the Norfolk coast is heaving with things for kids and grannies to do together. Families love the fact that there are so many opportunities for swimming and picnicking, and there's also crabbing, sailing, fishing and seal watching to keep everyone fully occupied.

To top it off, at the end of the day, with salt in your hair, you can go to sleep safe in the knowledge that there's nothing at all between you and the North Sea.

High Sand Creek Campsite, Vale Farm, The Greenway, Stiffkey, Norfolk NR23 1QP; 01328 830235

THE UPSIDE Romantic and picturesque marshes and, beyond these, the sea – just outside your tent.
THE DOWNSIDE It's not the biggest site but boy, is it popular; so at busy times there isn't a huge amount of space.
WHO'S IN? Tents, campervans, groups, dogs – yes. Caravans – no. No campfires, but barbecues raised off the ground are permitted.
THE FACILITIES No hook-ups, as the aim is to keep the site as old-fashioned as possible. There's a laundry for hand-washing clothes (but no washing machines), and 12 clean showers and 12 toilets divided into male and female blocks. Gas is available for sale, and there's a freeze-pack service (£1 deposit, 20p per freeze).
ONSITE FUN Part of the site is given over to ball games, and toys, tennis rackets, footballs and such like are available in reception. You can also borrow crabbing nets and buy bags of bait. The thick hedge that separates the site from the marshes is a favourite spot for children to explore.
OFFSITE FUN The coastal marsh is a haven for migrating birds, so expect to see a few birders twitching on the horizon. The Norfolk Coastal Path passes through Stiffkey, so the site's popular with walkers. A bridge across a creek, just beyond the site, is a prime spot for crabbing. Further afield is Bressingham Steam and Gardens (01379 686900; www.bressingham.co.uk), near Diss, with a great selection of vintage engines and 3 narrow-gauge railway rides around the gardens there. Hunstanton, on the west coast, is a classic Victorian resort with stripy cliffs and a good beach for rockpools and exploring.
IF IT RAINS Gressenhall Farm & Workhouse (01362 860563) has a traditional farmhouse, cottages and village

shop, and an adventure playground and cart rides around the farm. There's a leisure centre at Hunstanton, as well as a Sea Life Sanctuary (www.sealsanctuary.co.uk) with a good aquarium. There's a play centre with a ball pool in Wells, and cinemas in Cromer and Fakenham. Alternatively, Houghton Hall (01485 528569; www.houghtonhall.com) is an impressively grand place to shelter from the rain.

FOOD AND DRINK The village shop stocks basic groceries. The Red Lion pub (01328 830552; www.stiffkey.com) is within walking distance and does good food; there's also a playground nearby. Head to the fish stand at Morston for local cockles, and there are excellent dressed crabs for sale in Blakeney. The beautiful Stiffkey Stores (01328 830489; www.stiffkeystores.com) is just down the road from the campsite or, for a more scenic route, head right along the coast path for a shortcut through the fields and avoid the traffic. They serve tea, coffee and dainty cakes in their sun-drenched courtyard. Get your groceries (and water bombs) and papers here, too, and send a postcard from the tiny post office.

NANNY STATE ALERT There are muddy creeks across the marshes that could be dangerous for smaller children. Also beware the marsh tides – check the tide table displayed in the reception kiosk.

GETTING THERE Take the A149 into Stiffkey village. Go through the village, with the sea on your right. The site is just after the Red Lion pub, on the right.

PUBLIC TRANSPORT Thanks to the super-marvellous Coasthopper bus (01553 776980; www.coasthopper.co.uk), you can get the train to Sheringham from Norwich, then grab the 'hopper right the way to the campsite entrance.

OPEN March/April–October.

THE DAMAGE Family of 4 costs £18 per night.

haddon grove

What's the essential ingredient for successful camping with kids? More kids, of course! This site is likely to have plenty of them, so your juniors will be able to keep themselves occupied without your help, allowing you to sit back and relax.

With bags of room for the kids to roam, this back-to-basics campsite on a family-only field has great views thrown in. A short walk downhill and you're by the river, with its small weirs and shallow pools for creature spotting (look out for rare crayfish). As long as they've got space to run around in, the kids probably won't need much more than this. And it's a pretty safe bet that there'll be plenty of playmates to hand.

The field has lots of room for ball games, and the small wooded area separating the family field from its neighbour is good for hide-and-seek.

Although the kids probably won't appreciate this, you are pitched just a couple of fields away from the spectacular limestone gorge of Lathkill Dale – the far end of the field has the best views. What they probably will appreciate, though, is that the site is a short (albeit steep) walk from the river – which sometimes dries up in late summer – where the series of weirs and pools set the scene for picnicking and looking out for as many fish and river insects as you can count on 10 fingers.

This entire area is actually a haven for wildlife – Lathkill Dale is one of the five valleys making up the Derbyshire Dales National Nature Reserve, which is rich in all kinds of flora to tempt the local fauna. In the summer months the air around here is aflutter with the bright hues of butterfly wings, while all sorts of bird species set up their own camps in the trees above to breed.

Haddon Grove Farm, Bakewell, Derbyshire DE45 1JF; 01629 812343

THE UPSIDE Cheap and cheerful, back-to-basics camping in a family field with the river only a short walk away.
THE DOWNSIDE The family-only field is furthest from the toilets, so it's a bit of a trek. The nearest pubs are 2 miles away and shops are 4 miles away – so come prepared.
WHO'S IN? Tents, campervans, caravans, groups, dogs – yes.
THE FACILITIES Unmarked pitches are spread over 3 paddocks, although one of these is mainly for caravans. The best place for camping with kids is the family-only field at the far end of the site, although some clusters of families choose the larger field, for groups. The toilet and shower block is pretty basic (it's a working sheep farm) with 6 showers in total – including a family room. There are washing-up areas, too. Although there is no shop, David (the farmer) will usually find you some milk and teabags as he directs you back into Bakewell, where you can stock up on provisions. He can also refreeze icepacks and charge mobile phones.
ONSITE FUN Playing family games, hiding-and-seeking in the wood and hanging out with all the other kids.
OFFSITE FUN A short, but steep and sometimes rocky, path leads you down to Lathkill Dale, where you take a left along the river to reach the first of a number of small weirs and shallow pools; perfect for a riverside picnic.
IF IT RAINS The 12th-century medieval manor house Haddon Hall (01629 812855; www.haddonhall.co.uk) is a 15-minute drive away, while the home of the Duke and Duchess of Devonshire, Chatsworth House (01246 565300; www.chatsworth.org), with its array of shops and farmyard animals as well as beautiful gardens and stunning country pile, can be reached in less than half an hour by car.

FOOD AND DRINK Two good pubs are about 2 miles in either direction. Traditional pub food can be had at the Bull's Head (01629 812372; www.thebullsheadmonyash.co.uk) in Monyash. It is right next door to the village green and (more importantly) the excellent village playground, which caters for all kids, from tots to teens, and even has equipment adapted for kids with special needs. In the opposite direction, the Lathkil Hotel (01629 812501; www.lathkil.co.uk) at Over Haddon has food, including yummy puds, with a view.

NANNY STATE ALERT The ponies around the farm aren't for petting or feeding. But they do like to be admired.

GETTING THERE From Bakewell, take the B5055 towards Monyash and, after about 3 miles, turn left onto a long narrow lane, which is signposted 'Haddon Grove'. You'll find the campsite at the bottom of the lane. Travelling from Buxton, take the A515 and turn left onto the B5055. Go through Monyash and the lane to Haddon Grove is on your right after about 2 miles.

PUBLIC TRANSPORT Bus no. 172 runs to Matlock and Bakewell and stops about 10 minutes' walk from the site in the middle of the village.

OPEN March–October.

THE DAMAGE Adult £4 per night; child £2, under-6s and dogs free. Cars £2.

rowter farm

Ah – the highs and lows of camping! Spend the morning watching paragliders circling gracefully around Mam Tor summit, and then descend through the ravine of Winnats Pass for an afternoon's exploration of underground caves.

If you and your brood are active, outdoorsy types, and your kids enjoy nothing better than a good brisk walk scrambling up and down hills and rocks, then Rowter Farm deserves a visit. A short walk from the site takes you past Windy Knoll Cave, where prehistoric bones from wolves, bison, bears, hares and reindeer were discovered, to the summit of Mam Tor (or Mother Hill), once the home to some ancient Celtic tribes.

To give you some idea of the wonderful sense of space here, site owner Sarah Mark grew up on Rowter Farm and finds the wide-open landscapes of nearby Edale a bit 'claustrophobic'! The farm sits at the head of the Hope Valley, some 230 metres above sea level, and just above the spectacularly steep-sided Winnats Pass.

The site has unmarked pitches and can take up to five caravans and about 40 tents, although it only gets really busy here on Bank Holiday weekends. The facilities are quite basic, but nobody seems to mind; they're all too busy enjoying the space.

The best time to visit the farm is early summer, when the children can enjoy some country sights and sounds – sheep being rounded up for shearing, lambs frolicking in nearby fields and swallows swooping in and out of the farm buildings. The chickens scratching around the farmyard and goats and cows in the fields can be seen all year.

Given the ups and downs of camping, Rowter Farm should be high on everyone's list.

Rowter Farm, Castleton, Hope Valley, Derbyshire S33 8WA; 01433 620271; sarah.rowter@tesco.net

THE UPSIDE Wonderful sense of space, but bustling Castleton is just down the road.

THE DOWNSIDE It can get noisy on a busy Saturday night, despite its noise policy. As it's high up, it's exposed to winds.

WHO'S IN? Tents, campervans, caravans, dogs, groups – yes.

THE FACILITIES A dishwashing room, 2 toilets each for men and women, hand basins and 2 showers (50p-coin operated). The small shop sells eggs, long-life milk, chocolate and bread. It also has matches and disposable barbecues (which are allowed, although campfires are banned).

ONSITE FUN The middle of the camping field is perfect for family games of French cricket, football and rounders.

OFFSITE FUN Mam Tor – with superb views over the Hope Valley – is a short walk; a longer walk along the Limestone Way takes you into Castleton and its Peveril Castle (01433 620613).

IF IT RAINS With 10 miles of underground caves below the Castleton area, you're spoilt for choice (Speedwell Cavern, 01433 620512; Peak Cavern, www.devilsarse.com; Blue John Cavern, 01433 620638; Treak Cliff Cavern, 01433 620571).

FOOD AND DRINK Castleton has plenty of pubs serving food. Children are welcome at the Bull's Head (01433 620256), Castle Hotel (01433 620578) and the George (01433 620238).

NANNY STATE ALERT It's a working farm with machinery.

GETTING THERE On the way from Sparrow Pit to Castleton on the A6187 there's a metal gate on the right (just before you reach a fork in the road) leading to the track to the site.

PUBLIC TRANSPORT Take a bus to Bakewell, then take bus no. 173 from there to Castleton and walk to the site.

OPEN Easter–October.

THE DAMAGE Adult £6; child (12–16) £4, under-12 £3.

family festivals

If you love festivals, maybe your kids will too. Spend carefree summer days with them, dancing in a faraway field.

If you've picked up this book for research purposes, then your idea of an all-nighter has no doubt changed a bit over the years. Calpol and cocoa are probably the strongest things you want to get your hands on these days, but that doesn't mean that you have to hang up your dancing shoes altogether.

Let's face it, no one knows how to throw a party quite like we do, and the explosion of festivals across the country is colourful proof of the fact that becoming a parent – or even a grandparent – doesn't mean throwing in the party towel just yet. Of course, there are some parties that are best just left to the grown-ups. While it might not be that appropriate to take kids to a techno-festival like Glade, there are plenty of family-friendly festivals that have become as essential a part of the English summer as school sports day or strawberries and cream.

These days, punters are increasingly eschewing the big commercial events, with their onsite cashpoint machines and mobile-phone charging stations, for something a bit more handmade and authentic. Tiny boutique and family-orientated shindigs are cropping up across the UK. The festivals on the following pages are great places to take your children for a weekend of fun, whether they are babes in arms, tots, inbetweeners or sulky teens.

camp bestival

Baby sibling to Bestival on the Isle of Wight in September, Camp Bestival takes place at Lulworth Castle against the backdrop of the Jurassic Coast in Dorset. A quirky retro feel characterises this festival, which is really dominated by children. This is one for the family, and the kids' fields are fantastic, with the House of Fairy Tales, puppet shows, circus, Maypole and endless activities. There's a Dingly Dell trail, and the Breastival Mother and Baby Temple means that even the youngest family members needn't be left at home. The onsite farmer's market means that you never have to stray too far away from your comfort zone as there's good-quality food on offer, too.

Lulworth Castle, Dorset; 08448 884410 (ticketline); www.campbestival.net; July.

the larmer tree festival

Located at what was the site of a Victorian theme park, Larmer Tree is opened every year by Jools Holland and is a past winner of the Family Festival Award. It has a maximum capacity of 4,000, and there isn't a scrap of corporate sponsorship in sight, which is just as we like it. Dressing up is an essential part of the fun, so children love it, and there are usually at least six stages with a thumping selection of folk, roots, blues, jazz, reggae and country music. Larmer Tree has something for everyone, with a finale on Sunday night in which festival-goers, especially kids, parade in costumes they've made over the weekend.

Larmer Tree Gardens, nr Salisbury, Wiltshire/Dorset border; 01725 552300, www.larmertreefestival.co.uk; July

shambala

There are whispers that Shambala is the festival expert's festival and that it's maintained the sort of laidback vibe that was what all festivals used to be like before cashpoints, photo ID and monumental barriers spoiled all the fun. It's been going for over a decade and resides in Northamptonshire. There are few, if any, other festivals that have such a strong sense of community. Festivals with kids can be a bit fraught, but at Shambala you almost feel you could let your toddler toddle off for a dance on his own, and some kind girl dressed as a fairy would bring him back to you (probably not wise to rely on this, though!).

Northamptonshire; www.shambalafestival.org; last Bank Holiday in August.

guilfest

Guilfest triumphs in laying on a great musical line-up combined with circus tents, play areas, workshops and theatre clubs to entertain the children. As well as having a fabulous family area, the festival is packed with street theatre acts, including a Space Age children's carnival, who wander through the site. There's a lido just next door and an onsite Arts & Crafts Village, while the Kidzone team, who also work at other festivals, are especially adept at putting on activities your children will love, in particular the children's talent parades, fairground rides and all the usual acrobatics workshops, which make this a really special festival for a family outing.

Stoke Park, Guildford, Surrey; 01483 454159 (for more information); www.guilfest.co.uk; July.

wood festival

Wood is an affirmation of life, love and family; everything that's best about a homemade festival. It's a cosy event, with a largely acoustic line-up. It defines eco-chic, with showers heated by wood-burning stoves and a solar-powered main stage (the loos are, of course, composting). There are family workshops to keep your tribe happy, as well as puppet theatres and a cycle-powered cinema and disco, plus there's a smell of woodsmoke in the air and girls wear real flowers in their hair as children tumble among haybales. At Wood, there is some of the original spirit of Woodstock. Just on a very, very small scale.

Braziers Park, Oxfordshire OX10 6AN; 01235 821262; www.woodfestival.com; May.

just so

Possibly the most family-friendly of the lot, Just So festival began in 2010 and has captured children's imaginations in such a way as to make Peppa Pig jealous. Set in a magical woodland in the grounds of Cheshire's Rode Hall, the festival celebrates all that is creative and ensures that every event can be attended by both parents and children. From the midnight feasts, dance workshops, campfire singing, author talks and walkabout performers, the activities/shows are inclusive and delight kids while encouraging their creativity. Thoughtful touches such as a breastfeeding tent and baby changing areas provide the icing on the cake.

Rode Hall, Church Lane, Scholar Green, Stoke-on-Trent, Cheshire; 01625 410885; www.justsofestival.org.uk; August.

rosedale abbey

Fancy playing Tarzan? It's not exactly in the jungle, but this site does have lots of rope swings over the river. And when your kids have had enough of those, they can try a little dam building, tree climbing, stepping-stone jumping – or just plain paddling.

This really is a lovely spot for camping. The site meanders along the banks of the treelined river which, if you're lucky, you can pitch right next to, in a valley surrounded by sweeping hillside moors. And the pretty village of Rosedale Abbey is right there, close by. There is no abbey as such, but the village does have plenty to offer, including lots of yummy food, with a deli and two tea rooms around the green, as well as a couple of pubs.

Don't be put off by the somewhat corporate entrance to the campsite – this is not like the Flower of May's other holiday-park-style sites. It does have holiday cottages, statics and tourers, but there are two tent-only fields to fit about 70 tents on unmarked pitches. And the coolest part of the site is the smaller and quieter of the two fields, right at the end of the campsite, and with its own pond.

Kids will probably disagree with this assessment, as the first, larger, tents-only camping field (which has about 11 pitches with hook-ups) enjoys the widest, shallowest part of the river, where they can carry out all sorts of exploits involving dams, trees, rope swings and water.

And if, after you've worked your way through this list (and all the trappings of the playground with its monkey bars, slides and outdoor table tennis), you want more, there's the high-wire forest adventure course at Go Ape! in Dalby Forest.

Even the family pooch is catered for at Rosedale, with rather splendid views from the three-acre dog-walking field.

Rosedale Abbey Caravan Park, Rosedale Abbey, nr Pickering, North Yorkshire YO18 8SA; 01751 417272; www.flowerofmay.com

THE UPSIDE Riverside fun in a picturesque setting.
THE DOWNSIDE Purists will object to the tourers and statics. It can get busy at peak periods, so avoid Bank Holidays.
WHO'S IN? Tents, campervans, caravans, dogs on leads – yes. Groups – no. Campfires – no; barbecues off the ground okay.
THE FACILITIES There are 2 toilet/shower blocks with washing-up areas and a disabled/baby-changing room. One block has a laundry. There is a small freezer where icepacks can be refrozen (20p to refreeze each pack – this money goes to charity). The small shop sells a few basics and sweets.
ONSITE FUN Most kids seem to prefer the natural playground – the river – but there is also a large playing field for ball games (with basketball hoop) and a playground.
OFFSITE FUN Abbey Stores in the village is the National Park Information Point, hiring out bikes and selling maps.
IF IT RAINS Travel back in time (and about 4 miles) to Ryedale Folk Museum (01751 417367) in Hutton le Hole.
FOOD AND DRINK Abbey Stores sells the basics and has a tea room, while there is a deli counter and ice creams at Graze on the Green shop, tea room and gallery (01751 417468).
NANNY STATE ALERT Be aware of the river and pond.
GETTING THERE From the A170 between Pickering and Kirkbymoorside, turn off at Wrelton and follow signs, through Cropton, to Rosedale Abbey village. Pass the Caravan Club site and keep going until you see the 'Rosedale' sign, on the left.
PUBLIC TRANSPORT Train to Pickering, then the Moors bus service (01845 597000) to Rosedale.
OPEN April–October.
THE DAMAGE Family of 4 £13–£21. One pet per pitch.

masons

What a treat! A campsite that's actually run by campers who know all about choosing a great site. The river provides plenty of opportunity for wading and fishing, and you can make a dramatic river-entry via a rope swing, handily located on the bank.

In the heart of the Yorkshire Dales, by the banks of the River Wharfe and down the road from two good pubs, Masons is so good that even the owners still camp here. When their favourite campsite in the Yorkshire Dales came up for sale, Georgie and Grant bought Masons, and set about scrubbing up an already popular site.

You no longer have to walk a mile to the nearest shop. The campsite's 'office' (a 1969 Airstream caravan) stocks several basics, drinks and camping accessories as well as delicious local free-range eggs, milk, ice cream, bacon and sausages. Any barbecue items you might need can be pre-ordered for collection or delivery so that you'll be fully equipped for a sizzling time come evening.

The wide and mainly shallow river runs at the bottom of the two camping fields, with large, flat stones for paddling around. Try your hand at fly-fishing, while the kids happily pass the time catching crayfish with a bucket and net.

The level camping fields have plenty of space for kite flying, football, cricket and rounders, and lots of families bring lilos and dinghies. Although the campsite has open views over an area of outstanding natural beauty, Grant says that campers make straight for the steep hill over the road for an even better vista.

Masons Campsite, Appletreewick, Skipton, North Yorkshire BD23 6DD; 01756 720275; www.masonscampsite.co.uk

THE UPSIDE A top setting on the banks of a river, with open views over the Yorkshire Dales and lots of space for games, with 2 great pubs nearby.

THE DOWNSIDE With only 40 pitches on one field, and restrictions on the second limiting camping to 28 days a year, this site gets booked up well in advance – although if you are hikers or (pedal) bikers you won't be turned away.

WHO'S IN? Tents, campervans, caravans, dogs on leads – yes. No campfires on the ground, but barbecues off the ground are okay and there are a few fire pits available for hire.

THE FACILITIES There are allocated pitches spread across the main camping field, which caters for tents, campervans and tourers, with 40 hook-ups. In the second field, which is open most summer weekends, you can pitch where you like. The most popular spot for tenters is along the riverbank, leaving plenty of space for ball games in the rest of the large field. New facilities include a laundry room, disabled facilities, baby changing, coin-operated hairdryers and GHD straighteners. The washing-up room has 7 sinks, there are 10 showers in total (including one in a family room) and 9 loos. Tins, glass, plastics and paper are recycled. The onsite shop stocks plenty of quality produce as well as camping equipment. There are 10 rent-a-tents in a variety of sizes – pre-erected and fully equipped, as well as an Airstream caravan and 2 campervans available for hire.

ONSITE FUN Paddling and jumping in the river, crayfishing, ball games and tree climbing. The onsite chickens and ducks are popular with younger children.

OFFSITE FUN Footpaths lead directly from the bottom of the site along the river to Burnsall, which is a popular

picnicking and swimming spot, as well as to Appletreewick and Barden Bridge. Bolton Abbey (01756 718000; www.boltonabbey.com), with stepping stones over the river, walks, tea shops, cafés and the Embsay and Bolton Abbey Steam railway station (01756 710614; www. embsayboltonabbeyrailway.org.uk) is just up the road.

IF IT RAINS A noticeboard next to the showers tells you what's on at local cinemas, and Stump Cross Caverns in Nidderdale (01756 752780; www.stumpcrosscaverns.co.uk) is another good rainy-day option.

FOOD AND DRINK The 2 pubs in Appletreewick both serve food and are family-friendly. The New Inn (01756 720252; www.the-new-inn-appletreewick.com) has a selection of quirky beers, while the 16th-century Craven Arms (01756 720270; www.craven-cruckbarn.co.uk) has log fires, gas lamps and stone-flagged floors.

NANNY STATE ALERT The usual warnings about supervising children near water apply, particularly if dinghies and lilos are involved.

GETTING THERE From the A59 between Skipton and Harrogate, turn north on the B6160 at Bolton Abbey, signposted 'Grassington'. After about 3 miles take the first right after Barden Tower, signposted 'Appletreewick', and continue for around 2 miles to a T-junction. Turn left, into Appletreewick village, and continue until, less than a mile on, you reach Masons Campsite at the foot of the hill on the left.

PUBLIC TRANSPORT Bus no. 74 from Ilkley bus station drops off right outside the site (01756 753123; www.prideofthedales.co.uk).

OPEN April–October.

THE DAMAGE A standard pitch for a family of 4 starts at £24 per night, including a car. Dogs are free (max. 2 per pitch), but must be kept under strict control. Rent-a-tents £45 per night for 2 people to £80 per night for 5 people.

rukin's park lodge

Fire and water are the main attractions at this site: campfires on the grassy riverbank and tumbling waterfalls abound. Come nightfall, stargazers will be more than impressed by the beautiful clear sky.

Swaledale was pronounced by walking guru Alfred Wainwright as the most beautiful of the Yorkshire Dales. With this in mind, a better setting couldn't be wished for at this riverside campsite.

The river and waterfalls may be the main attraction for kids on this site, making the riverside pitches in the long narrow field at the bottom of the farm the most popular, but the views from the higher fields over the moors are spectacular. And even if you don't get to pitch on the riverbank, the village of Keld (meaning 'running water') has no fewer than five waterfalls surrounding it, so you can always pack up a picnic and set off to find a perfect waterside patch for a great afternoon of splashing around and paddling. (Wain Wath Falls is a top spot.)

As well as the long, narrow field by the river, with the most sought-after pitches, there is a large sloping field, and owner John can open up other fields as overflow. These actually have better views and more space for games than those by the river.

Campfires are allowed here, too. John and his wife Barbara, who farm the land in a way that's sensitive to the environment, were concerned that fires were contributing to the erosion of the riverbank. But John has come up with his own solution: four-legged fire boxes. These keep the fires off the ground: happy farmers and happy campers.

And if anyone's still awake when the campfire's embers finally fade, it's time to turn to the night sky for a truly awesome star display before tucking the kids into their sleeping bags.

Rukin's Park Lodge, Keld, Richmond, North Yorkshire DL11 6LJ; 01748 886274; www.rukins-keld.co.uk

THE UPSIDE Campfires by the river in stunning Swaledale.
THE DOWNSIDE The site can get overwhelmed on summer weekends – there are just 2 showers.
WHO'S IN? Tents only. Dogs – yes. Groups – no.
THE FACILITIES There are 2 showers, 4 toilets (a long walk from the riverside pitches) with hand basins, and a washing-up room. The tea shop at the site sells drinks plus bacon rolls and basics. It also sells logs, marshmallows and footpath maps.
ONSITE FUN It's only a short walk to the nearest falls, and kids can swim in the shallow pools along the river, paddle, mess about with fishing nets from the flattish rocks, or play on the rope swing on the small 'beach' just off site.
OFFSITE FUN Downriver, you can reach the most spectacular falls (Kisdon Force) via the Corpse Way.
IF IT RAINS Head into Hawes (about 8 miles) for the Dales Countryside Museum (01969 666210) with interactive displays. The Wensleydale Creamery Visitor Centre (01969 667664) has a museum, viewing gallery, cheese shop and restaurant.
FOOD AND DRINK A short walk up the road, Keld Lodge (01748 886259) has a restaurant and also does bar meals, while Tan Hill Inn (01833 628246), about 4 miles away, with resident animals, claims to be Great Britain's highest pub.
NANNY STATE ALERT The river has slippery rocks and deep water in places; there is a waterfall not far away.
GETTING THERE Keld is just off the B6270 between Kirkby Stephen and Richmond. The campsite is signed from the village.
PUBLIC TRANSPORT A bus to Keld leaves Richmond's market place 3 times a day.
OPEN April–end September.
THE DAMAGE Adult £6–£7 per night; £3 per child.

holme open farm

Let's make a *Cool Camping* cake. You'll find all the right ingredients here: the chance to get up close and personal with farm animals; glorious fell views all around; a river for paddling and – the icing on the cake – campfires allowed. Time to reserve your slice…

For a truly free-range camping experience, head to Holme Open Farm in the Lune Valley, cuddled between the Lake District and Yorkshire Dales national parks. While free-to-roam chickens are often to be found wandering through campsites, free-range pigs are not quite so common. But here, on this traditional Dales working farm, there are a couple to be found snuffle-shuffling around the farmyard and surrounding fields.

If you want to make friends with some of the other animals, owners David and Angela Metcalfe run bookable tours of their farm so you can meet the goats, ducks, pigs, kittens and pony, as well as hold and help feed lambs and chicks. The tour also includes playing in the indoor soft-play area and riding around on pedal tractors, but before you get too excited, this part is kids only – sorry. There are evening badger walks and a nature trail open to all, however, so campers young and old can discover a few members of the resident wildlife that form a part of the scenery on this 120-acre farm.

The campsite is a simple one: a large, flat field with glorious views over the dramatic greenery of the somersaulting Howgill Fells (which have been said to resemble a row of hippos' bottoms). The River Rawthey runs right alongside the field, with easy access from a picnic area for paddling and fishing. And (hurrah!) campfires are allowed – bring your own wood or buy bags from the farm – so don't forget to pack the marshmallows

Holme Open Farm, Sedbergh, Cumbria LA10 5ET; 01539 620654; www.holmeopenfarm.co.uk

THE UPSIDE Camping on a traditional Dales working farm with glorious views, campfires and the optional farm tours.
THE DOWNSIDE You have to share the farm with caravans, although they are in a separate field. Both the farm tour and the onsite café are closed on Tuesdays.
WHO'S IN? Tents, campervans, caravans (in separate field), groups (but no loud music allowed), fires – yes. Dogs – no.
THE FACILITIES Tents and campervans pitch on a flat, square camping field with a picnic area by the river. Caravans are in a separate field. There's a basic ablutions block with a couple of showers, separate men's and women's toilets and a washing-up sink and drainer in a farm outbuilding, a short walk from the camping field. The farm has a café (see Food and Drink, p241), a children's playground with swings and slides, and you can join a farm tour (see The Damage, p241) to meet the animals and use the indoor play area.
ONSITE FUN Join a farm tour, an evening badger walk or just follow the nature trail to find out more about the farm and its wildlife. You can paddle and fish in the River Rawthey or picnic on its banks. There's a playground just off the camping field and plenty of space in which to roam around and play.
OFFSITE FUN There are lots of good spots for paddling and even (if you can brave the icy water) wild swimming in the River Rawthey around Sedbergh, with flat, pebbled areas offering easy access to the water. Stonetrail Riding Centre (01539 623444; www.stonetrailridingcentre.com), halfway between Sedbergh and Kirkby Stephen, has horse riding and pony trekking through the fells for the over-12s. They also hire out mountain bikes.

IF IT RAINS The indoor play area comes in handy for families camping here with younger children on a rainy day. Otherwise, head into the 'book town' of Sedbergh to browse its many bookshops; or discover the history of nearby Dent at its Heritage Centre (01539 625800; www.dentvillageheritagecentre.co.uk).

FOOD AND DRINK The farm's Ewe Tree Café has homemade and locally sourced light meals (sandwiches, jacket potatoes and soups) as well as afternoon teas (open 11am–4pm; closed on Tuesdays). Otherwise head into Sedbergh for the award-winning Sedbergh Café traditional tea room (01539 621389; www.thesedberghcafe.com); 17th-century coaching inn, the Bull (01539 620264; www.bullhotelsedbergh.co.uk), which has an interesting menu and a large beer garden and play area; or stock up on Dales meats (and local cheeses) for the barbie at Steadmans Butchers (01539 620431; www.steadmans-butchers.co.uk).

NANNY STATE ALERT The usual warnings about working farms and washing hands after touching animals apply; and there's the river to be aware of.

GETTING THERE The farm is well signposted and lies about 4 miles from the M6. From the north, leave the M6 at junction 37 and follow signs for the farm on the A684, turning right at the Black Horse pub. From the south, leave the M6 at junction 36 and follow signs to Kirkby Lonsdale/Ingleton on the A65. Turn left at the sign for Holme Farm, onto the A683, go through Barbon and stay on A683 until you reach another sign for Holme Farm and turn right to go down the lane.

OPEN March–September.

THE DAMAGE £3 per person, £5 per tent and £2 per car per night. Farm tour: adult £6; child (aged 2–16) £5.50, under-2s free.

4 winds

Wild West meets North West on an idyllic Cumbrian campsite. With changeable weather in these parts – there's a good reason for all those lakes! – traditional Sioux tipis are perfect for a camping trip to the Lake District.

First-time campers? Rest of the family not completely convinced that camping in the notoriously rainy Lake District is such a great idea? Then 4 Winds Lakeland Tipis might just be the perfect pitch for your first under-canvas foray. It may not have some of the luxury extras afforded by other glamping sites – this is more back-to-nature tipi-ing – but the tipis are comfy, equipped and mean that you won't have to struggle to put up a soggy tent in the rain. In fact, this multicoloured tipi settlement will brighten up the dullest day.

The 12 brightly painted tipis form a colourful and eye-catching encampment in a corner of the National Trust's lovely Low Wray campsite on the shore of Lake Windermere. They come with just about everything but the kitchen sink, including a futon and air mats, rugs, cushions, gas cooker and heater, crockery, cutlery, washing-up gear, a coolbox with a couple of freezer packs – you can bring more of your own and freeze them at the National Trust reception – and tea-light lanterns for illumination. (You may want to pack a torch and will need to bring your own bedding and towels.)

Low Wray must surely be one of the most beautiful and diverse campsites in the country, with panoramic views over the surrounding fells, the lake's shoreline to wander along and, for the kids, woods to hide in and large fields to run around. But the main attraction for little ones here is bound to be the unforgettable experience of camping in a real tipi.

4 Winds Lakeland Tipis, Low Wray National Trust Campsite, Ambleside, Cumbria LA22 0JA; 01539 821227; www.4windslakelandtipis.co.uk

THE UPSIDE Ready-to-go tipi camping on an unforgettable lakeside site.

THE DOWNSIDE As to be expected, convenience and comfort comes at a price.

WHO'S IN? Families, couples, groups of up to 6 adults, campfires – yes. Tents, campervans, caravans, dogs – no.

THE FACILITIES Just a few metres from the tipis is a newly refurbished facilities block on the main campsite with toilets, showers and washbasins, and a couple of washing-up sinks outside. The site also has extensive recycling facilities, a laundry room, a disabled toilet and shower, 2 children's play areas, a lakeside beach and boating launch, a shop selling basics (and providing local info), and an upmarket catering van (see Food and Drink, p245).

ONSITE FUN Low Wray is next to Lake Windermere, so you can paddle, swim, feed the ducks or take a boat out on the lake. As well as the children's playgrounds, there's lots of space to run around, woods to hide in and you can have a fire right outside your tipi – so marshmallow-toasting fun aplenty.

OFFSITE FUN 4 Winds shares its corner of Low Wray with Long Valley Yurts (01539 731089; www.luxury-yurt-holidays.co.uk). They organise outdoor activities, departing from the site, including half-day mountain-biking and canoeing trips and moonlight canoeing with marshmallow-cooking over an open fire. A full day back-to-basics bushcraft course teaches you how to build shelters, forage for food, light fires, find water and make it safe to drink, and cook over an open fire.

IF IT RAINS The price of a complete tipi camping stay at 4 Winds includes free use of the 10-metre swimming pool,

sauna and gym at the nearby Windermere Manor Hotel on Rayrigg Road, Windermere. Ambleside Climbing Wall (01539 433794; www.adventurepeaks.com) is open daily from 10am to 9.30pm and boasts the best views in Ambleside from its Café Altitude. If you've already got wet, a rainy day might be the perfect time to hire kayaks from one of several companies (including www.windermerecanoekayak.com) operating on Lake Windermere or nearby Coniston Water.

FOOD AND DRINK If you want to stay on the site, but can't be bothered to cook, Yew Tree Farm's catering van provides hearty breakfasts using Heritage Meats (www.heritagemeats.co.uk) from 8.30 to 11am and afternoon teas and evening meals from 5 to 8pm (daily during the school summer holidays and weekends only at other times). You may have to book to get a table at the Drunken Duck Inn, about 2 miles away at Barngates (01539 436347; www.drunkenduckinn.co.uk), but it's more than worth it.

NANNY STATE ALERT Water, water, everywhere! Low Wray is right on the shore of Lake Windermere and there are also streams and marshy areas around the site.

GETTING THERE From Ambleside, take the A593 and turn left at Clappersgate, onto the B5286. Turn left at the sign for Wray and the site is less than a mile on the left. Directions to the tipis are provided on booking.

PUBLIC TRANSPORT The Coniston Rambler bus no. 505/506 from Ambleside or Windermere drops you to within a mile of the site.

OPEN Mid March–October.

THE DAMAGE From £235 for a midweek stay in a 16-foot tipi (sleeping up to 4 people) in low season to £495 for a week in high season. A smaller tipi is available for couples and there are large tipis that sleep up to 6, too.

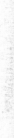

wild in style

The National Trust's Low Wray campsite on the shore of Lake Windermere has long been renowned as a pretty near-perfect spot for campers. And now you can glamp here, in fully equipped, luxury yurts nestling in woodland above the lake.

Banking's loss is definitely camping's gain. When Alex was made redundant from his IT job in the finance sector, he moved his family to the north west to set up a luxury yurt holiday site, Wild in Style, at Low Wray.

Four rather luxurious, cosy yurts, two of which have an extra sleeping area attached, come complete with comfy bed/settees, wood-burning stove and even a dining table and chairs. Bedding, cooking facilities, crockery and cutlery are all provided and there is a firepit or barbecue area with seating outside each yurt too. So, all you need to bring is 'a sense of adventure and a pocket full of fun' – and perhaps some waterproofs, walking boots and a kit bag for kayaking, canoeing and fishing.

Scattered among the woods at Low Wray – along with two gypsy caravans if Mum and Dad fancy a stay here someday without the kids in tow – the yurts are a short walk up the hill from the lake's shore and make for a wonderfully hassle-free, back-to-nature family holiday. Although the main campsite is large, with some 120 pitches, it manages to retain a wonderful air of tranquillity.

Adults will appreciate the opportunity to watch the sun rise over the lake, gaze at the stars through the yurt's central crown, and wander through the site to marvel at the views over the fells. For the kids, waking up in the yurt surrounded by woodland and having acres of lake, forest and fields to explore on this lovely Lake District campsite spells 'joy' with a capital 'J'.

Wild in Style, Low Wray National Trust Campsite, Ambleside, Cumbria LA22 0JA; 07909 446381; www.wildinstyle.co.uk

THE UPSIDE Cosy woodland yurt glamping right next to Lake Windermere.

THE DOWNSIDE There are only 4 yurts; although there are 2 gypsy caravans also.

WHO'S IN? Groups (though only 2 of the yurts are next to each other) – yes. Tents, campervans, caravans – no. Dogs – call ahead to check. Campfires in firepits.

THE FACILITIES Each yurt comfortably sleeps 4 and there are roll mats and Z-beds available on request. Just down the hill from the yurts is a newly refurbished facilities block that has plenty of toilets, showers and washbasins as well as a couple of washing-up sinks outside. Although bedding and cooking gear is provided, there is no fridge, so bring a coolbox and freezer packs (which you can refreeze at the site shop and reception), if you want an alternative to cooling your wine in the lake. Don't forget to bring a torch, too. Low Wray has extensive recycling facilities, a laundry room, a disabled toilet and shower, 2 children's playgrounds, a lakeside beach and boating launch, a shop selling basics (and providing local info) and an upmarket catering van for breakfasts, afternoon teas and evening meals.

ONSITE FUN Acres of fields and woods to run, play or cycle in, 2 play areas and, of course, the lake to wander around or get wet paddling, swimming, canoeing or kayaking. The National Trust site reception has a free Low Wray Wildlife Hunt to help younger children discover more about the birds, insects and animals that live on and around the site.

OFFSITE FUN Walk up the hill to Wray Castle and down to the lake to hop on a Windermere Lake Cruise (www.windermere-lakecruises.co.uk) to see Bowness,

Ambleside and the Lake District Visitor Centre at Brockhole (01539 446601; www.brockhole.co.uk). It has a soft indoor play area and an outdoor adventure playground with rope walks, slides, zip wires and scramble nets, and you can hire a kayak for £10 an hour. A walkers' ticket allows you to take a break at any of the stops and catch a later boat.

IF IT RAINS The Beatrix Potter Gallery in Hawkshead (01539 436355; www.nationaltrust.org.uk) is about 4 miles away and has a children's trail through displays of Beatrix Potter's watercolour paintings of Peter Rabbit and friends. Nearby, her house at Hill Top is also run by the National Trust. Or head to Zeffirellis in Ambleside for a movie and meal deal (see Food and Drink, below).

FOOD AND DRINK The Outgate Inn (01539 436413; www.outgateinn.co.uk) is about a 45-minute walk from the site and offers good food made with local produce. Try Zeffirellis (01539 433845; www.zeffirellis.com) or Fellinis (01539 432487; www.fellinisambleside.com) in Ambleside, where you can have a 2-course movie deal or a pizza-and-film deal; children's portions available.

NANNY STATE ALERT The wood-burning stoves are great for drying clothes, but make sure you keep the clothes a suitable distance away.

GETTING THERE From Ambleside, take the A593 and turn left at Clappersgate, onto the B5286. Turn left at the sign for Wray and the site is less than a mile on the left.

PUBLIC TRANSPORT The Coniston Rambler bus no. 505/506 from Ambleside or Windermere drops you to within a mile of the site.

OPEN March–November.

THE DAMAGE Prices range from £250 to £495 depending on length of stay, size of yurt and time of year.

fisherground

Marshmallow-toasting? Check. Water? Check. Playgrounds? Check. Trains? Check – all the things that make camping really cool for kids. And you can even arrive at the site's own station by steam locomotive.

This is a fantastic site for kids. It ticks all their campsite boxes, and probably a few more besides. Campfires are not only allowed, but are positively encouraged in selected areas, with bags of logs complete with kindling and firelighters sold on site each evening. Owner Mick takes a 'We like you to succeed' approach – just don't forget to pack the marshmallows.

The first thing that meets you on arrival is the pond, fed by a stream and usually full of children playing on tyre rafts – it makes a perfect focal point for kids to get to know each other. The playground has everything your young outward-bounder desires in the way of zip wires, climbing frames, tyre-rope swings and adventure courses. And there's an added extra: the site sits along the route of the Ravenglass and Eskdale steam railway line – a fab way to arrive if you're coming by public transport. So if you've walked into the nearby hamlet of Boot and there are some tired little legs as a result, hop on board for a scenic choo-choo trip back to camp.

For the adults, the site is in the heart of the Eskdale Valley, a quieter part of the Lake District, far from its hustle and bustle. Rugged, bracken-clad fells, woods and grazing sheep provide a splendid backdrop to rest your eyes on when you do eventually find time to relax.

Fisherground Campsite, Fellside Cottage, Eskdale, Holmrook, Cumbria CA19 1TF; 01946 723349; www.fishergroundcampsite.co.uk

THE UPSIDE A children's paradise with scenery for the adults. And no caravans.

THE DOWNSIDE It's at least an hour's drive from the M6.

WHO'S IN? Tents, campervans, dogs on leads, fires – yes. Caravans, single-sex groups without prior arrangement – no.

THE FACILITIES Unmarked pitches in 2 main areas: a larger field nearest to the children's playground and a smaller, quieter field nearest to the toilet/shower block, with wheel rims for campfires. The women's toilet block has 4 hand basins, 4 showers (50p-coin operated) and 5 loos; the men's are the same (except 4 toilets and 3 urinals), with 6 washing-up sinks outside. There is a washing machine, 3 tumble-dryers, a boot-dryer and a freezer. No shop on site, but you can buy logs, kindling and firelighters. The owners like to support the local village shop, which is ¾ mile away in Eskdale village. Noise after 10.30pm is not allowed.

ONSITE FUN Lots! As well as the playground and pond, there are rocks and trees for climbing on and plenty of space for ball games – there's a field next door for bigger games.

OFFSITE FUN If you manage to drag the kids off the site, go by steam train to Ravenglass or make the short trip to Dalegarth. From here you can walk into Boot or up to Stanley Force, following the tumbling beck up to the waterfall. A short walk towards Eskdale Green takes you along the River Esk, where a shallow area by the bridge is a good spot for a quick, if rather chilly, dip.

IF IT RAINS Hop in the pond! Kids who stay here don't seem to mind getting wet. But if you want to get out of the rain, take a tour of Eskdale Mill (01946 723335;

www.eskdalemill.co.uk) in Boot, one of the few remaining 2-wheel water corn mills in England. The mill also has a small honesty library.

FOOD AND DRINK The nearest shop is in Eskdale Green (01946 723229; www.eskdalestores. co.uk) for basics and there are 2 good pubs for food in Boot – the Brook House Inn (01946 723288; www.brookhouseinn.co.uk) and the Boot Inn (01946 723224; www.bootinn.co.uk). The King George IV (01946 723470; www.kinggeorge-eskdale.co.uk), a freehouse serving real ale and good food, is under new management, and it's only 300 metres away.

NANNY STATE ALERT The kids will be straight into the pond, rain or shine, before you've had a chance to even pitch your tent.

GETTING THERE Beware of using satnav if you want to avoid taking the white-knuckle ride over Hardknott and Wrynose Passes. From the south, leave the M6 at junction 36 and follow signs for Barrow, then 3 miles past Newby Bridge turn right towards Workington on the A5092. Keep on this road for around 10 miles then, beyond Broughton-in-Furness, turn right at traffic lights towards Ulpha. Turn left in Ulpha village to the steep hill signed 'Eskdale', follow the fell road to the King George IV pub and turn right to Boot. The campsite is 300 metres on the left. From the north, leave the M6 at junction 43 towards Workington/Cockermouth on the A595 then turn onto the A5086 to Cleator Moor and Egremont. Rejoin the A595, passing Egremont and Gosforth and driving through Holmrook. Turn left after the garage to Eskdale Green, follow the road to the next junction and turn right, then go through Eskdale village to the King George IV pub and turn left to Boot.

PUBLIC TRANSPORT Bus no. 618 from Ambleside and Windermere stops at Fell Foot around 5 times a day (08712 002233; www.stagecoachbus.com). To arrive in style, take a mainline train to Ravenglass, then the 'Ratty' steam train (01229 717171; www.ravenglass-railway.co.uk) to the site.

OPEN Early March–late October.

THE DAMAGE Adult £6 per night; child £3; vehicle £2.50. Visitors £2; campervan £4; gazebo/awning £2.50. There's a £5 supplement for large tents (6 berth and over) during the school holidays. Dogs £1.

solway view

Calling all pint-sized farmers, smugglers, intrepid explorers and eco-warriors. From tractor rides and nature trails to rockpools and rope swings, sustainability-conscious Solway View has it covered.

Run by affable owners Neil and Patricia, with a little help from their trusty wind turbine 'Tina Turner', Solway View is a small working farm in the kind of idyllic location that could have ambled its way off the pages of a *Famous Five* instalment. Overlooking the Dee Estuary, the farm is cradled by acres of woodland, with nature trails to explore and direct access over the fields to the sandy bay below. The sheltered cove makes a top spot for young sea dogs to let their imaginations run riot while becoming better acquainted with the numerous rockpools and their timid inhabitants.

The campsite itself is basic, but each of the 20 pitches is generous, with its own firepit and picnic area. For those after some home comforts, there are wooden wigwams, complete with electricity and heating, for hire in the neighbouring field.

When not running amok on the beach or adventure playground, kids can get stuck into impromptu games in the middle of the camping field. In the summer months, Neil organises tractor rides and tours of the farm for the little ones.

There's an all-weather cookhouse if you don't fancy campfire cooking, and the 'eco' boxes are ticked in the form of Tina, the solar-powered shower and toilet block (complete with, ahem, 'Steamy Windows'), recycling units and a clothes-drying tent. A trip to Solway View may not teach junior campers everything they need to know to save the planet, but it's a good start, with guaranteed fun and plenty of sea air to boot, m'hearties.

Solway View Holidays, Balmangan Farm, Ross Bay, Borgue, Kirkcudbright, Dumfries and Galloway DG6 4TR; 01557 870206; www.solwayviewholidays.com

THE UPSIDE Great rural location with doorstep beach access.
THE DOWNSIDE Canvas purists may be turned off by the site's 5 touring caravan pitches.
WHO'S IN? Tents, dogs on leads, campfires – yes. Large/stag/hen groups – no. Say that you're a *Cool Camping* fan on booking to ensure your pitch without having to join the Camping and Caravanning Club (site normally members only).
THE FACILITIES There's a solar-powered toilet and shower block with hot water and free showers. The block has baby changing facilities and a hairdryer in the ladies. Reception has a washing machine, and there's an eco-friendly clothes-drying tent. The kitchen has gas hobs, a kettle and dishwashing sinks.
ONSITE FUN Direct access to the beach, signed woodland walks and nature trails; space; playground and farm tours.
OFFSITE FUN There are plenty of family-friendly outdoor activities and attractions along the Solway Coast, including the Cream o'Galloway (www.creamogalloway.co.uk) and Caerlaverock Wildlife and Wetlands Trust (www.wwt.org.uk).
IF IT RAINS Head to the Cocoa Bean Chocolate Factory (www.thecocoabeancompany.com) on the edge of Twynholm.
FOOD AND DRINK No seaside break is complete without fish 'n' chips; try Polarbites (01557 339050) in Kirkcudbright.
NANNY STATE ALERT Be aware of machinery and livestock.
GETTING THERE Take the A75 south-west to Twynholm then briefly join the A711/A755 westward. Head to Borgue, taking the B727 towards the coast. Follow signs to Solway View.
OPEN All year.
THE DAMAGE Adult £5 per night; child £3, under-3s free. Wigwams (sleeping 4–5) from £35. Dogs £3 (max. 2 per pitch).

Caerlaverock Wildlife and Wetlands Trust

balloch o' dee

With horses for neighbours and chickens for playmates, Balloch O' Dee campsite is **eggs**actly *the kind of site for rural-loving families in need of space and stargazing opportunities as part of a back-to-basics camping experience.*

Balloch O' Dee's farm campsite is located in one of the Lowlands' most stunning areas — right on the edge of the fir-cloaked Galloway Forest Park, with its clear night skies (it's the only European designated Dark Skies forest). James and Hazel bought the place in 2010 and, just 12 months later, opened its gates to campers in search of a rural retreat. Their hard work has paid off, as the campsite is fast becoming a family favourite.

There's plenty of space (15 acres to be exact) and the large camping field offers spectacular views across the surrounding countryside. The atmosphere is relaxed and informal; kids can often be found paddling or trying to catch crayfish in the farm's tinkling burn before dragonflies appear at dusk. Communal campfires accompanied by evening sing-songs are commonplace, while in the morning campers are woken by the dawn chorus and get to throw open their tent doors to the sight of Culvennan Fell, framed in the morning mist.

Adjacent to the campsite is Balloch O' Dee's pony-trekking centre, offering a warm welcome to young riders. Tuition is available with qualified staff for every level, or there are regular supervised treks for the whole family through the forest. By day, kids will have a great view on horseback of the rare birds soaring overhead and the wild deer often spotted slinking through the trees and across the farmland. By night, they can keep watch for shooting stars and ponder what sort of fun campers might be having in another galaxy far, far away.

Balloch O' Dee Campsite and Trekking Centre, Kirkcowan, Newton Stewart, Wigtownshire, Dumfries and Galloway DG8 0ET; 01671 830708; www.ballochodee.com

THE UPSIDE Set in a stunning location at the foot of Culvennan Fell and on the edge of Galloway Forest Park (www.gallowayforestpark.com), so if the kids run out of things to do on site, they have Britain's largest forest park to explore – all 300 square miles of it.

THE DOWNSIDE Until the arrival of some facilities, even the most hardy of families may find it tough going with very young children in tow. There are plans afoot, though, so do check when booking.

WHO'S IN? Tents, campervans, touring caravans, dogs on leads, groups (so long as they respect their fellow campers) – yes. Campfires are permitted in previously used spots.

THE FACILITIES All pitches are grass and there are no electric hook-ups. Emphasis is on space, so there are only about 20 generous pitches in the large camping field. At the time of writing there were no showers or toilets, so if the planned facilities block has not yet been built when you're booking your pitch, bring plenty of wet wipes and be prepared to embrace a wild-camping experience. That said, fresh drinking water is available and campers can borrow one of several stone-built barbecues. There is a point for emptying chemical loos.

ONSITE FUN The pony-trekking centre should provide hours of fun for budding jockeys. Mum and Dad can also get involved by leading the rides, if they like. As well as the organised treks (£10 per hour or £15 for the day), children are welcome to stay at the stables for the day and groom the horses, learn more about their new four-legged friends and join in with the mucking out (bring wellies and waterproofs!).

There's also the opportunity to embrace the role of hunter-gatherer at breakfast time. Dozens of rare-breed hens roam freely round the site and the challenge is to find and collect their eggs each morning for a hearty omelette.

OFFSITE FUN Three Lochs Holiday Park (01671 830304; www.3lochs.co.uk) is a couple of miles down the road. Campers from Balloch O' Dee are welcome to use their facilities and book any of the activities on offer, from archery to mountain biking. You can book fishing at Loch Heron and Loch Ronald at the park's reception to go after pike as large as 13kg for supper.

IF IT RAINS In nearby Newton Stewart you'll find a swimming pool (01671 404301) and a community-owned cinema that regularly screens the latest releases as well as live theatre shows. In summer, the programme is usually family-orientated (www.nscinema.co.uk for listings).

FOOD AND DRINK Check out the House o' Hill Hotel at Glentrool (01671 840243; www.houseohill.co.uk). It has a fabulous location at the edge of Galloway Forest and a menu to match – crammed full of local produce with something tasty for even the youngest of diners – our firm family favourite were the homemade fishcakes.

NANNY STATE ALERT There is a relatively slow-running burn meandering through the farm. It may be shallow but care should still be taken, especially when it comes to very young children. Visitors to the trekking centre should also be mindful of the horses.

GETTING THERE Leave the M6, signposted for Stranraer (A75) and continue westward, past Newton Stewart, and on for a further 6 miles. Here you'll see a right turn for 'The Three Lochs'. Balloch O' Dee is about 1½ miles along this road, on the right.

PUBLIC TRANSPORT There is no direct public transport service to the site, but if campers can make their way via bus to Newton Stewart, the owners are happy to collect them (if pre-arranged).

OPEN All year.

THE DAMAGE It's a simple £6 per night for tents/£10 for motorhomes/caravans, regardless of occupancy numbers. Dogs free.

tibbie shiels

With its enviable lochside position, complete with fishing and water sports, the ancient campsite at the Tibbie Shiels Inn offers plenty of open space for kids to run amok, not to mention a cosy country pub for mums and dads.

Tibbie Shiels feels wonderfully remote yet is incredibly welcoming and has a definite hint of *Swallows and Amazons*. The camping field sits between St Mary's Loch and the 17th-century Tibbie Shiels Inn, which has proved a popular stopover for many illustrious Scotsmen over the years, including Robert Louis Stevenson.

St Mary's is the largest natural loch in the Scottish Borders and was formed at the end of the last ice age. It's a favourite haunt for watersports enthusiasts and many visiting families arrive with their own canoes strapped to the car roof for days of watery expeditions – the inn can provide picnics on request. If you're feeling brave enough to plunge into the loch's icy depths, do don a wetsuit. Meanwhile, younger campers might prefer to brave a tentative toe-dip from the end of the jetty. The loch is also well stocked with brown trout; fishing permits can be bought at the pub's reception, so the smell of barbecued fish is common in the evenings.

Alistair and Selina (and dog George) bought Tibbie Shiels a few years ago and have been busy transforming the campsite into a family-friendly zone. The trees overhanging the loch shore instantly morph kids into clambering monkeys and a rope swing invites mini-Tarzan impersonations all day long. They've also erected a tipi suitable for larger families and have created a tasty kids' menu at the inn. With its cosy wood-burning stove, it's an ideal spot for winding down at the end of a day's adventuring before you snuggle into sleeping bags.

Tibbie Shiels Inn, St Mary's Loch, Selkirkshire TD7 5LH; 01750 42231; www.tibbieshiels.com

THE UPSIDE As well as the site's fantastic location next to St Mary's Loch, it has one of the Scottish Borders' oldest and friendliest pubs on its doorstep. The inn is very child-friendly and the whole family will be spoiled for dining choice.

THE DOWNSIDE Campers stay at Tibbie Shiels for its location and back-to-basics charm; so don't arrive expecting a range of high-tech facilities or you'll be disappointed.

WHO'S IN? Families, walkers and outdoor enthusiasts in tents, campervans and caravans, with dogs on leads – yes, though the main clientele are tenters. Groups of 6 or less are permitted and only alcohol purchased at the inn can be consumed on site. Campfires are allowed but must be extinguished by midnight.

THE FACILITIES The camping field is licensed for 70 campers rather than a certain number of pitches. In addition to the camping area there is a large tipi that sleeps up to 12. The 4 showers and 4 toilets are housed in a Portakabin to the rear of the pub and have free pre-mixed warm water. There are several dishwashing sinks but facilities are limited.

ONSITE FUN Tibbie Shiels is all about the great outdoors. Wide-open spaces, plenty of good climbing trees, a few rope swings and access to a jetty, a fishing rod and a loch should ensure most outdoor-loving families are content. You can also bring your own canoes and kayaks, and what's more, the Southern Upland Way (www.southernuplandway.gov.uk) runs past the campsite with its easy access to bracing walks.

OFFSITE FUN Traquair House (01896 830323; www.traquair.co.uk), with its magnificent gardens, is 10 miles from Tibbie Shiels. Adults and kids alike love the giant hedged maze; it's a challenge to navigate, covering over half an

acre, and hosts a mighty egg hunt involving over 6,000 mini chocolate eggs every Easter Sunday for the under-10s. Grey Mare's Tail Nature Reserve at nearby Moffat (08444 932249; www.nts.org.uk) is also worth a visit – acres and acres of rolling countryside with wildlife to spot that includes feral goats and peregrine falcons. And its 60-metre waterfall should impress even the most discerning of youngsters.

IF IT RAINS The leisure centre at Selkirk (the nearest large town to St Mary's Loch) is open daily and has a 25-metre pool with inflatable fun at certain times (phone ahead to check: 01750 20897), as well as a café and soft play area for younger kids. Edinburgh is 2 hours away by car, and definitely worthy of a visit if the rain comes. There you'll find countless indoor attractions for the whole family (www.kidsedinburgh.com).

FOOD AND DRINK The number one choice has to be the Tibbie Shiels Inn, with its cosy bar area, additional dining room and conservatory overlooking the loch. Both the kids' and main menu offer a varied choice of hearty, home-cooked meals made from local produce wherever possible. The full Scottish breakfast with all the trimmings should set any camper up for the day ahead.

NANNY STATE ALERT With open access from the camping field to the loch, be vigilant with your young children around water.

GETTING THERE From Carlisle, take the M6 northbound, which becomes the A74(M) for 30 miles. Exit at junction 15 and follow signs for Moffat/Selkirk. Turn right onto the A708 and stay on it for 15 miles; this leads directly to the Tibbie Shiels Inn.

OPEN All year. Check in at the inn.

THE DAMAGE Adult £5 per night; child (under-16) £2.50, under-5s free. There are 5 electric hook-ups available at £5 per night.

culzean castle

Once upon a time, there was this rather large and really quite impressive castle called Culzean. It had vast grounds and an undoubtedly idyllic campsite right next door…

What child wouldn't be blown away at the idea of waking up next door to a castle? It's all about location at Culzean… You may find yourself rubbing shoulders with caravanners at the shower block, but don't let that ruffle your feathers. The whole family is going to have a blast here. Junior Knights of the Round Table and mini Rapunzels will be able to let their hair down while imaginations go into fairy-tale overdrive in the grounds of Culzean Castle.

This imposing building, complete with arresting ramparts and towering turrets, offers a spectacular backdrop to the campsite and provides acre upon acre of grounds ripe for exploration. Throughout the year, the walled gardens, swan pond, deer park and adventure playground are just some of the gems waiting to be discovered. And in the summer, there are guided ranger trails, kids' castle tours and plenty of organised family events.

The site itself is relaxed and geared towards families. Tents tend to congregate in an oval shape on the outside edge of the central green, leaving plenty of games-friendly space. There's a safe and convivial atmosphere, with kids forging instant friendships as soon as they tumble out of the car, and parents chatting over sizzling barbecues.

Culzean's facilities tend to be spotless. There's an onsite playground, which can be forgiven its basic nature with the Culzean Estate so close by. The doorstep country park, castle and miles of spectacular coastline should ensure that there's no time to grow tired of the site's slide and swings…

Culzean Castle Camping and Caravanning Club Site, Culzean, Maybole, Ayrshire KA19 8JX; 01655 760627; www.campingandcaravanningclub.co.uk

THE UPSIDE There's an actual castle next door! Campers have doorstep access to the castle grounds and the sandy beaches below, and the bonus of free admission to the country park throughout their stay.

THE DOWNSIDE As Culzean Castle is a National Trust property and the site is a Camping and Caravanning Club site, it can be incredibly busy during school holidays so it's best to plan your trip well in advance to avoid disappointment.

WHO'S IN? Tents, campervans, caravans, dogs (on leads) – yes. Large groups, stag or hen parties – no.

THE FACILITIES The site has a mixture of grass pitches and hardstandings, all generous in size, and electric hook-ups are available. Spotlessly clean large shower and toilet block with family and disabled rooms, as well as a covered dishwashing area and laundry facilities.

ONSITE FUN The kids' play area is quite basic: just a couple of swings and a slide. There is a grass area at the centre of the site where children can run around and play ball games, though.

OFFSITE FUN It's all about this magnificent cliff-top castle (www.culzeanexperience.org) and its country park. Canons and ramparts help to fuel imaginations, while the sprawling gardens, woodland trails, deer park and 13-acre swan pond with neighbouring adventure playground can help expend a little energy. Along the glorious stretch of shoreline below are sand dunes and numerous caves and rockpools.

IF IT RAINS The Heads of Ayr Farm Park (01292 441210; www.headsofayrfarmpark.co.uk) is a great day out with lots of additional indoor activities on top of the outdoor farm

Culzean Castle

Culzean Castle

attractions. Many of the reptiles and animals are housed indoors, along with the play barn and its ride-on super diggers and electric tractors.

FOOD AND DRINK There's a family-friendly café and restaurant at the castle, but if you'd rather venture further afield, try the Minishant Inn (01292 442483) at nearby Maybole for good, wholesome food in a cosy setting. They have a varied kids' menu and the staff are very cheery.

NANNY STATE ALERT The entrance to the campsite and the country park are adjacent to one another and lie off the busy A77, so in high season there can be increased traffic using the shared access road.

GETTING THERE Take the M77 southbound from Glasgow. This eventually becomes the A77 and is signposted for Kilmarnock. At the village of Maybole, turn right, following the signs to Culzean. Both campsite and country park are clearly signposted.

PUBLIC TRANSPORT There is a regular bus service operating between Ayr and Girvan (Western Scottish, no.60) that stops opposite the campsite entrance.

OPEN April–October.

THE DAMAGE For non-members, a pitch for a family of 2 adults and 2 children costs £25–£31 per night, depending on season. Dogs free.

seal shore

Your own private beach on a little Scottish island, complete with seals, otters and basking sharks... now that's pretty cool. Throw in a few fossils and plenty of outdoor-loving young playmates, and you're guaranteed a top-notch family camping break.

Located at the southern tip of Arran, Seal Shore is in the sunniest and driest area on the island. Unfortunately it's also the windiest, but that helps to blow the midges away – along with any cobwebs! Its private beach is a huge draw, making the site incredibly popular with young families. All day long, little Robinson Crusoes can be found combing the beach for fossils, building sandcastles of epic proportions and investigating any crustacean that moves – or doesn't – in the copious rockpools.

The views afforded from the shore-side pitches are spectacular; looking out towards the majestic Ailsa Craig (a 300-metre-high rocky plug from a long-extinct volcano) and Pladda Island with its working lighthouse. On a clear day, keen-eyed campers can even see Ireland. And then there's the wildlife: regular sightings include one or two of the campsite's eponymous seals, as well as otters and basking sharks, in the glistening waters.

Arran is nicknamed 'Scotland in miniature', as within one small island it manages to replicate most of the landscape found throughout Scotland, from the Lowlands to the Highlands. Circumnavigating it by car shouldn't take longer than an afternoon, but it's a worthwhile excursion. Places to explore include castle ruins, waterfalls and nature trails, before its time for you and your little rascals to return to Seal Shore for a communal barbecue or campfire on the beach. These happen frequently over the summer; just bring a pound of sausages and be prepared to join in with a sing-song or two.

Seal Shore Camping & Touring Site, Kildonan, Isle of Arran KA27 8SE; 01770 820320; www.campingarran.com

THE UPSIDE A private island beach with marine life to spot.
THE DOWNSIDE The site can be incredibly busy during the school holidays. So, all bookings must be made in advance.
WHO'S IN? Everyone, plus dogs, in tents, caravans and caravans – yes. Groups are asked to keep noise levels down.
THE FACILITIES There are 43 grass pitches and 8 hook-ups available. There are 4 new showers to help free up the other showers; laundry; washing-up sinks; an undercover cooking area, a TV room (with board games) and barbecue stands are available for campers to borrow. Campfires on the beach only.
ONSITE FUN The beach provides the main entertainment.
OFFSITE FUN Enjoy a 2-mile walk from the beach around the coast to the Black Cave, reputed to be the island's largest, and a popular haunt for 18th-century smugglers.
IF IT RAINS Head back up the coast to Brodick and the Auchrannie Resort (www.auchrannie.co.uk). It has a fantastic play barn, a swimming pool and activities such as archery.
FOOD AND DRINK The Auchrannie Resort has several dining options, including a Brasserie with a wide selection of kids' meals. Closer to Seal Shore, check out the Kildonan Hotel (01770 820207) or the Pierhead Tavern (01770 600418).
NANNY STATE ALERT The sea is near and the rocks slippy.
GETTING THERE From the ferry terminal at Brodick, turn left and follow the coastal road south for 12 miles. At the sign for Kildonan, turn left and follow the track down to Seal Shore.
PUBLIC TRANSPORT Take the Arran Bus no. 323, which runs regularly from Brodick to Kildonan. Then walk for 2 minutes.
OPEN March–October.
THE DAMAGE Tent per night: 4-/5-/6-man £4/£5/£6. Adult £6; child (5–15) £3, under-5s free. Dogs £1. Hook-ups £3.50.

comrie croft

Adventure-loving families scramble, run and jump this way… Comrie Croft has forest to roam around, mountain bike trails to race along and a small loch to fish. An opportunity to truly embrace the great outdoors from the moment you pitch your tent.

Eco-friendly Comrie Croft welcomes campers, hostellers and even the occasional worm or two… It's run by a group of outdoorsy locals who wanted to make the most of the croft's farmland. The result: a cosy hostel and a naturally beautiful and friendly campsite that allows tenters to get as close to a wild camping experience as possible, with the added bonus of doorstep facilities and activities.

There are three camping areas to choose from – a spacious field next to the reception that's ideal for larger tents; a birch glade offering the thrill of true woodland camping; and an elevated meadow, whose views across the Perthshire countryside more than make up for the extra walk to the loos and showers.

For something a little more luxurious, and an experience that both kids and parents are guaranteed to love, Comrie also has Swedish kåtas. These pre-erected tipi-style tents are pitched in the woodland and come complete with log-burning stoves and alpine beds with sheepskin throws that should fuel the imagination of even the youngest would-be cowboy or Indian.

There are too many tempting activities here to list, but some family favourites include: nature trails, bike tracks with a range of difficulty levels, a small fishing loch, fruit picking and den making in the woods. In the school holidays there are even kids' recycling workshops, where all ages can get involved in making cool stuff from old things, ranging from go-karts to bunting, and even worm hotels. There's no such thing as boredom at Comrie Croft.

Comrie Croft, Braincroft, Crieff, Perthshire PH7 4JZ; 01764 670140; www.comriecroft.com

THE UPSIDE All the best bits of wild camping combined with all the best bits of regular camping – you're deep in rural Perthshire yet the facilities are great and the site is only a few miles from the picturesque village of Comrie on one side and the bustling small town of Crieff on the other.

THE DOWNSIDE It's a firm favourite for families during the school holidays, so be warned that you may encounter lengthy morning queues for the showers. Good news, though: there are plans to install more showers and loos, which should be in place by the time you read this.

WHO'S IN? Tents, dogs (on leads), campfires – yes. Campervans, caravans, stag or hen groups – no.

THE FACILITIES There are 4 kåtas for hire and 34 tent pitches without hook-ups. Ablutions-wise, there are 4 toilets and 3 solar showers with plans for further bush showers and new compost loos. Mirrors and electric sockets can be found in the bathrooms, and lockers with internal phone chargers are available for hire (£1/24 hours). Campers have use of the microwave, fridge and freezer, and there are double sinks for hand-washing clothes and pulleys for drying. Campfires are encouraged in the site's firepits – £5 for a bag of logs and kindling. There is also a communal area with a campfire that's sheltered from the elements by a parachute strung across the branches of an overhanging tree.

ONSITE FUN Lots and lots… a natural playground with trees for climbing and rope swings galore. There's a small loch for fishing, bikes for hire and trails to explore in and around the forest. There are also plans for a mountain bike skills area suitable for older kids. Building dens in the woods is a popular pastime, while grown-ups laze in one of the

site's many hammocks. During the school holidays there are kids' workshops in operation (see www.remakescotland.co.uk), inside and out, depending on what recycled contraptions are being created on that day.

OFFSITE FUN A firm family favourite is the Auchingarrich Wildlife Park (www.auchingarrich.co.uk) on the other side of Comrie village. It caters for all ages, with plenty to see and do, indoors and out. If the weather turns, there's a play barn with a soft-play section for younger visitors. Outside, there's an adventure playground, crazy golf, flying fox and ride-on tractors. Oh, and don't forget the wildlife: this place is home to many creatures, great and small, from Highland 'coos' and pot-bellied pigs to meerkats and llamas.

IF IT RAINS Auchingarrich (above) has plenty to offer on a rainy day, but so does Comrie Croft if you'd rather stay closer to your tent. The farm's outbuildings host many gatherings over the course of the season, from campsite ceilidhs and craft workshops to games of 5-a-side footie, basketball and table tennis. Keep an eye on the website for organised events.

FOOD AND DRINK Eggs can be gathered from the site's coop and there's an 'edible hedge' that produces wild fruit in abundance. Essentials are available to purchase from reception, which boasts a real coffee machine and fresh goods such as rolls, croissants, and sausages and bacon from the local butcher, as well as the all-important marshmallows. Comrie village is only 2 miles away and home to the Deil's Cauldron (01764 670352; www.deilscauldron.co.uk), which specialises in local produce and has a tasty children's menu and outdoor terrace. The Royal Hotel (www.royalhotel.co.uk) on the Square in Comrie is worth a visit for a more formal dinner.

NANNY STATE ALERT The road from Crieff to Comrie village runs past the bottom of Comrie Croft's driveway. Keep a careful watch on younger children if you're heading out onto the road for a family cycle.

GETTING THERE Take the A85 from Crieff to Comrie. Comrie Croft is clearly signposted on your right.

PUBLIC TRANSPORT There's a bus stop opposite the site's entrance. Nos. 15 and 15A from Perth pass on a regular basis.

OPEN All year.

THE DAMAGE Adult £7 per night Sunday–Thursday, £9 Friday–Saturday; child (under-16) half price, under-5s free. Kåtas sleep 4–6 people; weekend breaks start from £88. Dogs free.

iona campsite

The rugged and windswept Isle of Iona lies just off the coast of Mull and has some of the UK's most wonderful and virtually deserted beaches. And now it has a campsite (the island's one and only), called… Iona Campsite! Are your bags already packed?

The approach to Iona is stunning. A short ferry crossing takes foot passengers across the mile-long stretch of water between the isle and Mull's south-west coast. Dotted along the shoreline is sheltered inlet after inlet, just waiting for little feet to run over the white sands, dip their toes and paddle in the crystal-clear waters.

The island itself is only one mile across and three in length, but the beaches and rocky outcrops that speckle Iona's grassland – inviting intrepid pint-sized explorers to scramble up and conquer – more than justify a few days' stay. Until recently, there wasn't a single campsite here, but at long last Iona Campsite has thrown open its gates to tents.

The site itself is very basic. A mile's walk from the ferry – half of it uphill – it's really just a field located behind Cnoc-Oran B&B. The sparse facilities take the form of a small toilet and shower block, but then, what more do you need when there are so many beaches waiting to be discovered just a short walk away?

There are no designated pitches or hook-ups, but plenty of level patches of grass are interspersed among the hills and rocks that provide welcome shelter from Iona's winds and a little privacy from other campers. A couple of picnic tables await alfresco diners and you'll spy a few hens and sheep roaming around: amusement for the little ones while Mum and Dad pack up the day sacks before the whole family hits the beach.

Iona Campsite, Cnoc-Oran, Isle of Iona PA76 6SP; 01681 700112; www.ionaselfcateringaccommodation.co.uk

THE UPSIDE The only campsite on a gorgeous island and a great option for the budget-conscious family.

THE DOWNSIDE The camping field is in an elevated position so, while it offers fantastic panoramic views back across to Mull, it also leaves it a little exposed to the elements. Thankfully there are quite a few raised rock formations providing some shelter for tenters, and solar-powered wooden wigwams have recently been built, which will offer plenty more shelter from the elements.

WHO'S IN? As non-residents aren't allowed to bring vehicles over to Iona, it's tents only. Dogs on leads – yes. No campfires permitted, but barbecues are allowed if they're raised off the grass.

THE FACILITIES Very basic. There is a small toilet block with 3 hot electric showers and 3 toilets.

ONSITE FUN Open space for kids to run amok and plenty of rocks to scramble up. It's really all about those beaches…

OFFSITE FUN Fantastic beaches. The bays dotted along Iona's coastline are sandy Shangri-Las for families. The shimmering white sands caressed by clear waves are sheltered from coastal breezes – perfect for paddling and swimming – while rockpools aplenty await scrutinising by young eyes. Iona is best explored by bike; Finlay Ross (01681 700357) have bicycles suitable for all ages to hire, including helmets and child seats, if required. Those with sea legs should hop aboard a traditional wooden sailboat with Alternative Boat Hire (01681 700537; www.boattripsiona.com) to spot seals and learn about the sea birds. For a spot of history and culture, Iona Abbey (01681 700512; www.isle-of-iona.com) has daily guided tours. It's a focal point on the island and played a

View from the ferry over to Iona

strong role in the history of Christianity in both Ireland and Scotland. It's also the burial ground of many ancient Scottish and European kings, as well as John Smith, the Labour Party leader in the early 1990s.

IF IT RAINS Put on your waterproofs and get down to those beaches anyway! If the weather isn't too bad, then a boat trip in some light rain can still be worth taking. Staffa Trips (01681 700358; www.staffatrips.co.uk) sail to awe-inspiring Fingal's Cave, with its 59-million-year old basalt columns. En route, passengers often spot dolphins and otters and, occasionally, whales and basking sharks.

FOOD AND DRINK Both the diminutive isle's Argyll Hotel and Martyr's Bay restaurant have decent menus with kids' options. The Argyll (01681 700334; www.argyllhoteliona.co.uk) is over 140 years old and specialises in home-grown and local produce (fantastic home-baked goods are on offer). It's worth booking in advance in the summer months. Overlooking the harbour, Martyr's Bay (01681 700382; www.martyrsbay.co.uk) is Iona's only pub and serves a great range of hearty, traditional meals and speciality seafood dinners, as well as coffees and snacks.

NANNY STATE ALERT The rocky outcrops scattered around the camping field may be fun for older kids to scramble up and over, but might be a little ambitious for less-sure-footed toddlers. Watch out in case they attempt to follow big brother or big sister!

GETTING THERE As visitors aren't permitted to bring vehicles onto the island, they can only visit Iona as a foot passenger via the Caledonian MacBrayne (08000 665000; www.calmac.co.uk) ferry service from Fionnphort on Mull. The crossing takes about 10 minutes. From the ferry, turn left at the end of the pier and follow the single-track road for about 1 mile. It hugs the coastline before turning right and heading up the hill, over a small crossroads. Cnoc-Oran is signposted, on your right.

PUBLIC TRANSPORT There is a taxi service on the island. To book, call Iona Taxi on 07810 325990; they can carry up to 6 and will also take passengers on a tour of the island, if desired.

OPEN April–October.

THE DAMAGE Adult £5 per night; child (5–12 years) £2.50, under-5s free. There are also tents and camping kit available to hire from £10 per night for a tent – phone for more details and to enquire about availability.

calgary bay

In the furthest flung corner on the far-flung Isle of Mull, a wee gem of a beach campsite glimmers, cunningly disguised as a wild camping spot. They say the best things in life are free – Calgary Bay provides supporting evidence, in buckets and spades.

Calgary Bay is a special campsite for would-be pirates and smugglers. It's incredibly basic, but has a million-dollar location on the north-west coast of the Isle of Mull. The most unbelievable thing about this hidden gem is that it's absolutely free! That's because it's a campsite that isn't really a campsite… There are no shower blocks, no electric hook-ups, no cooking facilities and no reception. It's simply a patch of machair (sandy grass) bordering one of Scotland's finest beaches and just longing for imaginative re-enactments from Stevenson's classic, *Treasure Island*.

The bay faces west, towards Tiree, and is well sheltered by low hills, making it uncharacteristically warm for Scotland. The beach is truly spectacular, with white sands stretching into the distance and holiday-brochure waters inviting toes to take a dip. Children tend to roam the beach all day: building sandcastles and burying their treasure, creature-spotting in rockpools and flying their kites… with the occasional break for paddling or swimming.

The cliffs just beyond the bay provide an excellent spot for permit-free fishing – there's plenty of pollack waiting to be caught and cooked over the campfire for supper. The area is also teeming with wildlife, so keen-eyed family members are sure to spot some of the local otters or the sea eagles soaring overhead. If you can tear mini pirates away from the beach, Tobermory (aka *Balamory*) is a 12-mile drive and worthy of a visit – if only to go in search of PC Plum and Josie Jump.

Calgary Bay, by Dervaig, Isle of Mull; www.calgarybay.co.uk

THE UPSIDE Definitely one of the finest campsite locations in all of Scotland.

THE DOWNSIDE In order to preserve the machair, campers are asked to keep their stay to 2 or 3 nights. Be warned, it's going to be hard to drag the kids away.

WHO'S IN? Tents permitted on the machair and small campervans allowed in the adjacent lay-by. Caravans – no. Dogs on leads, small groups – yes. Beach campfires only. Please consult the wild camping code of conduct before visiting (www.outdooraccess-scotland.com).

THE FACILITIES The grassy camping area has a scattering of picnic benches and there's a toilet block across the road – 1 men's loo, 1 ladies'. Here you'll find cold running water that can be boiled for cooking. At Tobermory there's a modern facility at the harbour (www.tobermoryharbour.co.uk) with hot showers and a laundry room. There are camping guidelines on a noticeboard but, in general, campers are asked to respect their surroundings and to take anything they bring to the site away with them.

ONSITE FUN One of Scotland's finest beaches just outside your tent should ensure plenty of fun for the whole family all day long. There's also a rope swing on one of the trees overhanging the camping area and plenty of driftwood for campfires on the beach. The option to be sociable and join in a sing-song around one of the beach campfires is there most summer evenings. It's not compulsory to bring a guitar, but it certainly won't be frowned upon if you do.

OFFSITE FUN There are ruins of ancient buildings and old stone forts along the coastline, which make for some fun exploration. Tobermory, the island's capital, is 12 miles away

Tobermory

by car (the roads are windy and often single-track so this can take 40 minutes) is worth a trip. From its famous harbour you can take a family boat tour with Sea Life Surveys (01688 302916; www.sealifesurveys.com) and hopefully spot a few whales, dolphins and basking sharks. Discover the island on two wheels – families can hire bikes and helmets for the day from Brown's shop on Tobermory Main Street (01688 302020; www.brownstobermory.co.uk). The shop itself is one of the island's oldest and an Aladdin's cave, stocking everything from hardware to musical instruments, malt whiskies and local fishing permits. For any toddlers in tow, a walk around the village will have them spotting houses from *Balamory*.

IF IT RAINS The Old Byre Heritage Centre (01688 400229; www.old-byre.co.uk) near Dervaig is a good rainy-day option. It's open Wednesday–Sunday from April to October and has a pretty tea room that serves Scottish puddings as well as a covered play area for toddlers with bright murals of Tobermory's seafront, playhouses, climbing toys and a dressing-up box, too.

FOOD AND DRINK The Am Birlinn (01688 400619; www.ambirlinn.com) is only a few miles away from Calgary Bay and offers a wonderful kids' menu, including Mull stew and local linguine, with a special early dining slot (6–7.30pm) for families with young children. The added bonus is the complimentary minibus service laid on for diners coming from any of the nearby villages. Tobermory has a selection of cafés and restaurants by the harbour and, for something more indulgent, there's the Tobermory Chocolate Factory (01688 302526; www.tobermorychocolate.co.uk), housed in the building where *Balamory*'s Edie McCredie once dwelled.

NANNY STATE ALERT A small burn runs between the site and the beach and, of course, there's open access to the sea.

GETTING THERE From the Oban to Mull ferry, turn right and head north to Tobermory. On entering the village, turn left at the first roundabout and follow signs for Dervaig. Continue through Dervaig and on to Calgary Bay. Much of the road is single-track. The campsite is on the right, opposite the toilets.

PUBLIC TRANSPORT There are several daily buses that run from Tobermory to Calgary Bay, via Dervaig. For timetables for no. 494, see www.bowmanstours.co.uk.

OPEN All year.

THE DAMAGE It's free! Leaving plenty of spare pennies for purchasing the obligatory *Balamory* memorabilia in Tobermory.

borlum farm

Wanted: Monster Hunter. Must be brave, with good eyesight and binoculars… If searching for the elusive Loch Ness Monster isn't enough in the way of adventure for young heroes and heroines, how about some horseback fun on a trusty steed?

Borlum Farm is a heaven for kids who are into horses. It's a 400-acre working farm and equestrian centre with a basic camping field right next door to the stables. Riding lessons are available for all ages and abilities, or campers can trot out on one of the organised hacks through neighbouring woodland, and there are plenty of opportunities to don wellies and give a hand mucking out the stables. Thankfully, the onsite hot showers ensure any *eau de cheval* stays outside the tent…

The farm is also well placed for intrepid monster hunters who are eager to scan the mystical waters of Loch Ness, steeped in myth and legend, for a certain alleged inhabitant. The loch is just a two-mile walk from the campsite, so in no time at all you can be on its shores, binoculars at the ready.

Resident monster-hunter Steve Feltham has been living in a not-so-mobile library van beside the loch for almost 20 years, hoping to catch a glimpse of Nessie in all her grandeur. He's been the subject of nearly as many documentaries and articles as the mysterious Nessie herself; and if you take the 30-minute trip to his home at Dores, he will happily tell you about his experiences so far. In return, you could purchase one of his very cute Nessie models.

But be warned, if you manage to spot Nessie before him, he'll be pretty peeved. Keep your eyes peeled, though, just in case.

Borlum Farm, Drumnadrochit, nr Inverness, Inverness-shire IV63 6XN; 01456 450220; www.borlum.com

THE UPSIDE A Nessie's tail-length away from iconic Loch Ness. Horse-loving kids are going to be able to walk to the stables straight from their tent, every morning.

THE DOWNSIDE The owners prefer not to take advance bookings so an early arrival is recommended in order to bag yourself a good pitch.

WHO'S IN? Tents, campervans, caravans, dogs (on leads) – yes. Barbecues are allowed if raised off the ground but no campfires permitted.

THE FACILITIES There are 35 grass tent pitches spread across 2 camping fields without hook ups. Next to the stables are 12 hardstandings, all with electric hook-ups. The top camping area offers spectacular views down to Glenurquhart; the bottom field is more level, although it can get boggy after heavy rain. There's a covered dishwashing area. Two toilet and shower blocks, one in each field. Showers are coin operated – 20p for 5 minutes. There are also washing machines and tumble-dryers; tokens for these can be bought at reception.

ONSITE FUN Horses to ride and lots and lots of mucking out to be done – messy fun that definitely calls for wellies and waterproofs. Plenty of wide-open space for kids to enjoy, as well as an abundance of trees, such as horse chestnut and Scots pine.

OFFSITE FUN Loch Ness Monster hunting along the shores of Loch Ness and visiting Nessie expert Steve at Dores village. Urquhart Castle, only half-a-mile's walk from Borlum (01456 450551; www.historic-scotland.gov.uk), dates back to the 13th century and is one of Scotland's largest castles, with commanding views over the loch. You can learn all about its bloody history through centuries of Highland conflict at the

Stables adjacent to the site

Monster-hunter Steve Feltham at Dores

visitor centre. If you're still determined to find Nessie for yourselves, board the Nessie Hunter boat (01456 450395) for a guided tour of the loch with George, who will regale the whole family with tales of monsters galore.

IF IT RAINS At Drumnadrochit village, you can immerse yourself in all things Nessie for a few hours. Visit the Loch Ness Centre & Exhibition that charts the history of the loch and Nessie through folklore and research (01456 450573; www.lochness.com). At Nessieland Castle Monster Centre (01456 450342; www.nessieland-castle-monster-centre.co.uk) you'll find a fun presentation about Nessie, as well as a monster-themed adventure playground and a café.

FOOD AND DRINK The Loch Ness Inn is only a 5-minute walk from the campsite and serves tasty, locally sourced food, has a kids' menu and a child-friendly beer garden (01456 450991; www.staylochness.co.uk). If you make the trip to Dores to meet Steve then you should definitely check out the Dores Inn (01463 751203; www.thedoresinn.co.uk). It's a family-run pub and restaurant whose friendly staff greet children especially warmly. There's a lovely beer garden overlooking the loch and a varied selection of dishes on offer, including vegetarian and speciality seafood. It's advisable to book a table at either pub in advance in the summer months.

NANNY STATE ALERT As Borlum is a working farm with lots of horses, children need to take care in and around the farm machinery and livestock.

GETTING THERE From Inverness, head south on the A82, signposted Fort Augustus. Drive through the village of Drumnadrochit and, just past it, you'll find Borlum Farm, on your right.

OPEN All year.

THE DAMAGE Adult £6 per night; child (under-16) £4. Electric hook-up £3. If there's no one around at reception, it's a case of pitch and pay later.

index

4 Winds Lakeland Tipis, Low Wray, Ambleside, Cumbria 242–45
Aberaeron, Ceredigion 175
Aberdovey (Aberdyfi), Gwynedd 180, 184
Abergavenny, Monmouthshire 145
Aberystwyth 171
Acorn Events 210
Ailsa Craig 268
Aldeburgh, Suffolk 196
Allen Valley, Cornwall 46
Alternative Boat Hire, Iona 274
Ambleside, Cumbria 249
Ambleside Climbing Wall, Cumbria 245
Appletreewick, North Yorkshire 232
Arran, Isle of 268
Arthur's Field, Cornwall 38–41
Arvor Sea Kayaking, Cornwall 34
Astro Clear View Campsite, Herefordshire 142–45
Auchingarrich Wildlife Park, Perthshire 273
Auchrannie Resort, Isle of Arran 268
Aylsham Fun Barns, Norfolk 209

Badgworthy Water, Devon 78
Baker Street Cinema, Abergavenny 145
Balloch O' Dee Campsite and Trekking Centre, Dumfries & Galloway 256–59
Barden Bridge, North Yorkshire 232
Barn Climbing, Milton Abbot, Devon 65
Bath 84
Battlefield Line Railway 190, 192
Beatrix Potter Gallery, Hawkshead, Cumbria 249
Beechenhurst Lodge, Coleford, Glos 128, 131
Beer Quarry Caves, Devon 72
Bexhill Leisure Pool, Bexhill-on-Sea, East Sussex 108
Bexhill-on-Sea, East Sussex 108
Big Blue Surf School, Cornwall 42
Big Pit National Coal Museum, Wales 152
BIG Sheep, nr Bideford, Devon 57
Birdland, Bourton-on-the-Water, Glos 119
Bishop's Castle, Shropshire 188
Black Cave, Isle of Arran 268
Black Mountains, Wales 142
Blickling Hall, Norfolk 209
Blue John Cavern, Derbyshire 224
Blue Lagoon Water Park, Pembs 167
Bluebell Railway 103
Bodmin Moor, Cornwall 44, 49
Bolton Abbey, North Yorkshire 232, 235
Boot, Cumbria 250, 253
Borlum Farm, Inverness-shire 282–85
Borth, Ceredigion 180
Bosworth Battlefield Heritage Centre and Country Park, Leicestershire 190, 195
Bosworth Water Trust, Warwickshire 190–91, 192
Bourton-on-the-Water, Glos 119, 123
Bowness, Cumbria 246
Brancaster, Norfolk 206, 215
Branscombe, Devon 72
Branscombe Beach, Devon 72
Brecon and Monmouthshire Canal 150
Brecon Beacons National Park 141, 152
Brendon Manor Riding Stables, Exmoor, Devon 81
Bressingham Steam and Gardens, nr Diss, Norfolk 216
Brighton 96, 99
Britchcombe Farm, Oxon 116–19
Broadstairs, Kent 113

Brodick, Isle of Arran 268
Brown Willy, Bodmin Moor, Cornwall 46
Bude, Cornwall 52, 55
Burnsall, North Yorkshire 232

Caerlaverock Wildlife and Wetlands Trust 254
Caffyns Farm, Lynton, Devon 74–77
Calgary Bay, Isle of Mull 278–81
Cambrian Mountains 171
Camel Trail 44, 49
Camp Beaumont 148
Camp Bestival, Dorset 228
Cantref Adventure Farm Park, Powys 150
Caravanserai 38
Carbis Bay Beach, St Ives, Cornwall 28
Cardigan Bay 157
Carew Castle, Pembs 157
Carnllidi mountain, St David's 162
Carreg Cennen Castle, Carmarthenshire 152
Castell Henllys Iron Age Fort, Preseli Hills 157
Castleton, Derbyshire 224
Celtic Camping, Pembs 164–67
Centre for Alternative Technology (CAT), Machynlleth, Powys 183, 184, 187
Cerenety Eco Camping, Cornwall 52–55
Chained Library, Hereford Cathedral 179
Charleston, Firle, East Sussex 104, 107
Chatsworth House, Derbyshire 220
Cheltenham, Glos 120
Chilterns 114
Cholwell Riding Stables, Mary Tavy, Devon 62
Chysauster Iron Age village, New Mill, Cornwall 27
Clearwell Caves, Coleford, Glos 131
Cliff House Holiday Park, Suffolk 196–97
Clippesby Hall, Norfolk 198–99
Cloud Farm, Devon 78–81
Clyst river 68
Cobbs Hill Farm, East Sussex 108–9
Cocoa Bean Chocolate Factory, Twynholm, Dumfries & Galloway 254
Colerne, Wiltshire 84
Comrie, Perthshire 270
Comrie Croft, Perthshire 270–73
Coniston Water, Cumbria 245
Coombe View Farm Caravan and Camping Site, Devon 72–73
Corinium Museum, Cirencester 127
Cornish Way 52
Cornish Yurts, Cornwall 50–51
Corpse Way 236
Corris Railway 187
Cors Caron National Nature Reserve, Tregaron, Wales 175
Cotswold Farm Park, Glos 120–23
Cotswold Way 120
Cotswolds 120
Crealy Adventure Park, Exeter 71
Cream o' Galloway 254
Crieff, Perthshire 270
Cromer, Norfolk 206, 209
Cubert Common, Cornwall 42
Culvennan Fell, Dumfries & Galloway 256
Culzean Castle Camping and Caravanning Club Site, Ayrshire 264–67

Dale Hill Farm, Pembs 158–61
Dalegarth, Cumbria 250
Dales Countryside Museum, Hawes, North Yorkshire 236
Dandelion Hideaway, Leicestershire 192–95
Dartmoor 62, 65, 66, 149
Dawlish, Devon 68
De La Warr Pavilion, Bexhill-on-Sea, East Sussex 108
Dee Estuary 254
Denmark Farm Conservation Centre 172, 175
Denmark Farm Eco Campsite, Ceredigion 172–75

Dent Heritage Centre, Cumbria 241
Derbyshire Dales National Nature Reserve 220
Devil's Bridge, Ceredigion 171
Devon Yurt, Devon 62–65
Didcot Railway Centre, Oxon 119
Dinas Head, Pembs 157
Dinosaur Adventure, Weston Park, Norfolk 204
Dinosaur Museum, Dorchester 88
Ditchling, East Sussex 96
Dolaucothi Gold Mine, Carmarthenshire, 152
Dolgoch Waterfalls, Gwynedd 187
Dome Garden, Glos 128–31
Donkey Sanctuary, Sidmouth, Devon 72
Doone Valley, Devon 78
Dorchester, Dorset 88
Dores, Loch Ness 282
Dover, Kent 113
Dovey Valley 180
Dragon Hill, Oxon 116
Drover Holidays, Hay-on-Wye 141
Drumnadrochit, Inverness-shire 285
Drusillas Park zoo, nr Alfriston, East Sussex 107
Dunster Castle, nr Minehead, Somerset 81
Dunwich Heath Coastal Centre and Beach, Suffolk 196
Dymchurch miniature railway, Kent 113

East Onny river 188
East Runton, Norfolk 206, 209
Edale, Derbyshire 224
Eden Project, Cornwall 46, 49
Egg Theatre, Bath 84
Eglwysfach RSPB reserve, Powys 183
Elemental Adventure, Swanpool, Cornwall 34
Embsay and Bolton Abbey Steam railway 235
English Channel 107
Erwlon Caravan and Camping Park, Carmarthenshire 152–53
Esk river 250
Eskdale Green, Cumbria 250
Eskdale Mill, Boot, Cumbria 250, 253
Eskdale Valley 250
Eweleaze Farm, Dorset 88–89, 90
Exe river 68
Exeter, Devon 68, 71
Exmoor 74, 77, 78, 81
Exmoor Zoo 81
Exmouth, Devon 68

Fakenham, Norfolk 219
Falmouth, Cornwall 34, 37, 41
Fantasy Farm Park, Ceredigion 175
Farmer Gow's Activity Farm, Oxon 119
Felbrigg Hall, Norfolk 210
Fingal's Cave 277
Firle House, East Sussex 107
Fisherground Campsite, Cumbria 250–53
Fishguard, Pembs 157
Flambards, Helston, Cornwall 30, 33
Flushing, Cornwall 37
Folly Farm Adventure Park & Zoo, Pembs 161
Ford, nr Bath 84
Forest Adventure, Forest of Dean 131
Forest of Dean 128
Forestry Commission 128

Galloway Forest Park 256
Geevor Tin Mine, Cornwall 28
Giffords Circus 124
Gigrin Farm Red Kite Centre, Powys 179
Gilfach Farm Nature Reserve, Powys 176
GL1 Leisure Centre, Gloucester 127
Glenurquhart 282
Glyndebourne 104
Glyndwr's Way long-distance path 176
Go Ape!, Dalby Forest, Yorkshire 230
Golden Valley, Glos 124, 142

Goodrich Castle, Herefordshire 132
Goonhilly Earth Station, Cornwall 50
Grandma's Garden, Machynlleth, Powys 183
Great Yarmouth, Norfolk 198
Green Caravan Park, Shropshire 188–89
Gressenhall Farm & Workhouse, Norfolk 216, 219
Grey Mare's Tail Nature Reserve, Moffat, Dumfries & Galloway 263
Grogley Woods, Cornwall 44
Guilfest, Stoke Park, Guildford, Surrey 229
Guiting Power, Glos 120
Gwerniago Farm Camping, Powys 180–83

Haddon Grove Farm, Derbyshire 220–23
Haddon Hall, Derbyshire 220
Hastings, East Sussex 108
Hawes, North Yorkshire 236
Hay-on-Wye, Powys 141, 145
Heads of Ayr Farm Park 264, 267
Helford Estuary, Cornwall 34
Henley-on-Thames, Oxon 114
Hereford 141, 145, 179
Hereford Cathedral 137, 179
High Sand Creek Campsite, Norfolk 216–19
Higher Moor, Cornwall 42–43
Higher Pentreath Farm, Cornwall 30–33
Highfield Farm, Devon 68–71
Hill Top, nr Sawrey, Cumbria 249
Hoarwithy, Herefordshire 134
Holkham Beach, Norfolk 210, 215
Hollywood Cinema, Dereham, Norfolk 204
Holme, Norfolk 215
Holme Open Farm, Cumbria 238–41
Holt, Norfolk 209
Hope Gap, East Sussex 107
Hope Valley, Derbyshire 224
Houghton Hall, Norfolk 219
The House!, Overstrand, Norfolk 148
Howgill Fells, Cumbria 238
Howletts Wild Animal Park, Kent 110, 113
Hunstanton, Norfolk 216, 219

International Centre for Birds of Prey, Newent, Glos 134
Iona Abbey 274, 277
Iona Campsite, Isle of Iona 274–77

Jurassic Coast 72, 88, 228
Just So festival, Rode Hall, Stoke-on-Trent, Cheshire 229

Keld, North Yorkshire 236
Kelling Heath Holiday Park, Norfolk 210–11
King Arthur's Labyrinth, Corris Craft Centre, Machynlleth 183, 187
Kingsand, Devon 56
Kisdon Force, North Yorkshire 236

Lake District 242, 246, 250
Lake District Visitor Centre, Brockhole, Cumbria 249
Lake Windermere, Cumbria 242, 245, 246
Lampeter, Ceredigion 175
Land's End, Cornwall 44
Larmer Tree Gardens, Wiltshire/Dorset border 228
Lathkill Dale, Derbyshire 220
Lee Abbey, Devon 74
Lee Bay, Devon 74
Lewes, East Sussex 107
Limestone Way 224
Lion Royal Hotel, Rhayader, Powys 176, 179
Little Stour river 110
Lizard Lighthouse, Cornwall 50
Lizard Peninsula, Cornwall 50
Llandovery, Carmarthenshire 152
Llangorse Activity Centre, Powys 141, 150
Llangrannog Beach, Ceredigion 171

Llawhaden Castle, Pembs 157
Llys-y-Fran reservoir, Pembs 157
Loch Heron, Dumfries & Galloway 259
Loch Ness 282
Loch Ness Centre & Exhibition,
 Drummadrochit, Inverness-shire 285
Loch Ness Monster 282, 285
Long Mynd, Shropshire 188
Long Rock, Cornwall 24
Long Valley Yurts, Low Wray National Trust
 Campsite, Ambleside, Cumbria 242
Low Wray National Trust Campsite, Cumbria
 242–45, 246–49
Lulworth Castle, Dorset 228
Lune Valley 238
Lydford Gorge, Devon 65
Lynton–Lynmouth cliff railway, Devon 77

Ma Simes Surf Hut, Whitesands Bay, Pembs
 162
Machynlleth, Powys 183, 184
Maenporth Beach, Cornwall 34
Majestic Cinema, Kings Lynn, Norfolk 215
Maker Camping, Cornwall 56–57
Mam Tor, Derbyshire 224
Manor Farm Caravan and Camping Site,
 Norfolk 206–9
Mappa Mundi, Hereford Cathedral 137, 179
Marazion, Cornwall 24
Margate, Kent 113
Marshfield, Glos 84
Marteg river 176
Masons Campsite, North Yorkshire 232 ·35
Mayrose Farm Glamppod and Camping,
 Cornwall 46–49
Merry Maidens stone circle, Cornwall 27
Middle Farm, Firle, East Sussex 107
Milky Way adventure park, Devon 81
Minack Open Air Theatre, Cornwall 27
Minchinhampton Common, Glos 124
Miniature Pony Centre, Dartmoor 66
Minsmere RSPB bird reserve, Suffolk 196
Monkey Business, Lewes, East Sussex 107
Monkey World Ape Rescue Centre, Dorset 90
Morston, Norfolk 210
Motiva Adventure Tower, Beechenhurst Lodge,
 Coleford, Glos 128, 131
Mounts Bay, Cornwall 24
Muckleburgh Collection, Weybourne,
 Norfolk 209
Mull, Isle of 274, 278–81

National Marine Aquarium, Plymouth 56
National Maritime Museum, Falmouth 37, 41
National Seal Sanctuary, Gweek, Cornwall 27
National Space Centre, Leicester 195
National Trust 65, 72, 103, 164, 196, 210,
 242, 246, 249, 264
Nature's Path Tipi and Yurt Holidays, Norfolk
 204–5
Naturesbase Holidays, Ceredigion 168–71
Nessie Hunter boat 285
Nessieland Castle Monster Centre,
 Drummadrochit, Inverness-shire 285
Nethergong Nurseries, Kent 110–13
Newgale, Pembs 157
Newport, Monmouthshire 157
Newport Sands, Pembs 157
Newquay, Cardigan Bay 180, 183
Newquay, Cornwall 42
Newton Stewart, Dumfries & Galloway 259
Noongallas, Cornwall 24–27
Norfolk Broads 198
Norfolk Coastal Path 216
North Norfolk Railway 209
North Pembrokeshire Islands 167
Northdown Farm, Dorset 88

Oasis, Swindon, Wiltshire 119

Odds Farm Park, Oxon 114
Offa's Dyke Trail 188
Old Byre Heritage Centre, Isle of Mull 281
Onny Valley 188
Over the Wall camps 148
Oxford 119

Padstow, Cornwall 44
Paradise Park wildlife sanctuary, Hayle,
 Cornwall 27, 28
Peak Cavern, Derbyshire 224
Pecorama, Beer, nr Seaton, Devon 72
Pembroke Castle, Pembs 157
Pembrokeshire Coastal Path 164, 167
Pembrokeshire Heritage Coast 158
Pembrokeshire Sheepdogs 167
Penberi mountain, St David's 162
Pencarrow House, Cornwall 44
Pencelli Castle Caravan and Camping Park,
 Powys 150–51
Pendennis Castle, Cornwall 37, 41
Pensthorpe nature reserve and gardens,
 Norfolk 215
Penzance, Cornwall 24, 27
Perranuthnoe Beach, Cornwall 30
Perrygrove Railway, Coleford 134, 137
Peveril Castle, Castleton, Derbyshire 224
Pitt Rivers Museum, Oxford 119
Pladda Island 268
Plymouth 55
Poldark Tin Mine, Cornwall 28
Polzeath, Cornwall 44, 49
Port Isaac, Cornwall 49
Porth Joke, Cornwall 42
Porthcurnick beach, Cornwall 41
Porthcurno, Cornwall 24
Portscatho, Cornwall 38, 41
Praa Sands, Cornwall 30
Puzzlewood, nr Coleford, Glos 132
Pwllheli, Gwynedd 183

Quackers Play Barn, Newbridge-on-Wye 179
Quantock Hills 82

Rame Peninsula, Cornwall 56
Ramsgate, Kent 113
Raven Surf School, Cornwall 42
Ravenglass and Eskdale steam railway 250
Rawthey river 238
Rhayader Leisure Centre, Powys 179
Ridgeway 116
Ringstead Bay, Dorset 90
River and Rowing Museum, Henley-on-
 Thames 114
Rock, Cornwall 44, 49
Rocks East Woodland, nr Bath 84–87
Roman Baths, Bath 84
Roscuick Organic Farm, Cornwall 50
Rosedale Abbey Caravan Park, nr Pickering,
 North Yorkshire 230–31
Roseland Peninsula, Cornwall 38
Rosewall Camping, Riding and Lakes, Dorset
 90–91
Ross-on-Wye, Herefordshire 132
Rough Tor, Bodmin Moor, Cornwall 46
Rowter Farm, Derbyshire 224–25
Royal Pavilion, Brighton 99
Royal Regatta, Henley-on-Thames 114
Royal Victoria Park and Botanical
 Gardens, Bath 84
RSPB 183, 196
Rukin's Park Lodge, North Yorkshire 236–37
Runnage Farm, Devon 66–67
Ruthern Valley, Cornwall 44–45
Ryedale Folk Museum, Hutton le Hole,
 North Yorkshire 230

Safari Britain Campsite, Sussex 104–7
St David's, Pembs 157, 162, 164
St Ives, Cornwall 28

St Mary's Loch, Scottish Borders 260, 263
St Mawes, Cornwall 37, 41
St Mawes Castle 41
St Michael's Mount, Cornwall 27, 30
Sandworth, Weymouth 88
Scolton Manor, nr Haverfordwest 157
Scottish Borders 260
Sea Life Sanctuary, Hunstanton, Norfolk
 198, 219
Sea Life Surveys, nr Dervaig, Isle of Mull 281
Seal Shore Camping & Touring Site,
 Isle of Arran 268–69
Sedbergh, Cumbria 238, 241
Selkirk 263
Seven Sisters Country Park, East Sussex 107
Shambala Festival, Northamptonshire 228
Sheffield Park, East Sussex 103
Sheringham, Norfolk 206, 209
Showcaves, Dan-yr-Ogof, Wales 152
Sidmouth, Devon 72
Skokholm nature reserve 158
Skomer nature reserve 158
Smugglers' Adventure Caves, Hastings,
 East Sussex 108
Snibston science and technology
 museum, Leicestershire 195
Snowdonia National Park 184
Solway Coast 254
Solway View Holidays, Dumfries & Galloway
 254–55
Somerset Yurts, Somerset 82–83
South Downs National Park 96, 99, 116
South Downs National Trail 107
South Foreland Lighthouse, Kent 113
South West Coast Path 38, 88
Southern Upland Way 260
Southwold, Suffolk 196
Speedwell Cavern, Derbyshire 224
Splash Leisure Centre, Sheringham,
 Norfolk 209, 215
Staffa Trips 277
Stanley Force, Cumbria 250
Stanway, Glos 120
Stiffkey, Norfolk 216
Stiperstones Ridge, Shropshire 188
Stodmarsh Nature Reserve, Kent 110
Stonetrail Riding Centre, Cumbria 238
Stoneywish Nature Reserve, East Sussex
 96–99
Strikes, Dereham, Norfolk 204
Stump Cross Caverns, Nidderdale,
 Yorkshire 235
Sussex Downs 104
Swaledale, Yorkshire 236
Swiss Farm Touring & Camping, Oxon 114–15
Symonds Yat, Herefordshire 132

Tamar Valley 62
Tank Museum, Bovington, Dorset 90
Tarka Trail 65
Tate St Ives, Cornwall 33
Taunton, Somerset 82
Thames and Severn Canal 124
TheCanoeman Canoe and Tipi Adventures,
 Norfolk 200–203
Three Lochs Country Park, Dumfries &
 Galloway 259
Thrigby Hall Wildlife Gardens, Norfolk 198
Tibbie Shiels Inn, Selkirkshire 260–63
Tide Mills, nr Seaford, East Sussex 107
Tintagel Castle, Cornwall 44, 49
Tir Bach Farm Campsite, Pembs 154–57
Tobermory, Mull 278, 281
Tom Brown's School Museum, Uffington,
 Oxon 119
Topsham, Devon 68, 71
Trago Mills, nr Newton Abbot, Devon 66
Traquair House, Peeblesshire 260
Treak Cliff Cavern, Derbyshire 224
Trebarwith Strand, Cornwall 49

Treehouse, Powys 184–87
Treen, Cornwall 24
Tregaron, Ceredigion 175
Tregedna Farm Holidays, Cornwall 34–37
Trehenlliw Farm, Pembs 162–63
Tresseck Campsite, Herefordshire 132–33
Trethorne Farm, nr Launceston, Devon 65
Trevalyor Woods, Cornwall 24
Trevarno Gardens, Cornwall 27
Truro, Cornwall 37
Twycross Zoo 190, 192
TYF Adventure, St David's, Pembs 167

Ultimate Activity Company, Hereford 142
Urquhart Castle, Inverness-shire 282, 285

Venture Centre, Isle of Man 149
Verderer's Trail 128
Viaduct Barn, Glos 124–27
Voyages of Discovery, St David's, Pembs 167

Wain Wath Falls, North Yorkshire 236
Walberswick, Suffolk 196
Wantage Leisure Centre, Oxon 119
Wapsbourne Manor Farm, East Sussex
 100–103
Watermouth Castle, nr Ilfracombe, Devon 77
Wayland's Smith Neolithic burial chamber,
 Oxon 116, 119
Wells-next-the-Sea, Norfolk 219
Wensleydale Creamery Visitor Centre,
 Hawes, North Yorkshire 236
West Dale, Pembs 158, 161
West Runton shire horse centre, Norfolk 209
West Somerset Railway 81
Westerley Campsite, Cornwall 28–29
Weybourne, Norfolk 209
Weymouth, Dorset 88
Wharfe river 232
White Horse of Uffington 116
Whitcsands Bay, Pembs 162
Whitsand Bay, Cornwall 56
Whitstable, Kent 113
Wickedly Wonderful, West Sussex 149
Wild in Style, Cumbria 246–49
Wild Luxury, Norfolk 212–15
Wild Rock Climbing, Far Peak, Glos 123
WildWise, Devon 149
Wilmington church, East Sussex 107
Windermere Lake Cruise 246
Windermere Manor Hotel, Cumbria 245
Windy Knoll Cave, Derbyshire 224
Wingham Wildlife Park, Kent 113
Winnats Pass, Derbyshire 224
Wood Festival, Braziers Park, Oxon 229
Woodhouse Farm, Powys 176–79
Wray Castle, Cumbria 249
Wriggles Brook Gypsy Wagons, Herefordshire
 134–37
Wye river 131, 132, 138
Wye Valley 134
Wye Valley Canoes 141

Yellow Wood Bush Camps, Herefordshire/
 Powys 138–41
Yorkshire Dales 232, 236

Zeffirellis, Ambleside, Cumbria 249

Cool Camping: Kids (2nd edition)

Series Concept and Series Editor: Jonathan Knight

Researched, written and photographed by: Sophie Dawson,
Jonathan Knight, Andrea Oates, Hayley Spurway, Clover Stroud,
Alexandra Tilley Loughrey, Ally Thompson, Dixe Wills,
Harriet Yeomans

Managing Editor: Sophie Dawson

Design and cover template: Kenny Grant

Artwork: Harriet Yeomans

Proofreaders: Nikki Sims, Leanne Bryan, Catherine Greenwood

Marketing: Shelley Bowdler

Published by: Punk Publishing, 3 The Yard, Pegasus Place,
London SE11 5SD

All photographs © Sophie Dawson/Jonathan Knight/
Andrea Oates/Hayley Spurway/Clover Stroud/
Alexandra Tilley Loughrey/Ally Thompson/Harriet Yeomans/
Dixe Wills/Keith Didcock except those on the following pages
(all reproduced with permission; t = top, b = bottom, r = right,
l = left): 23 bl © Ruthern Valley Holidays; 57 t, bl © Maker
Events; 63–64, 65 tl © Julia Martin/Devon Yurt; 91 © Ellie
Maguire; 105–107 © Dan Renton/Safari Britain; 123 t ©
Cotswold Farm Park; 155, 157 t © Tir Bach Farm; 195 b ©
The Dandelion Hideaway; 199 © Clippesby Hall; 229 © Just So
Festival; 233, 234 bl 235 t © Grant and Georgie/Masons; 234 t,
235 b © Daniel Start; 247 © Wild in Style; 257–259 © Balloch
O' Dee; 11 tr, 19 bl, 23 br, 271–272, 273 b © Comrie Croft.

Front cover: Astro Clear View © Alexandra Tilley Loughrey.

Map p9 © MAPS IN MINUTES™/Collins Bartholomew (2012).

The publishers and authors have done their best to ensure the
accuracy of all information in *Cool Camping: Kids*. However,
they can accept no responsibility for any injury, loss or
inconvenience sustained by anyone as a result of information
contained in this book.

Punk Publishing takes its environmental responsibilities seriously.
This book has been printed on paper made from renewable
sources and we continue to work with our printers to reduce our
overall environmental impact. Wherever possible, we recycle, eat
organic food and always turn the tap off when brushing our teeth.

A BIG THANK YOU! Thanks to everyone who has written and
emailed with feedback, comments and suggestions. It's good to see
so many people at one with the Cool Camping ethos.
Thanks to all the lovely models whose happy faces grace the
pages of this book. We'd especially like to thank our own little
helpers: Jimmy Joe and Dolly, Milini and Suriya, Libby and Isaac,
Oli and Leo, Arthur and Lily, and Dicken and Lettice.

HAPPY CAMPERS?

We hope you've enjoyed reading *Cool Camping: Kids* and that it's inspired you to get out there.

The campsites featured in this book are a personal selection chosen by the Cool Camping team. We have visited hundreds of campsites across the UK to find this selection, and we hope you like them as much as we do. However, it hasn't been possible to visit every single British campsite. So, if you know of a special place that you think should be included, we'd like to hear about it. Send an e-mail telling us the name and location of the site, some contact details and why it's special.

We'll credit all useful contributions in the next edition of the book, and senders of the best e-mails will receive a complimentary copy. Thanks, and see you out there!

kids@coolcamping.co.uk